D1068688

CHINA AND THE ORIGINS OF THE PACIFIC WAR, 1931-1941

CHINA AND THE ORIGINS OF THE PACIFIC WAR, 1931-1941

Youli Sun

St. Martin's Press
New York

First published in the United States of America 1993
Printed in the United States of America

ISBN 0-312-09010-2

Library of Congress Cataloging-in-Publication Data

Sun, You-Li, 1955-
China and the origins of the Pacific War, 1931-1941 / Youli Sun
    p. cm.
Includes bibliographical references and index.
ISBN 0-312-09010-2
1. World War, 1939-1945—Causes. 2. World War, 1939-1945—China.
3. World War, 1939-1945—Japan. 4. China—Foreign relations—Japan.
5. Japan—Foreign relations—China. 6. China—Foreign relations 1912-1949.
7. Japan—Foreign relations—1912-1945.
I . Title.

D742.C5S85   1993
940.53'11'0951—dc20   92-36305
                                                            CIP

CONTENTS

To Todd and Paul

ACKNOWLEDGMENTS

The research for this book began in 1987 when I was a graduate student at the University of Chicago. There I worked under the supervision and guidance of Professor Akira Iriye and, as his first student from the People's Republic of China, benefited immensely from his knowledge, encouragement, and criticism. It was under Professor Iriye that I learned something about the meaning of historical objectivity and changed many of my previous biases. My deep gratitude also goes to Professor Guy Alitto, who has helped me throughout the years in modern Chinese history, and professors Tsou Tang, Arthur Mann, and Michael Geyer, who have either taught me or offered criticisms on my dissertation.

I am also deeply grateful to Professor Bill Kirby at Washington University in St. Louis (where I spent a year improving the manuscript), who has offered all kinds of assistance. The one-year fellowship at the Washington University History Department made it possible to finish the manuscript. I have also benefited from the criticisms of Dr. Ramon Meyers and Dr. Thomas Metzger of the Hoover Institution on War, Revolution, and Peace.

Research grants from Colby College and the University of Southern Mississippi provided me with the necessary income and release time that enabled me to do further research and writing.

Assistance from librarians and archivists has been crucial in my research and I wish to thank those professionals at the Far Eastern Library at the University of Chicago, the Library of Congress, the Hoover Institution, the Archival Section of Butler Library at Columbia University, the National Archives, and the Franklin Roosevelt Library.

I wish to thank Professor Denis Sinor for his gracious permission to use an article published in the *Journal of Asian History,* a different version of which appears here as Chapter Two.

Finally, as Benjamin Franklin wisely said, "He who wants to thrive must ask his wife." It simply would have been impossible to finish my degree and the manuscript without the help of my wife, Xiaoyan Zhang, who not only assisted me in her capacity as a librarian but more importantly cared for two newborn sons after 1989.

A NOTE ON ROMANIZATION

Chinese romanization is perhaps the most confusing task faced by scholars. To date, some prefer the Wade-Giles system and some the Pinyin. Asian libraries have to provide charts of comparison between the two systems. I have decided to adopt the Pinyin system for the most part. However, for the sake of convenience, some well-known names of people and places are retained in their old usages, whether Wade-Giles or customarily adopted. The following is a list:

Names adopted	(Pinyin)
Chiang Kai-shek	(Jiang Jie-shi)
Wellington Koo	(Gu Wei-ju)
H. H. Kung	(Kong Xiang-xi)
T. V. Soong	(Song Zi-wen)
Peking	(Beijing or Beiping)
Tientsin	(Tianjin)
Nanking	(Nanjing)
Canton	(Guangzhou)
Yangtze River	(Yangzi River)

INTRODUCTION

Since the late nineteenth century, China had been reduced to an object of imperialist rivalry and of balance-of-power struggles in the Far East. Japan's effort to establish a new order in this part of the world by conquering Manchuria in 1931 and thus nullifying the Nine Power Treaty went essentially unchallenged by the powers. Oddly enough, China, the object of power politics, became the only country that did not acquiesce to Japan's new order and eventually resisted it both by necessity and by choice. The decade of the 1930s witnessed an active Chinese diplomacy. The decision to fight Japan in 1937 altered China's status from an object to a player, thus adding a new dimension to the Far Eastern power configurations. The Sino-Japanese conflict during this decade was not only crucial for China but also one of the most important events precipitating the conflict between Japan and other powers and thus leading to Pearl Harbor.

Important as it was, China's foreign policy has not received as close scholarly attention as that of other players, such as Japan and the United States. Partly because of the lack of available archival materials, China was treated by diplomatic historians as a marginal factor.[1] In the 1980s, two excellent studies of China's bilateral relations with Germany and the Soviet Union greatly broadened our understanding of the Chinese side of the story. In particular, John Garver's book on Sino-Soviet relations relied primarily on government documents newly published by Taiwan and revealed to us the active and shrewd diplomatic maneuvers of the Chinese government from 1937 to 1945. Similarly, two earlier studies of the peace movement also used Chinese materials to illuminate the views of the minority faction on Chinese foreign policy. Yet much more needs to be done in this field. The best study of China's relations with Japan, from the perspective of internal Chinese politics from 1931-1937, is Parks Coble's *Facing Japan: Chinese Politics and Japanese Imperialism, 1931-1937.* Coble's book is the most detailed treatment of Chinese politics available in the English language and, while still following a somewhat traditional approach, sheds much light on Chiang Kai-shek's policies toward Japan.[2]

If comparatively little has been written on China's foreign policy of this period, even less has been done to conceptualize it and to understand the rationale behind such active diplomacy. Past studies focused heavily on internal politics, and foreign policy appeared simply as a function of domestic power struggles. Obviously this kind of treatment omits China's perceptions and calculations about international politics. To some extent, one can argue that domestic politics was a function of these perceptions and calculations.

In this period, there seemed to exist a highly consistent and widely accepted belief system among the Chinese regarding international politics in general and the Sino-Japanese conflict in particular. It consisted of two major perceptions: first, that Japan's aggression in China threatened Western interests, and that conflicts between imperialist powers to control China (Japan on the one hand and the powers on the other since 1931) were inevitable; second, that it was practical for China to seek anti-Japanese alliances not only as a way to defend the country but also as a means for the government to concentrate its military resources on domestic opponents. The study of these fundamental perceptions of international politics and their impact on Chinese diplomatic behavior forms the central thesis of this enquiry. It argues that the rationale of Chinese foreign policy during this decade was influenced directly or indirectly by these perceptions.

Chapter One deals with the Chinese concept of imperialism and the changing perceptions of international relations in the 1920s and 1930s. It stresses the transforming role of the Manchurian Incident in changing Chinese perceptions, the rise of the alliance idea, and the belief in the inevitable war between Japan and other powers. It also tries to show that these perceptions were the most dominant and were widely shared by the Chinese public and the government leaders alike.

The first impulsive try to form an anti-Japanese coalition in the immediate aftermath of the Manchurian Incident is the focus of Chapter Two. The futility of this attempt, mainly due to the unwillingness of the powers to confront Japan, led to a practical retrenchment from 1933 to 1935, generally known as the policy of appeasement. Chapter Three deals with the rationale of such a policy and points out that the term *gradualism* rather than *appeasement* captured the real intent of the Chinese government.

The rising public protest against gradualism and its demise is the subject of Chapter Four. The convergence of Soviet popular front strategy and Chinese nationalist fervor formed a barrier to the gradualist policy. Nanking, too, responded to the Soviet gestures through secret diplomacy and became determined to counter Japan's further encroachments. All these factors prevented any Sino-Japanese accommodation and pushed the government further toward confrontation.

In the next chapter the political debates concerning the dilemma of the Sino-Japanese War, which erupted in July 1937, are analyzed with an emphasis on the divergent views of the international situation especially in the critical year of 1938. The hopes for eventual intervention either by the Soviet Union or by the powers prevailed; the victory of the war faction and the defection of Wang Jing-wei, the leading peace advocate and second in command in the Chinese government, made it extremely difficult for a peaceful settlement of the undeclared war.

The last two chapters deal with China's relations with the Soviet Union and the United States, respectively. In both cases the Chinese belief that Japan would eventually conflict with these powers was a governing concept and, psychologically, the only hope in these relations to be seen at almost every major turn of events. Repeatedly, the Chinese beliefs resulted in proposals for formal alliance between China and these powers. As time went on, the Chinese counted heavily on the United States, "The Last Best Hope." The coming of Pearl Harbor thus became the redeeming event that Chinese leaders had prayed for; it seemed to have vindicated the Chinese beliefs about the inevitable conflict throughout the past ten years.

1

The World in the Chinese Mind, 1920s and 1930s

In postwar studies of diplomatic history and international relations, increasing attention has been paid to the images and perceptions nations have had of each other and their impact on the formation of foreign policy. Some scholars, such as Akira Iriye, have viewed international relations as intercultural relations. Political scientists' writings on cultural perceptions and images are numerous. Such terms as "cognitive maps," "belief systems," "perceptions," and "images" connote more or less the same meaning. Ole R. Holsti, for instance, characterized the belief system as "a set of lenses" with which to look at the outside world.[1]

This kind of approach calls attention not only to individual perceptions of the outside world, but also to those held by society in general. In his *World in Their Mind,* Yaacov Y. I. Vertzberger summarizes the political science research on this point as follows: "Decision-making by individuals and groups cannot be fully understood apart from the broader societal-national environment, culture, and experience."[2] Whether concentrating on the broad cultural canvas or on individual case studies, this approach offers us a different perspective to understand foreign policy behavior that was inadequately covered by traditional approaches. The cultural lenses through which the Chinese collectively saw international relations provide us with a framework of reference for China's foreign policy during the 1930s.

Puzzling facts in China's foreign policy also call for this kind of approach. For example, it is indeed a mystery that given the obvious disparity between China's and Japan's military power, the Chinese government decided to fight a war rather than to make concessions in 1937 and to fight alone for the next four years without formal commitment of alliance from any power. It will be beneficial to probe the world of the Chinese mind, namely, the images and perceptions of relationships between China and major powers in the Far East and of those among the big powers themselves. A discussion of these general beliefs, cumulatively formed in previous decades, to see how they may have influenced foreign policies of this period is a good starting point.[3]

CONCEPT OF IMPERIALISM AND ITS IMPLICATIONS

Nothing characterizes the Chinese attitude toward, and perceptions of, international relations better than the term *imperialism*. In fact, imperialism had became such an emotion-laden generic name for the major powers that it indicated intense nationalist resentment of foreign domination of China. A unique feature about the concept of imperialism was that by the 1920s it had become predominantly economic-determinist among the Chinese regardless of their political persuasions, whether Communist or Nationalist. This concept of imperialism was derived from two main sources: Chinese historical experiences and imported theories of imperialism.

Since the Opium War, Westerners coming to East Asia had been seen as motivated by a search for trade and markets; the use of military power and imposition of the unequal treaty system were seen only as means to subdue China for profits. In fact, "economic imperialism" was a term widely used to describe Sino-foreign relations. By 1935 several dozen books had been written with the approximate title, *A History of Imperialist Aggression in China,* and many were specifically devoted to the subject of "economic imperialism." For example, between 1927 and 1929 Tang Shou-chang, Chen Tong-he, and Huang Xiao-xian each wrote a book on this subject. Not only did they have the same title but also supported their charges of Western imperialism with the same historical evidences: defeats of China, losses of sovereignty and economic rights, and so on. Imbued in these accounts of history was the notion of China as a rich source of raw materials and an indispensable market for the West. Chen Tong-he, for instance, wrote that iron deposits alone amounted to 10 trillion tons, and, consequently, China was "a chunk of fat and fresh meat" for every imperialist nation.[4] The Kuomintang (KMT) ideologue Dai Ji-tao, reflected this widespread Chinese belief in the China Market and Western economic imperialism in his explanation of Sun Yat-sen's doctrines.[5] Indeed, Western ownership of Chinese railroads, mines, and factories were constant reminders of economic imperialism. As John Gittings has observed, when the Chinese talked about imperialism, they were merely "attempting to describe a situation with which they were only too familiar."[6]

One inherent theme of the Chinese notion of imperialism was that competition and rivalry among the imperialist powers could be manipulated for China's benefit. A case in point was the Triple Intervention by Germany, France, and Russia after the Sino-Japanese War of 1895, which forced Japan to give up the Liaodong Peninsula. Utilizing the powers lay at the foundation of Li Hong-zhang's secret alliance with Russia as a defense against Japan. A more persuasive example would be the Open Door Policy, which revealed to the Chinese eye the notion of the China Market and the conflicts among foreign powers to control it. The Chinese officials during this period consciously used the lure of the China Market as a mechanism to play the United States against other powers so as to maintain China's integrity.[7] The Open Door Doctrine had long been considered a product of conflicts between those imperialists who desired China's partition and the United States, which wanted to preserve China's integrity for its commercial interests.

At the theoretical level, the Chinese understanding of imperialism went through a change from a Social Darwinist to an economic interpretation. In the early 1900s, Liang Qi-chao, the famous reformer of 1898 whose views influenced generations of Chinese, considered imperialism a result of a Darwinist competition among nation-states or races. His term for it was "National Imperialism." Liang acknowledged that he was influenced by foreign works on imperialism, such as Franklin Henry Gidding's *Democracy and Empire* and Ukita Kazuomi's *Imperialism,* both pro-imperialist. To Liang and his generation imperialism was motivated by racialism in the Darwinian sense of the word.[8]

There was an economic aspect to Liang's analysis of imperialism. Liang at one point mentioned that the development of trusts in the United States was chiefly responsible for imperialism. In his polemic engagements with the Chinese Nationalists under Sun Yat-sen, Liang called attention to economic aspects of imperialism and advocated the development of Chinese capitalism to counter it, whereas Sun and his disciple, Hu Han-min, welcomed foreign investments in China as wholesome for economic development.[9] Even up to 1919, some leading KMT theorists like Zhu Zhi-xin still held that imperialism was fundamentally an outgrowth of militarism, not capitalism.[10] However, economic interpretation appeared to be spasmodic and certainly not most important at this stage. Those who held a noneconomic view of imperialism were definitely in the minority afterwards.[11]

The economic view of imperialism gained ascendancy and then dominance in the 1920s. The Soviets had an impact on the concept of imperialism. The Chinese Communists believed in the Leninist economic interpretation of imperialism as an article of faith— whatever their beliefs had been earlier.

As for the Nationalists, after Sun Yat-sen's acceptance of Soviet assistance and reorganization of his KMT Party, Sun and his followers changed their views on Western imperialism and began to denounce it in terms of the economic oppression of China. In his lectures on nationalism, Sun defined imperialism as political and economic oppression of other nations, though he appeared not to have accepted Lenin's theory in toto.[12] Therefore, after Sun's death, Wang Ching-wei, Liao Zhong-kai, and Hu Han-min, the three most important contenders for the KMT leadership, were able to explain imperialism in economic as well as political terms. For example, Wang defined imperialism as "a country that by its superior political and military force practiced economic aggression against other countries or regions or nations."[13] In the same year Liao Zhong Kai offered exactly the same definition in a public lecture on imperialism.[14] He considered economic imperialism more detrimental to the Chinese than any other form of aggression. Even after the Chinese Communist Party (CCP)-KMT split, Hu Han-min in 1928 still showed a trace of the economic interpretation as he viewed imperialism as a combination of bureaucracy, capitalism, and militarism.[15]

The notion of imperialism as revealed in books and magazines clearly showed the influence of both Lenin and Leonard Woolf on the subject. The first major Marxist treatment of imperialism, *China under the Iron Heel of Imperialism,* was published in 1925 and it was prefaced by Tang Shao-yi, who served as prime minister under the warlord Yuan Shi-kai, by Xu Qian, a KMT leader, and by Guo Mo-ro, the famous writer who had just become converted to Marxism-Leninism. As Gittings pointed out, this indicated a diversity of support for the author's characterization of imperialism.[16] Perhaps the best and most systematic treatise of imperialism was written by Ma Zhe-min. This author became interested in imperialism when he was still a student in 1925 and finished his *General Theory of Imperialism* four years later. Ma regarded imperialism as the last stage of monopolistic capitalism. He literally accepted Lenin's five features of imperialism without any change.[17]

Leonard Woolf's interpretation of imperialism as motivated by commercial interests also found a large audience. By 1935 there existed in China four different translations of Woolf's *Economic Imperialism* (1920). In 1928 an author by the name of Yang You-jong acknowledged his debt to Woolf's views. Of the factors responsible for imperialism, the economic one was considered the most important. Furthermore, Yang argued that it was a stage in the development of capitalism, somewhat echoing Lenin's points, too. Other books published in the 1920s on this subject tended also to be economic determinist.[18]

This economic view of imperialism appeared to have been accepted by most Chinese, not just the Communists or the leftists. Even after the

Communist-Nationalist split, Dong Lin, a KMT scholar of foreign relations, still considered Marxist theories on imperialism most attractive and
important. "Indeed, the development of modern imperialism was driven by
capitalism," Dong wrote in 1929.[19]

These theories on imperialism strongly reinforced Chinese historical
experiences with the foreign powers and provided a timely and new
rationalization for the anti-imperialist movement. Economic exploitation
of China and the big power rivalry, which composed the meaning of
imperialism, were accepted as givens whenever the phenomenon was being
discussed. Some popular political terms reflected semantically the Chinese
notion of imperialism. For example, establishing hegemony in China by
one power was referred to as *Duzhan,* literally meaning "occupying alone";
opposition to these kinds of hegemonic attempts by other powers due to
their interests was given the word *Gongguan,* meaning "joint management"
of China, or sometimes *Guafen* (partition) in the anti-imperialist literature
of the 1920s and 1930s. These terms were quite indicative of Chinese
perceptions of imperialist conflicts of interests in China.

Hence the Chinese concept of imperialism contained a built-in diplomatic
mechanism: China could ally with the powers to ward off threats from any
particular one of them that attempted to disregard China's integrity and to
establish hegemony. China supplied a new rationale to old diplomatic tactics
of playing barbarians against each other when its own defense was weak.
Indeed, when Japan occupied Manchuria, it was described in China as a
Duzhan power whereas other occupying countries were described as
Gongguan powers. Even in 1990, Hu Sheng, a Chinese historian, still
regarded the Pacific War as a result of Japan's attempt to *Duzhan* (establish
hegemony in) China and the Anglo-American powers' reaction to it, a
standard view of the Chinese in the 1930s.[20]

THE CRISIS AND PERCEPTIONS

The Manchurian Incident has been described by many historians already. The
concern here is with the impact of this event upon China's domestic politics and
Chinese perceptions of international relations. By invading China and creating
a puppet regime in Manchuria, Japan made itself the sole target of Chinese
nationalism. The invasion aroused a deep sense of national crisis, in fact, the
gravest in nationalist China. About 6.7 million square miles of territory and 30
million people fell under Japanese control. The gravity of the crisis was well
expressed in Fu Si-nian's words: "The Manchurian Incident was the most serious

national crisis since our birth and it was also the greatest turning point in East
Asia for the last hundred years and at the same time was one of the biggest events
in world history in the twentieth century."[21] Feng Yu-xiang, a powerful warlord
in retirement at this time, regarded it as "the gravest danger for the country" and
called for a new army to fight Japan.[22]

This sense of grave crisis produced two major results. First, it set a new
rule of the game for domestic politics as far as propaganda was concerned.
Various anti-Nanking forces championed the anti-Japanese and nationalist
causes by demanding resistance and denouncing Chiang Kai-shek, who
headed the Chinese government in Nanking. Undoubtedly, advocating resistance to Japan was now the best way to play the political game. The most
effective advocates would get the most benefit. An intense wave of patriotism
was emerging among students and intellectuals, and it eventually played a
decisive role in forcing the Nanking government to play the same game.

The second obvious result was that the vehement anti-imperialism of
the previous decade gave way to anti-Japanism. The decade of the 1920s
was marked by violent protests against all imperialist powers throughout
China. Only four months prior to the Manchurian Incident, the Nanking
government issued a mandate abolishing all the unequal treaties, and public
anti-imperialist sentiments were riding high. In view of the new circumstances, Nanking quietly dropped its anti-imperialist policies. The powers
were now to be co-opted in order to deal with Japan.

One way to understand the new Chinese perceptions after the Manchurian
Incident is to examine the Chinese concept of imperialism again. The
pre-Manchurian Incident beliefs and attitudes toward the imperialist powers
may be regarded as the old paradigm that emphasized economic exploitation
and political domination of China by the powers. Therefore, ridding China
of the unequal treaty system was necessary for China's liberation. The
Japanese aggression in Manchuria made the old paradigm impractical and
effected a change of emphasis to other beliefs with which the Chinese
rationalized international politics and China's foreign policy. As mentioned
already, in both historical experiences and theoretical analyses, the imperialist conflicts in China due to competing economic interests were an integral
part of the concept of imperialism. The Chinese considered Japan's effort to
dismember China a violation of the Open Door Policy and a probable cause
of conflicts among the powers. Now the unique term *Duzhan* (establishing
hegemony) was applied to Japan's policy, which supposedly would cause
conflicts with the powers who desired *Gongguan* (joint management). The
basic beliefs in the new paradigm included: 1) that the economic interests of
the Anglo-American powers and Japan were incompatible, as the former

tried to maintain the Open Door Policy and the latter to establish hegemony; 2) that war between Japan and the Anglo-American powers was inevitable as a result; 3) that war between the Soviet Union and Japan was inevitable because of Japan's anticommunism and occupation of North China; and 4) that it was probable China would achieve international alliances against Japanese expansion. The majority of the Chinese public shared these beliefs to various degrees.

THE TALK OF ANTI-JAPANESE ALLIANCES

In post-1931 China, there seemed to be a fetish of talking about anti-Japanese alliances with the powers. In magazines, newspapers, and public discussions, many such ideas and strategies were discussed by people of different political persuasions. The expectations of the Chinese public reflected perhaps more about the Chinese psychological state of mind than about the realities of international politics. Yet the unprecedented scope of these discussions indicated a new attitude toward the imperialist powers and a new outlook on international relations. Alliances with imperialist powers had never been the subject of public discussion in the previous decade, when the tactic of anti-imperialist diplomacy only made a distinction as to which power to attack first and which to attack later.[23] And yet by the 1930s, the idea was to form alliances with all the powers for a single objective: to resist Japan. Without alliances with the imperialist powers, as the consensus went, the nation would not be able to survive Japan's designs to conquer China.

Various ideas for seeking foreign alliances were summarized in 1938 by Zhou Geng-sheng, a KMT scholar of foreign relations, as four major approaches: the German-Italian line, the League of Nations line, the Anglo-American line, and the Soviet line.[24] The German-Italian approach probably never figured as significantly as the other approaches. Germany was a source of military supplies and advisers and a spiritual model for KMT's version of the regeneration of China, but few expected it to be a strategic factor in the Pacific, except as a bridge to reach accommodations with Japan. The approach to the League of Nations was mainly the position of Nanking and certain intellectuals sympathetic to the government. Chiang Kai-shek pursued this approach in the immediate aftermath of the Manchurian Incident, to no avail. Until 1939, the League of Nations was merely a place to win international moral support. Hu Shi was among the minority who argued that moral help from any international source would be better than none and would isolate Japan diplomatically.[25]

The real Chinese hopes for alliances in the early 1930s were placed with the Soviet Union and the Anglo-American powers, who were viewed as adversaries of Japanese expansionism. China's relations with the Soviet Union had deteriorated since the CCP-KMT split in 1927; even diplomatic relations were severed. The Japanese aggression produced incentives for a better and closer relationship with the Soviet Union and resulted in a sudden change of attitude. This can be best illustrated by the Chinese magazine *The Soviet Russia Review,* which was established several days before the Japanese invasion. In its introductory issue, the magazine divided imperialism into two kinds, Red and White, the former referring to the Soviet Union and the latter to Western powers. China was regarded as being bullied by both. The purpose of the magazine was to study Red imperialism.[26] But in its subsequent issues, the anti-Soviet tone was dropped, and it carried articles arguing for restoration of diplomatic relations and even for an alliance with the Soviet Union.[27]

This change of attitude toward Soviet Russia was typical. Moreover, many advocated a close relationship because they were attracted to Lenin's theory of national liberation. One article in *Diplomatic Monthly* divided the world into three parts: imperialist countries, colonies and semicolonies, and the socialist country. For China, a semicolony, the only way to avoid extinction by imperialist countries was to ally itself with the Soviet Union.[28] An *Eastern Miscellany* editorial explained that the Soviets advocated two kinds of revolution, national and social. The former meant anti-imperialism, and the Chinese crisis needed just that, though not the social revolution. In short, cooperation with the Soviets was considered the best policy.[29]

In addition to the pro-Soviet attitudes of the Communists and the leftists, the anticommunist and conservative elements also saw much strategic virtue in approaching the Soviets, though they constantly warned of overoptimism and the dangers associated with such an approach. For example, the *Diplomatic Monthly* organized a forum at the Association of Returned Students from Europe and America (O Mei Tong Xue Hue) in 1933 to discuss China's Soviet policy and, as Wang Yue-bo, head of the journal put it, to "offer opinions for both the public and the government to consider." Participants were mostly well-known intellectuals and experts in foreign affairs such as Hu Shi, Dewey's student and best known philosopher, and Jiang Ting-fu, a historian of foreign relations, both of whom entered the government services in the mid-1930s. Two kinds of opinion dominated the forum. The moderate one, championed by Hu Shi and Zhang Jun-mai, head of the National Socialist Party, argued that China could not afford to have two enemies— Japan and Russia—and had to befriend Russia while avoiding total reliance. The less moderate opinion was advanced by Wang Qi-pu, a foreign affairs expert, and Wang Yue-bo, who desired a strategic anti-Japanese partnership. The Soviet support for the Nationalist movement in China, Wang Yue-bo pointed out, was a common basis for cooperation. Wang Qi-pu advocated an outright alliance. He argued that Russia, being a hypothetical enemy of Japan in the Pacific, was a natural diplomatic ally. He suggested that China could deal Japan an economic blow by replacing Japanese goods with Russian imports and that Russia would be a vital source of supplies during war when Japan blockaded China's coastal lines. It is noteworthy that of the major speakers at the forum, Jiang Ting-fu was the only voice that doubted the value of a closer relationship with the Soviets because they were not "in a position of strength." However, Jiang Ting-fu carefully mentioned that China should consider an alliance with the Soviets if a world war broke out. Indeed, Jiang Ting-fu advised Chiang Kai-shek to form a close relationship with the Soviet Union and was appointed ambassador to Moscow in 1936-1937. At the forum, the subversive Soviet support for the Chinese Communists was generally thought to be a minor issue.[30]

Forming close ties with the Soviet Union was clearly a national consensus. This was adequately expressed by one Northeast organization: "As enemy troops are menacing Chinese territory and as the state and people are being insulted, it appears to be urgently necessary for us to be friendly with our northern neighbor."[31] The government took steps to improve relations with the Soviets. It announced its decision to restore relations and to conclude a pact of nonaggression in the summer of 1932. By the end of that year, China reestablished diplomatic relations with Russia.

Among those advocates of alliance with the Soviet Union were many KMT leaders who had lost power and resented Chiang Kai-shek, such as Li Lie-jun, Cheng Qian, Chen You-ren, and Sun Ke (the son of Dr. Sun Yat-sen), who had all pressured Nanking to have closer relations with the Soviet Union as early as 1932. The chief pro-Soviet voices in the government were Sun and Feng Yu-xiang, who served as vice commissioner of the KMT Military Affairs Commission (the commissioner being Chiang Kai-shek), throughout the 1930s. For example, Feng believed that among Japan's enemies—Britain, America, and Russia—the last was the only anti-imperialist country that also shared Japan's threat geographically with China. Though he applied the aphorism "An enemy's enemy is my friend" also to the Anglo-Americans, Feng consistently argued and pushed for cooperation with the Soviets as the basis of China's foreign policy.[32]

The position of the government differed essentially little from this public expectation of closer Sino-Soviet relations. Of course it was concerned with the Soviet support for the Communists as it was trying to eliminate the Red

Army before 1937. After restoration of relations with the Soviets, Zhang Chong, a KMT official who played a role in later KMT-CCP and Sino-Soviet relations, warned of Soviet ideological subversions in *Shishi Monthly,* a CC Clique publication. (The CC was an important faction under Chiang Kai-shek whose head, Chen Li-fu, was instrumental in establishing a wartime alliance with the Soviet Union.) Yet he hoped that Moscow would send experts to investigate the Chinese situation and would not believe the groundless reports by the CCP, so that cooperative relations could be formed. In the same issue of the magazine, another author complemented Zhang by saying that China should give the Soviet Union the benefits of China's market and trade to force it to abandon the CCP. Then the two countries could join hands against Japan.[33] Previously Chiang Kai-shek had slaughtered hundreds of Communists in the 1927 coup that ended the Soviet influence in China, and until 1937 he had been conducting military campaigns to wipe out the CCP and Red Army. Yet, in spite of his bad relations with Moscow and his public hostility toward the Soviet Union, Chiang secretly proposed a Sino-Soviet military alliance as early as 1935.[34]

Similarly, the United States and Britain were widely considered as possible allies against Japan. The Chinese in the 1930s always put the Anglo-American powers into the category of Open Door imperialism. However, the national crisis resulted in a change of attitude. For example, in a forum organized by *Diplomatic Monthly,* Wang Diao-pu, a columnist, showed almost blind faith in America's Open Door Policy and Nonrecognition Doctrine, which, according to him, protected both American economic interests and China's integrity. Since the United States was the only Western power sympathetic to and supportive of China, he urged that the anti-imperialist slogans such as "American cultural aggression," "religious aggression," and "economic imperialism" be dropped from descriptions of the United States.[35]

Geopolitical analysis also put the United States in the category of alliance. "To befriend distant countries and to attack nearby ones" was an old Chinese geopolitical dictum. It was revived and commonly used in discussions about foreign policy. Hu Huan-yong, a professor of geography at National Central University, did a geopolitical analysis of international relations and concluded that Japan was a predestined enemy of China whereas the United States was the opponent of Japan's designs on China.[36]

American-educated diplomats and intellectuals were most active in propagating pro-American policies. Among them were Hu Shi, Wellington Koo, and T. V. Soong (brother-in-law of Chiang Kai-shek and finance minister). Jiang Ting-fu, a graduate of Oberlin and Columbia, contended that the United States was the only country that dared to challenge Japan and that foreign aid from imperialist powers was crucial for China's survival. "If any foreign aid comes," he predicted, "it will be from the Nine Power Treaty countries. The Nine Power Treaty and the preservation of China's territorial and administrative integrity were beneficial not only to China but also to these powers."[37] It was exactly along this line of thought that the secretary general of the Chinese Military Staff, Dr. Yu, asked for American help. He further argued that Japan was a potential enemy of the United States and consequently it would be to the advantage of the United States to assist China.[38] Even though Stimson's Nonrecognition Doctrine received some criticism, it was generally appreciated in China. The failure to deter Japan's aggression in Manchuria, for example, was blamed on British non-co-operation with the United States. Britain was generally viewed as a partner with the United States in the Far East, though many people still had strong confidence in the role Britain could play by itself.

Different emphases and biases notwithstanding, a common denominator in these discussions was very clear: foreign alliances were indispensable for China's survival. For most people, the international coalition against Japan meant cooperation with two major Pacific powers, the Soviet Union and the United States, and, only to a lesser extent, with Britain. Zhang Zhong-fu, a diplomatic historian who became a foreign policy adviser to Chiang Kai-shek during the war, proposed tripartite cooperation among China, the Soviet Union, and the United States. "Under the premise of resisting the Japanese," he wrote, "the cooperation among these three countries is really necessary. If this anti-Japanese effort is to have important effects, then every country in this tripartite cooperation is indispensable."[39] This hope for a common alliance against Japan explains why the Chinese hailed the restoration of relations between the United States and the Soviet Union in 1933. It is not difficult to see the link between China's security and the improvement of relations with Japan's potential adversaries. During the height of the appeasement period in 1934, Sun Lin-sheng, a well-known columnist, articulated the beliefs and hopes of many Chinese in the *Eastern Miscellany*:

> At present, China, for its own survival, has to take advantage of the conflicts between Japan and the Soviet Union, Japan and the United States, and to ally with Russia and America to contain Japan. Moreover, China should actively prevent rapprochement between Japan and the United States, Japan and the Soviet Union. Making Russia and America our allies in the common struggle against Japan is the only diplomacy for China.[40]

The government leaders were not immune to these widespread perceptions. They might not have been so outspoken about it for fear of provoking

Japan, which was accusing China of playing the powers against it. However, evidence suggests that their views were not very different from those discussed above. Wang Ching-wei, the premier who was responsible for foreign policy from 1932 to 1935, was publicly known as an appeaser of Japan. Yet, in his view, there were two functions of diplomacy, the positive and the passive. The passive function was to reduce the number of enemy countries, as Bismarck did during the German unification. Bismarck isolated his enemy, Denmark, and befriended Austria and other countries. The positive function of diplomacy, according to Wang, was to increase one's allies. His favorite example was France after the Prusso-French war. France was in every way inferior to Germany, but France allied herself first with Russia and England and then with Italy and the United States. The consequence was victory over Germany during the first world war.[41] However, he could not openly advocate playing the powers against Japan for fear of provoking Japan's further aggression. As he once wrote, "If we harbor a scheme against another, it is dangerous to let it be known."[42] Wang favored a gradualist course of building up national strength first and opposed any premature showdown with Japan. Yet he never really abandoned the idea of approaching the powers until after the Sino-Japanese War broke out in 1937.

On the KMT left, Feng Yu-xiang favored immediate national mobilization against Japan. In his repeated suggestions to Chiang, Feng urged that China should send top officials to the Soviet Union and the United States to work out anti-Japanese cooperation.[43] Hu Han-min, a major opponent of Chiang Kai-shek, assailed Nanking's foreign policy in his publication *Sanmin Zhuyi Monthly* from 1931 to his death in 1936 due to his bitter power struggle with Chiang. In fact, he was highly in favor of allying with the imperialist powers to resist Japan. In an interview with a Western reporter, Hu even urged Britain, the Soviet Union, and the United States for closer cooperation.[44]

INEVITABILITY OF WAR

Interestingly enough, the above ideas were proposed and discussed in a period when responses to the Chinese request for help from the United States, Britain, and the Soviet Union were far from satisfactory, and the formation of anti-Japanese alliances was out of the question. Then the question remains: In such an unfavorable situation, how could the Chinese conceive and sustain the idea in the first place? In a nutshell, the idea of seeking anti-Japanese alliances was based ultimately on a commonly shared stereotypical belief that conflict between Japan and the Anglo-American powers and between Japan and the Soviet Union was inevitable.

Psychologically, the fear of Japan's ambitions and power was partially responsible for this belief. Plagued by the worldwide depression and pressured by its large population, the Japanese expansion into Manchuria and then all of China appeared to the Chinese only too obvious. Even before the Manchurian Incident occurred, most Chinese believed in the existence of a Japanese blueprint of conquest, the Tanaka Memorial, which was widely publicized and supposed to be the core of the Japanese continental policy.[45]

The Japanese occupation of Manchuria and then North China did much to promote such Chinese fear. The Tanggu Truce of 1933 legitimized Japan's control of China north of the Great Wall; the Amau Statement of 1934, which was called the Asian Monroe Doctrine, proclaimed that Japan had a special duty to maintain order in East Asia; and the He-Umetsu Agreement of 1935 drove Chiang's Central Army from North China. To the Chinese eye, facts like these indicated that the Japanese were carrying out their preconceived plan of conquest.

This fear was coupled with the awareness of China's inability to defend herself. Chiang Kai-shek's assessment of the relative strength of China and Japan led him to the conclusion that Japan could destroy China in a short time. Chiang's point was not merely to justify his non-resistance policy and to carry out war against the Communists. There was some truth in his belief.[46] Others might not have agreed with his pessimism, but not even his opponents disputed Japanese military and economic superiority. Partly responsible for this pessimistic outlook was China's political division. C. Martin Wilbur rightly characterized this period of Chinese history as "military separatism."[47] Little wonder that in a country divided and ruled by many power-holders, unity was considered a precondition to resist Japan by both Chiang and his opponents, though means to achieve it differed. While the CCP and other opponents, much for their own self-interests, demanded unity and an end to the civil war, Chiang Kai-shek desired unity by force and was determined to wipe out the CCP and other regional warlords before confronting Japan.

Hence, expecting Japan's foes to challenge its expansionism became a psychological necessity for the public and a political necessity for the government. The collapse of the postwar world order as symbolized by Japan's invasion of Manchuria undoubtedly encouraged the Chinese hope. Many Chinese believed that Japan and Germany had destroyed the balance among the powers of the Versailles and Washington systems (e.g., the Nine Power Treaty). The powers had entered into a new period of redividing the world.[48]

The uncertain and chaotic international situation formed the basis for a common belief in China that war among the imperialist countries, especially between Japan and the United States, was inevitable. At work here was the economic interpretation of imperialism, according to which the powers depended on China for resources and markets. The Great Depression sped up the conflicts among these powers. It was under these circumstances that Japan's expansion in China occurred and threatened to destroy the Open Door Policy championed by the Anglo-American powers. The Chinese saw the conflict in terms of Japan's determination to "occupy China alone" and the powers' desire to jointly exploit it. Therefore, this conflict of economic interests would necessarily lead to war. For evidence, they pointed to the Stimson Doctrine, the Amau Doctrine, the disagreements over the Naval Treaty, and so on.[49] Ma Xing-ye, a journalism professor who became press director for the Ministry of Information after Pearl Harbor, was among those who believed in the inevitability of war. Like most Chinese, he argued that "the China question is the center of the Pacific problem for China, the United States, and Japan whereas the naval question is only the surface." After observing naval development in Japan and the United States, Ma concluded: "The United States not only cannot avoid the war but will probably be the first to start it." Ma's view represented a general consensus, though predictions about the timing of this world war differed.[50]

The other focus of the so-called inevitability of war idea was on Soviet-Japanese relations. Nearly everybody in China viewed socialism as totally incompatible with capitalism; a war between the two systems was just a matter of time. The Japanese expansion in China accompanied by the anticommunist rhetoric made such a conflict seem more imminent. In fact, Japan's occupation of Manchuria was seen as the first step toward attacking the Soviet Union.[51] In spite of Soviet conciliatory overtures to Japan, relations between the two countries never improved and both prepared for war. The Soviets had been steadily strengthening their Far Eastern military capability since 1931. Tensions along the Soviet-Manchurian border tended to worsen as time went on. The Comintern's call for a popular front against the Fascist powers was in part related to these tensions. It is understandable that the Communists, partially following the Soviet rhetoric, accepted the idea of an imminent Japanese attack on the Soviet Union.

Some conservative opinion leaders also regarded the Soviet-Japanese conflict as inevitable. For example, in the opinion of Fu Si-nian, a member of the *Independent Review* group and a member of the National Defense Council after 1937, the Soviet efforts to reduce hostilities through peace diplomacy were just tactics to build up its economy and its military for the eventual showdown with Japan or the other powers. Though also fully aware of the Soviet problem of a two-front war, Fu still thought that a Soviet-Japanese war would break out at any moment.[52]

These beliefs were the rationale for seeking anti-Japanese alliances. For most Chinese, the world in the 1930s was a battlefield between two camps: the peace-loving camp (the Soviet Union, the democracies, and China) and the aggressor camp (Japan, Germany, and Italy). China needed foreign assistance from the peace camp, without which it would not be able to fight to recover its lost land. It therefore appeared quite logical that China should in some way take advantage of the situation and become an ally to the opponents of Japan. Little wonder that one lecturer at Qing Hua University said that "only when Japan is at war with another country can we take advantage of it and force Japan out of our Manchuria." Similarly, another person even openly advocated world war and entitled his article "We Need a Second World War."[53]

Consequently, between 1931 and 1936 there was an unusual obsession with a second world war, and predicting its outbreak became something of a political fashion. In 1932, the *Shenbao Monthly* sponsored a forum on the Manchurian Incident and the possibility of another world war.[54] World war was such a popular subject in the following year that the *Eastern Miscellany* also called on well-known intellectuals to offer their opinions on the possibility of a Pacific war.[55]

There were numerous books and hundreds of articles predicting the next great war. The Chinese concerns with and predictions of such a war, especially a Japanese-American war, reflected the influence of Japanese and Western writings on this subject. For example, H. C. Bywater's *The Great Pacific War,* which described a possible Japanese-American conflict, was translated into Chinese and widely read. So was John Steel's *Second World War.* There were many writers in Japan forecasting an inevitable war between Japan and the United States. Some of these books, such as Chuko Ikezaki's *Discourse on Pacific Strategy* (1932), were also translated into Chinese. Most prophets of war also regarded the year 1936 as the most likely time for the war to start. So widespread was such a belief that an author adopted *1936* as the title of his book and a 1936 Association was even formed at Peking University, making the study of war and its prediction its main business.[56]

Of course such predictions of a 1936 war lost their credibility when the year arrived; the forecasting of war itself did not. An article in the *Independent Review* argued that the war was merely postponed and conditions were not yet ready. "The angel of peace has never been a match for the god of war." According to the author, when the Soviet Union rid itself of its Western worries, when Japan destroyed all American interests, and when Stimson's big navy program was complete, the armed forces of these countries would eventually attack Tokyo.[57]

The idea of inevitable war between Japan and other powers was part of Chiang Kai-shek's mentality. As a matter of fact, three days after Japan attacked Manchuria, Chiang considered the act the "beginning of the Second World War" and wondered whether other world leaders had realized the seriousness of the situation.[58] A clearer indication was a speech Chiang gave to the army staff college in 1932. He asserted, "How many years do we have to prepare for the Second World War? What kind of plan shall we prepare? In my opinion, it is 1936 when the second world war will probably break out. Therefore, we have only five years to prepare." If preparations were made well and early, Chiang continued, a new China would emerge from this world war.[59]

Chiang also held that the Sino-Japanese conflict would give birth to the coming world war. He consistently emphasized that the Sino-Japanese conflict was a world problem because "China was a subcolony, that is, a joint colony of the world [powers]. Therefore, to completely control China, Japan will have to fight other powers."[60] Chiang was so confident that in 1934 he described the following war scenario in his diary:

1. Japan wants to conquer China without resorting to force;
2. To conquer China by using threats and by supporting its puppets;
3. Militarily attacks China in the end;
4. China then resists;
5. (The Sino-Japanese War) causes international invention and thus causes the world war.[61]

These kinds of perceptions of Japan's conflict with the powers provided the basis for the Chinese quest for anti-Japanese alliances during the 1930s.

There was, of course, a small minority that considered such ideas simplistic. For example, Wang Ching-wei, premier and foreign minister for four years, was disappointed with the powers after 1933 and did not believe that China would benefit from a world war. Nonetheless Wang never denied the imminent danger of war and stressed long-term reconstruction of the country as the most effective way to deal with Japan rather than relying totally on foreign powers. But Wang was in the minority and even his position in the government depended on Chiang's support.

These perceptions appeared to be proven correct by the ensuing events that culminated in Pearl Harbor. Yet in the first half of the 1930s, they were perhaps illusions more than anything else, certainly not accurate predictions of war. Significantly enough, the Chinese had become captives of their own creations and acted according to these perceptions. "If men define situations as real, they are real in their consequences."[62] Therefore, the most realistic policy of reaching some kind of accommodation with Japan immediately after the Manchurian Incident was excluded as an option. Later, the gradualist approach was also rejected by the nation. Pursuing anti-Japanese alliances, clandestinely or openly, was the only diplomatic strategy. These perceptions of inevitable conflicts between Japan and other powers furnished China with hope and can explain in part why China fought Japan against all odds after 1937. It was their persistent, though at times precarious, efforts to hang on in war that made conflicts between Japan and the powers difficult to resolve and finally led to war. These consequences would have been different had the Chinese not had these perceptions of imperialist conflicts. The following chapters will trace how this idea of forging anti-Japanese alliances fared in the 1930s and how the internal and external political conflicts affected the pursuit of this idea.

2

The International Approach to the Manchurian Crisis, 1931-1933

On the night of September 18, 1931, the Japanese Kwantung Army attacked the Chinese troops. Subsequently it occupied all of Manchuria and set up a puppet regime, Manzhouguo, in early 1932. In response, the Nanking government steadfastly pursued an international solution to the Sino-Japanese conflict. It relied on the League of Nations, counted on the support of Anglo-American powers, and tried to bring in the Soviet Union as a counter-weight to Japanese expansion on the Asian continent.[1] Though somewhat immature and inconsistent, Nanking's attempt at forming an international coalition against Japan was very indicative of Chinese perceptions and foreshadowed China's diplomacy in the 1930s.

REACTIONS TO THE MANCHURIAN INCIDENT

The invasion of Manchuria confirmed China's worst fears about Japanese imperialist ambitions. Yet, the Nanking government under Chiang Kai-shek found itself unable to deal with the crisis. Faced with challenges to his power from Communists and other militarist groups, Chiang acknowledged in his diary that "there is no way of remedying the situation." On September 21, Chiang immediately organized a Special Foreign Affairs Commission. Dai Ji-tao, a KMT ideologue and longtime friend of Chiang Kai-shek, was selected to be chairman and T.V. Soong, Chiang Kai-shek's brother-in-law, to be vice chairman. Its membership included about a dozen people. Chiang also ordered military operations against the KMT Canton regime and the Communists to be temporarily halted.[2]

Nanking's initial military response to the crisis was a preconceived policy of nonresistance. Two months before the Manchurian Incident, Chiang had instructed Zhang Xue-liang, commander of the Northeast Army, to avoid conflict with Japan.[3] Zhang, who fully concurred with such a policy, was also keenly aware that China would lose in a war with Japan at this time. Japan might use such a war not only to demand indemnity but more importantly, Zhang feared, to seize territories, possibly all of Manchuria. Therefore, Zhang considered it "absolutely necessary to avoid conflicts."[4]

In the immediate aftermath of the incident, Chiang issued no orders for active military resistance. Instead, he constantly urged his generals to refrain from escalating the conflict and to wait for an international settlement. In late September, at a meeting of KMT party members in Nanking, Chiang asked them to "fight might with right and to fight barbarity with peace. We must . . . tolerate oppression so as to wait for international justice."[5] At the ceremony of Wellington Koo's inauguration as acting foreign minister two months later, Chiang further articulated the same theme. Not only did he reiterate the diplomatic solution as "ten, a hundred, or a thousand times more effective than a military solution," but also emphasized the need to quell the internal Communist revolution first.[6] Formally this became known as the Policy of Internal Pacification before External Resistance (*an nei rang wai*), to which Chiang adhered until the Sian Incident of 1936. The emotional public, however, refused to accept such a policy. From the beginning of the crisis to the outbreak of fighting in Shanghai in January 1932, students in major cities, especially in Peking and Shanghai, opposed the government, sometimes with violence. Foreign Minister Wang Zheng-ting was beaten by students. So were other government officials such as Cai Yuan-pei, a famous and well-respected intellectual and minister of education, and Chen Ming-shu, the acting premier, in late December 1931. The KMT headquarters in Shanghai was attacked by students, and its mayor, Zhang Qun, had to resign because of the protest movements. Chiang Kai-shek, under pressures from the KMT Canton faction and public anger, also had to resign in December. Petitioning students from all over the country came to Nanking demonstrating against the policy of nonresistance. At a news conference held in Nanking in mid-December, students demanded China's withdrawal from the League of Nations and severance of diplomatic relations with Japan.[7]

The students were not alone. Practically every section of the population found fault with the government policy. Many kinds of anti-Japanese organizations issued public circular telegrams and statements demanding decisive action from the government. In Shanghai alone, there were 523 such public declarations before December 31, about 10 percent of which asked for a declaration of war. Labor unions, university associations, and even a Christian salvation society joined the outcry for resistance war.[8] As Dong Lin recalled, the "nonresistance policy was disliked by an overwhelming majority of the population, whose support could no longer be maintained merely by words without deeds in respect of the preservation of the territorial integrity against Japanese aggression."[9]

RELIANCE ON THE LEAGUE AND WESTERN POWERS

The decision to rely on the League of Nations was made by Chiang Kai-shek on September 20, 1931, the day he returned to Nanking. There seemed to be some opposition to this approach within the Special Foreign Affairs Commission. Dai Ji-tao, T. V. Soong and Wellington Koo all seemed to favor direct negotiations with Japan because they doubted the League's ability to halt Japanese advances. On the morning of September 19, the day after the Manchurian Incident started, the Japanese minister, Shigemitsu Mamoru, called upon T. V. Soong in an attempt to resolve the problem locally. A preliminary understanding seemed to have been reached that a joint commission be established with three members each from China and Japan to prevent deterioration of the situation and to find a solution. The understanding was welcomed by Foreign Minister Shidehara of Japan.[10] However, Chiang Kai-shek convened a meeting of high officials on September 21, which Soong also attended, and made the final decision to appeal to the League. He asserted: "In my opinion, we should first take the case of Japanese aggression in the Eastern provinces to the League of Nations and signatories of Kellogg-Briand Pact. At this time we can only resort to international justice."[11] Chiang Kai-shek explained his decision later to Zhang Xue-liang: "The reason why the central government tried to use the League to solve this problem is to maintain China's international status and to reduce the direct Japanese pressure on Chinese forces. This is the only way out." He was confident that Japan would not dare to ignore the League's resolution of September 30 urging the withdrawal of Japanese troops.[12]

The Japanese aggression caught Chiang Kai-shek's Nanking government in a serious dilemma. He was ruling over a divided party in a divided country where national authority was limited by independent political-military power centers. The Canton KMT faction openly defied him by setting up a rival regime; the Chinese Communists were expanding their bases in Jiangxi province, and both were determined to overthrow Nanking. To fight Japan would mean that Nanking would lose militarily to either the Canton regime or the Communists;

not to fight would indicate capitulation and result in defeat on domestic propaganda fronts against Nanking's enemies. However, to escape this dilemma Chiang could wage a diplomatic war against Japan by invoking international assistance. If Japan was checked by the powers, Nanking could claim some credit for its foreign policy without losing control of the domestic situation.

Once Chiang decided to rely solely on the League, Soong was forced to abandon his understanding with Shigemitsu. He informed the Japanese consul general in Nanking that the government had decided to appeal to the League of Nations because Japan's actions were "warlike operations on a large scale"—more serious than a local clash—and a joint commission could no longer deal with the situation. By now, Nanking had obviously closed the door to bilateral direct negotiations, on which Japan was insisting, for fear of a Carthaginian peace.[13] Others, like Wellington Koo and Luo Wen-gan, who was to become foreign minister in 1932, believed that direct negotiations would be inevitable. In their opinions, a historical precedent such as the solution of the Shandong problem at the Washington Conference could serve as a formula for direct Sino-Japanese negotiations with a third power present. The presence of a third party would cushion Japanese pressures and consequently benefit China. But like Chiang Kai-shek, majority members of the Special Foreign Affairs Commission opposed such a move and placed faith in the League of Nations.[14] The predominant official sentiments were expressed by Huang Fu, Chiang's close friend and a former KMT foreign minister. "We cannot have war, nor can we have peace," he wrote Chiang. "The only way out is to rely on international sanctions and at the same time unify our country."[15]

With direct bilateral negotiations ruled out, the business of the Special Foreign Affairs Commission was primarily to direct diplomatic efforts toward the League and other powers. As early as September 19, Nanking instructed Shi Zhao-ji, Chinese delegate to the League of Nations, to request that the League force a Japanese withdrawal from occupied Chinese territories. Shi was also instructed to state that "China will abide by any decision the League of Nations makes with regard to this matter."[16] Shi spoke on the same day at the League Council, to which China had been elected a member only five days earlier. Shi invoked Article 11 of the League Covenant that obligated the League to take "any action that may be deemed wise and effectual to safeguard the peace of nations." After many discussions and debates, the Council passed a resolution on September 30, calling on Japan to withdraw all its troops "as speedily as may be." [17]

The withdrawal of Japanese forces was crucial not only to China's sovereignty but also to the prestige of the Nanking government. China therefore insisted on the withdrawal of troops and the participation of a third party as preconditions for opening negotiations with Japan. On October 19, Chiang Kai-shek and key members of the Special Foreign Affairs Commission added a timetable of ten days for a complete withdrawal of Japanese troops.[18] This was so important to China that, at one point, T. V. Soong was even willing to concede to Japan economic domination in Manchuria and control over railroads already built and still under construction in exchange for the withdrawal of troops.[19] At the League, Shi Zhao-ji was instructed by the Special Foreign Affairs Commission to push for the passage of a resolution stipulating a timetable of Japanese troop withdrawal before the current session adjourned. On October 24, the League Council did pass a resolution asking the Japanese government to completely withdraw its troops before November 16.[20]

In its effort to secure foreign assistance, the Chinese government also approached the United States. Immediately after the Manchurian Incident, the Chinese representative in Washington urged the United States to "take such steps as will insure the preservation of peace in the Far East and the upholding of the principle of peaceful settlement of international disputes."[21] Before the United States was formally invited to participate in the League of Nations' deliberations on the Manchurian crisis, Wellington Koo, acting foreign minister, requested that the United States send an observer to the League Council. T. V. Soong and Yan Hui-qing, a veteran diplomat and a member of the Special Foreign Affairs Commission, each independently asked the United States to call a conference either on the basis of the Kellogg-Briand Pact or the Nine Power Treaty.[22] Though the United States opposed Japan's expansion and was even willing to cooperate by sending an American observer to the League meetings, no American commitment of any kind was in the offing. Nor did the United States have any intention of invoking either the Kellogg-Briand Pact or the Nine Power Treaty, which would obligate it to intervene.

China's international approach was ultimately based on the perceptions of the relations among powers mentioned earlier. For example, Japanese expansionism was thought to necessarily threaten the interests of the Anglo-American powers, who would not tolerate Japan's hegemony and would uphold the Open Door Doctrine and the Nine Power Treaty. Consequently, it was believed that these powers would intervene on China's behalf, as they had done many times in Chinese history, to face the common enemy. Chiang Kai-shek echoed the predominant opinion when he said: "China is a common colony of all powers. If Japan wants to occupy China, it will have to fight these powers. If it cannot defeat them, it cannot establish hegemony in East Asia and hence cannot extinguish us."[23] Little wonder that in his diary

Chiang Kai-shek characterized Japan's action in Manchuria as "the beginning of the Second World War."[24]

The expectation that the powers would counter Japanese expansionism was at the core of a November report by the Special Foreign Affairs Commission. The Commission firmly believed that the League powers Britain and France, due to their own interests in the Far East, would "aim at preventing the success" of Japanese expansion in China. The League, as the only postwar international organization, could still play a significant role in world affairs. Similarly, it considered the United States another stumbling block in Japanese expansion. Traditionally, the United States had been viewed as the champion of the Open Door Policy and of China's territorial integrity. Manchuria threatened to close the door, and in the eyes of the Nanking leaders, "the United States, though avoiding expressing opinions, would possibly resort to the Nine Power Treaty and effectively resist Japan when necessary."[25] In 1931 and 1932, the Nanking government clung tenaciously to these sanguine assumptions.

FOREIGN POLICY OF THE SUN REGIME

Critics of the Nanking government all appeared ultranationalistic in their declarations, but they had no better solution to China's crisis than that of Chiang Kai-shek. After the Manchurian Incident two rival KMT regimes, Nanking and Canton, decided to bury the hatchet, at least on the surface. A Canton-Nanking reconciliation conference was held from the end of October to mid-December 1931, and Wang Ching-wei, chief representative for the Canton side, expressed his wish for diplomatic unity. Both sides viewed Chiang's international approach as the most effective policy. The conference asserted, "Our people should understand that Japan is now in isolation. . . . We should promote the League to realize its spirit of justice."[26]

There was, however, one change in policy: partial resistance should be offered instead of nonresistance. Chiang, who resigned during the negotiations but was still in charge of the government, sent a squadron of planes to reenforce Zhang Xue-liang and ordered him not to retreat from Jinzhou. After Chiang formally stepped down, Sun Ke's regime in Nanking gave by far the most unequivocal order to resist militarily Japan's further attacks.[27]

Hu Han-min, another veteran KMT leader, together with Wang and Chiang, who had just been released from house arrest by Chiang Kai-shek, had a different opinion. Knowing fully well that Chiang had decided to rely on the League of Nations, Hu advised Dai Ji-tao that the central government should negotiate with Japan formally and suggested that a conference of foreign consuls be convened. He criticized Nanking's policy as "no means, no responsibility, and no resistance."[28] Refusing to join the government, he was free to embarrass Chiang and bore no responsibility for any policy failure. Hu's criticism was a result of animosity toward Chiang rather than a responsible policy recommendation. In spite of Hu's opposition, the majority of the KMT leaders seemed to have reached a consensus over Nanking's foreign policy.

With Chiang, Hu, and Wang failing to reach a political compromise, a government headed by Sun Ke was established on New Year's Day of 1932. The new foreign minister, Chen You-ren, who had been a vehement anti-imperialist in the same post in the 1920s, was now more interested in fighting his rivals in Chiang's faction than Japanese imperialism. Both before and after the Manchurian Incident, Chen had negotiated with Japanese officials for a peaceful settlement of the Manchurian crisis. The purpose was to limit Chiang's influence in Manchuria (Zhang Xue-liang was following Chiang at this point). Now in power, Chen continued his contacts with Inukai Tsuyoshi, now Japan's prime minister, in early January hoping to solve the crisis. These attempts failed by January 8, when the Japanese government proved unable to restrain the Kwantung Army.[29] Out of frustration, Chen dramatized this policy in mid-January by proposing to sever diplomatic relations with Japan.[30]

Chen's proposed policy differed little from that of the previous government except for his radical talk of cutting off diplomatic relations. Oddly enough, Chen intended the severance of diplomatic relations as a means to reach agreement with Japan. As he explained, China could then send its army to fight the Communists in Jiangxi as a peace gesture to Japan. Thus, China and Japan might reach a resolution of the current crisis.

However much Chiang relied on the League, he did not see any benefit in escalating the Sino-Japanese crisis. Chiang Kai-shek attacked Chen's rash idea in a speech he gave during his retirement. Not only did he continue to favor a diplomatic solution, but also warned his fellow countrymen with a quotation from Dr. Sun Yat-sen: "If China breaks diplomatic relations, Japan can destroy all of China within ten days." Chiang also wrote letters to those in Nanking trying to stop Chen You-ren's reckless policy.[31] Partly because of Chiang's statement and behind-the-scenes maneuvers, Chen's policy was quickly denied by Sun's regime even though he had secured endorsement earlier. Chen Ming-shu, the vice premier and commander in chief of the 19th Route Army who was neutral between Canton and Nanking factions, shifted to Chiang's side and began to oppose Chen's policy. So did Zhang Ji, a top

KMT figure who had played a key role in bringing about Canton-Nanking reconciliation. Severing diplomatic ties, to most people, would worsen rather than improve relations. Chen's idea did not receive any support from responsible circles. Tientsin *Dagongbao* commented: "If the severance of diplomatic relations was followed by a declaration of war, it is logical; if one cannot declare war, one should not sever diplomatic relations."[32]

The foreign policy of Sun's regime was seemingly in disarray due to the Chen controversy. However, upon close examination, the policy of international cooperation and limited resistance remained in effect. Even Chen himself emphasized the League sanctions and the Nine Power Treaty. If anything, Chen's proposal for severing diplomatic relations with Japan was just a variation of the nonresistance theme, since the Sun-Chen regime had no control over the armed forces and thus had never contemplated a military solution. Like Chiang Kai-shek, Chen relied on international help to solve the Sino-Japanese conflict. As Chen's vice minister, Fu Bing-chang, explained in the *Canton Daily News*, "We proposed severance of diplomatic relations with Japan in order to create a new aspect to the (Sino-Japanese) question with the hope of persuading the signatories of the Nine Power Treaty pact to enforce Articles 15 and 16 of the League."[33]

THE CHIANG-WANG GOVERNMENT AND "RESISTING WHILE NEGOTIATING"

Among the three top leaders of the KMT, Wang Ching-wei and Chiang Kai-shek struck a deal in mid-January 1932, and Hu was forced out. From this point onward, Wang and Chiang cooperated for the next five years. Wang became the premier of the Nanking government and Chiang took charge of military operations against the Communists as well as limited defense against the Japanese. In the Wang-Chiang partnership, nobody had any doubt that the real power was in the hands of Chiang.

The foreign policy of the Wang-Chiang regime was expressed in Wang Ching-wei's slogan "resisting while negotiating." On the surface, it was different from the nonresistance policy, as it supported simultaneously both armed resistance and diplomatic efforts. In actuality, limited resistance was largely for public consumption. The real priority still remained "negotiating" (diplomatic solution) over any military confrontation. The Shanghai war was just such an example. Tension in Shanghai between the Japanese and the Chinese had been escalating since the Manchurian Incident. Contrary to Nanking's conciliatory policy, the 19th Route Army generals opted for resistance on January 28, 1932, and surprised the world by fighting against the Japanese forces. Yet Nanking was still not enthusiastic about the war efforts, though Chiang did send two divisions of his troops to reinforce the 19th Route Army. During a Military Affairs Commission meeting, Chiang and War Minister He Ying-qin opposed the majority opinion to completely support the 19th Route Army and insisted that the war should be localized. When the British and American consuls offered to mediate, He Ying-qin cabled Mayor Wu Tie-cheng to accept the mediation and asked the 19th Army to obey the order not to escalate the war. Chiang's orders to Cai Ting-kai, the 19th Army commander, read "The 19th Route Army should take advantage of its victorious position in the last dozen days, avoid decisive fighting with Japan, and end the war now."[34]

In the meantime, the Chinese government intensified its appeals to the Anglo-American powers. Even before the fighting started, Wang Ching-wei had told the American consul in Nanking that for their own interests, the powers should intervene in Shanghai. It was held among the Chinese that Shanghai was vested with so many Western commercial interests that the powers would not tolerate war in this area. When the fighting began, Foreign Minister Luo Wen-gan requested that the American minister come to Nanking immediately. In keeping with the earlier principle that no negotiations with Japan should be held without the presence of a third party, China repeatedly asked the powers to take part in the negotiations between Japan and China not as observers but as participants.[35] A group of KMT central committee members in Shanghai, including T. V. Soong, Sun Ke, Chen You-ren, and H. H. Kung, were inclined toward resistance and looked to the United States for support. Following the American Nonrecognition Doctrine, Sun Ke and Chen wrote in a newspaper that only a combination of the Anglo-American powers could coerce Japan. They believed that Japan's action in Shanghai was a menace to American security and interests in the Pacific as well as to her prestige. Consequently, the United States would eventually intervene militarily. Such a belief resulted in a government request to the United States to lend China her surplus war materials. However, the United States was unwilling to get involved and did not respond to China's efforts.[36]

The position this Shanghai group took was somewhat different from that of government leaders in Nanking. They insisted to Nanking, and later during negotiations with Japan, on linking the Shanghai war with the Manchurian problem. Such a linkage might have been conceived as a means to involve the powers to solve the Manchurian problem. They opposed the central government's desire to localize the Shanghai conflict and put strong pressure on

Nanking by publicly demanding "unshakable and complete resistance," and "reinforcements to the 19th Route Army and other air, navy, and army forces to defend Shanghai." They even demanded counterattacks to recover Manchuria.[37]

By comparison, Chiang Kai-shek and his followers desired a speedy diplomatic settlement of the Shanghai war. They worried that with new enforcements, Japan now was in a better military position in Shanghai and that linking the Shanghai war with the Manchurian problem would not benefit China. They, too, insisted on the participation of the powers as "the most important strategy" for China, "in order not to be isolated when it comes to the solution of the entire problem."[38] This basic tendency to win the goodwill of the powers and the League of Nations was reflected in China's general willingness to accept mediation. In the negotiations facilitated by the powers in March and April, China demanded a fixed schedule for the withdrawal of Japanese troops and the restoration of the status quo ante. A truce agreement was finally signed on May 5 by which Japan agreed to withdraw troops to the settlement area, but without a timetable, and Chinese troops were to remain in their present positions until the situation became normal. As measured by the moderate demands of the Nanking government, this compromise was to a certain degree satisfactory. The Manchurian problem, however, was left for the League of Nations to reach a verdict on at a later date.

The truce agreement did not meet the radical demands of Nanking's opponents and thus came under attack. The Southwest Political Council, the former Canton government, the KMT central committee members in Canton, and Chen You-ren all denounced it as an insult to the nation and accused the government of betraying its own policy of limited resistance and of deceiving the public. More important, they demanded that Japan withdraw from all of China and criticized the government for having acquiesced to the status quo in Manchuria by separating it from the Shanghai settlement.[39]

PLAYING THE SOVIET CARD?

The Manchurian Incident also caused a change of attitude toward the Soviet Union. Geopolitically, the Soviet Union occupied a unique position during the Manchurian crisis. Though it was not a member of the postwar international system, both China and the League of Nations acknowledged its strategic significance and sought its participation in the solution of the crisis. In addition, Japan's anticommunist policies made Soviet Russia even more attractive to China as a counterweight to Japanese expansion.

China's relations with the Soviet Union had been strained since the CCP-KMT split in 1927. Moreover, anticommunism in China resulted in the severance of diplomatic relations, and a border war was fought in 1929 over the Chinese Eastern Railway. Negotiations were being conducted before the Manchurian Incident, but no serious efforts were made to improve relations. Now the Japanese aggression produced a change of attitude and incentives to better relations with the Soviets.

The government was reevaluating its Soviet policy. The KMT leftists, such as Sun Ke, demanded a reorientation of policy. By early 1932, the KMT Central Political Council (CPC), which was temporarily influenced by Sun, passed a resolution to restore diplomatic relations with the Soviet Union. The decision was clearly a response to the national mood. It was designed to bring in Soviet participation as a component of the international solution of the Manchurian problem. To further maximize the Soviet role, it was also decided to conclude a treaty of nonaggression as a first step in normalizing relations.[40] They thought that the restoration of relations and conclusion of nonaggression treaty would strengthen China's position vis-a-vis Japan and expected the Soviet Union to respond positively since in so doing the Soviets could break their international isolation.

The change of governments in January and February slowed down the process of establishing relations with the Soviet Union. Wang Ching-wei was not as enthusiastic about the Soviets as Sun Ke. At the KMT's Second Plenary Session of the Fourth Congress from March 1 to 6, Sun and Chen You-ren insisted on the restoration of Sino-Soviet diplomatic relations as a major topic of discussion, but the matter was tabled for the time being. Chiang Kai-shek, however, favored establishing ties with the Soviet Union and requested that Wang Ching-wei and Foreign Minister Luo Wen-gan prepare such a plan.[41] Perhaps because of Chiang's direct intervention, on May 19 the CPC's foreign affairs committee passed a resolution to restore relations with the Soviets in principle and ordered Luo Wen-gan and Jiang Zuo-bin, a KMT veteran general and diplomat, to recommend concrete steps toward such a goal.[42]

Although in principle everyone in the government agreed to the restoration of relations with the Soviets, there were apparently two different approaches to this problem. Besides KMT leftist politicians, career diplomats like Wellington Koo were also in favor of an active Soviet policy to establish close relations without any preconditions so that China could win the Soviet Union to her side. Koo, then the Chinese official assessor accompanying the Lytton Commission of Inquiry in the spring of 1932, was afraid that the Soviets and the Japanese might strike a deal in Manchuria. While in

Manchuria, Koo was alarmed by "flirtations" between Japanese and Russian officials. Koo warned that if China failed to approach the Soviet Union quickly, it would become "passive" and might, for its own interests, recognize Manzhouguo and compromise with Japan. Once that happened, according to Koo, it would cause serious global repercussions. Japan would grow bolder and ignore any action the Anglo-American powers might take to help China. Koo's fears were shared by many in the government. The Soviet Union had repeatedly proposed a nonaggression pact with Japan after December 1931. If such a pact were assigned and there were a Sino-Japanese war, the staff officers of Chiang's Military Affairs Commission feared that the consequences would be disastrous beyond imagination. Furthermore, any possibility of Soviet-American cooperation in the Far East against Japan would be lost. Consequently, they all wanted a speedy rapprochement with the Soviets.[43]

On the other hand, Chiang and Wang Ching-wei favored a much more cautious approach. Wang feared that close Sino-Soviet ties might trigger negative reactions from Western powers who avoided diplomatic relations with the Soviet Union. The image of the Sino-Soviet alliance against the imperialist powers from the mid-1920s was only a few years old. Moreover, moving too close to the Soviets might lend credence to Japanese propaganda about the Sovietization of China. Thus, it would cost China the sympathy of these countries, on which China's international solution of the Manchurian crisis was based. Therefore, the policy Luo Wen-gan and Jiang Zuo-bin recommended emphasized the necessity to assure the Anglo-American powers that China would not politically or militarily ally with the Soviet Union. This policy resulted in an unfeasible proposal that China, Japan, and the Soviet Union conclude a tripartite nonaggression pact with an international guarantee. The restoration of relations was conditional upon signing such a pact. The proposed formula, according to Wang Ching-wei, would bind both Japan and the Soviet Union to respect China's territorial integrity, and, at the same time, China would not be suspected of being procommunist.[44] In June, Wang actively pushed for this tripartite nonaggression pact and tried to secure an international guarantee by urging Lord Lytton to play a role in this scheme. Wang obviously tried to link his Soviet policy to China's reliance on the League of Nations as a comprehensive international solution.[45]

Nanking did have plenty of reasons to promote a nonaggression treaty. First, the Soviet Union had already brought Outer Mongolia under firm control and might take advantage of the Sino-Japanese conflict to further extend its control to Xinjiang. Second, it worried about Soviet support for the Chinese Communists. A nonaggression treaty would restrict Soviet activities in these regions and in support of the CCP.[46] Chiang Kai-shek gave his support to Wang's handling of the Soviet policy when they met at Guling, his summer residence, in June 1932. Chiang insisted not only on a nonaggression treaty as a precondition to a restoration of diplomatic relations, but also on Soviet recognition of China's sovereignty in Outer Mongolia. Even if in July Wang appeared to have abandoned these preconditions, Chiang still held his opinions in the next two months.[47]

Once this policy was established, the Foreign Ministry immediately ordered Wang Ceng-si, a Chinese official in charge of trade negotiations in Moscow, to relay the message to the Soviet government and to start negotiations. The response was not enthusiastic, even though the Soviets had expressed the desire to restore relations as early as December 1931. Wang Ceng-si was ignored for a month and was not received by the chief of the China section of the Far Eastern Division in the Soviet Foreign Ministry until June 20, 1932.[48]

From the very beginning, Wellington Koo objected to any kind of precondition to restoring relations. He not only urged the government to realize the common interests of China and the Soviet Union, but also took up personal diplomacy to advance his cause. In June, with the consent of Foreign Minister Luo Wen-gan, he took the initiative of sending his personal representative, Harry Hussey, to Moscow to see Karakhan, Soviet deputy commissar of foreign affairs, whom Koo had known since the 1920s. Hussey, a Canadian architect who had worked in China since the 1910s and who also knew Karakhan, was in Koo's service. Though he instructed Hussey to present the tripartite nonaggression pact, Wellington Koo wanted the Soviets to know that China would "serve as a bridge" between the Soviet Union and the United States and that cooperation among the three countries could be established to the benefit of all. Clearly, Koo was implying an anti-Japanese Far Eastern coalition of China, the Soviet Union, and the United States.[49]

Wellington Koo's new initiative did not change the Soviet attitude. Hussey arrived in Moscow but was unable to see anybody in July. Though Hussey finally managed to see Karakhan and transmit the Chinese government's proposals, the Soviet position remained unchanged. The Chinese delegate to the League of Nations, Yan Hui-qing, had several talks with Maxim Litvinov, Soviet commissar for foreign affairs, who headed the Soviet delegation to the World Disarmament Conference in Geneva. The main barrier in these preliminary negotiations was China's insistence on the tripartite nonaggression treaty as a precondition for restoring diplomatic relations. The Soviets objected to such a precondition. They were very suspicious of Nanking's idea of a tripartite pact and viewed it as a scheme to draw the Soviet Union into the Far Eastern conflict.

Since the Soviets feared that supporting the Chinese initiative would create the impression of a Sino-Soviet understanding against Japan, Litvinov repeatedly rejected the proposal.[50]

This cautious approach showed Chinese wishful thinking. The idea of balancing the Soviet Union and Japan in a tripartite arrangement may sound like a plausible strategy, but in reality it was next to impossible to implement given the animosities among Japan, China and the Soviet Union. In September 1932, China dropped this impractical precondition because of Japan's overtures to the Soviets and the possibility of a Japanese-Soviet nonaggression treaty.[51] By December 1932, diplomatic relations were finally normalized between China and the Soviet Union. Though the normalization had very little impact on the solution of the Manchurian crisis, Chiang Kai-shek, like many Chinese, still claimed victory. He wrote in his diary that "restoring relations with Russia is enough to make the Japanese afraid and adds strengths to our national salvation."[52]

WINNING PUBLIC SUPPORT

In January 1932, in order to manipulate public opinion, the government invited well-known intellectuals and prominent people to attend a national conference on the crisis and to offer solutions.[53] Apparently, exposing the public to China's difficulties was a good strategy to win sympathy. For that purpose, Wang Ching-wei dictated three topics to be discussed in the conference: 1) defending the nation against external humiliations; 2) famine relief; and 3) pacification of internal rebels.[54] The message was that fighting Japan and the Communists simultaneously was impossible, and, therefore, that reliance on an international solution was the only sound policy. In order to secure an endorsement of its foreign policy, Wang's government gave public opinion a nominal say in the decision-making process. Once resolutions sympathetic to the government policy were adopted, critics could be silenced.

Most intellectuals of the country did not want to be treated as decorative objects and two-thirds of the invitees, primarily from Peking, Tientsin, and Shanghai, openly refused to participate in the conference. Those who did participate tended to be either progovernment or appreciative of the difficulties the government faced.

Professor Jiang Ting-fu, a prominent scholar on international relations, was among those sympathetic to the government's foreign policy. In an article entitled "How to Utilize the League and the World Powers in Long Term Resistance," he equated the League to a collective security bureau from which China might benefit and argued that it was an important source for China's modernization. He also believed that for their own economic interests, the powers would not allow Japan to prevail in China. In Jiang's view, it was suicidal for China to fight Japan until it became modernized. Consequently, the government's international approach presented no problem for him. Not until the Japanese invasion of Rehe Province later in February 1933 did Jiang Ting-fu begin to reconsider his internationalist position.[55]

Fully aware that the conference on national crisis might not solve any problems, Professor Jiang considered it nonetheless a duty of the conference to lend support to the government in its time of crisis.[56] For the most part, the conference, which was held in the summer of 1932, endorsed the policy of "resisting while negotiating," and yet still demanded better military and diplomatic performances. For example, Gong De-bo, a well-known journalist, demanded that the government send special units to Manchuria as volunteers, reinforce Rehe Province, and even sell national treasures in the Forbidden City to finance the war.[57]

The conference affirmed support for the international approach to the Sino-Japanese conflict. One proposal specifically insisted on the convening of a second Nine Power Treaty conference to guarantee China's territorial and administrative integrity. There were altogether eight proposals on foreign policy. Virtually all of them talked about a strategy of alliance with Japan's foes. The United States was seen as the most likely ally of China in these schemes. Gong De-bo proposed that the government send high officials to Washington to conclude a secret military alliance. He asserted that Japan had been the imaginary enemy of the United States for a long time and that the reason that the United States hesitated on the Manchurian question was the fear that China would not cooperate with her. Such ideas were purely wishful thinking, and yet some participants sincerely believed them.[58]

The conference also reflected a national consensus on Soviet policy. As mentioned before, the government was reluctant to move quickly toward a close relationship with the Soviet Union for fear that capitalist powers would become apprehensive. Against such a fear, some delegates argued that the powers would become more friendly to China if a close tie was formed with the Soviet Union, for such a relationship would create political and commercial competition between the Soviets and the capitalist countries for China's market and for political control.[59]

China's foreign policy was tested before public opinion when the Lytton Commission published its report in October 1932. By then, the impotence of the League as an effective agency of collective security had been fully revealed to the Chinese. Reflecting its desire not to offend any party, the

Lytton Report was a masterpiece of ambiguity. It implicitly designated Japan as an aggressor and yet it gave special consideration to Japanese interests in Manchuria by recommending the creation of a "highly autonomous region." This autonomous Manchuria was to be run by an advisory body made up of foreigners in which the Japanese would have a strong voice. Although it did not advocate the restoration of the status quo ante, it tried to please the victim by upholding Chinese sovereignty over Manchuria, which meant in effect nonrecognition of Manzhouguo.

Nanking's reaction was by and large favorable. Chiang Kai-shek considered the first eight chapters of the report fair descriptions of the Manchurian situation and was willing to accept them because in the report Japan's military action in Manchuria was considered an act of aggression. However, he could not accept the proposed solutions in chapters nine and ten, which afforded Japan some measure of control in the area. Chiang was even willing to consider the suggestions in the report that Manchuria be demilitarized and that China and Japan sign a nonaggression pact. Yet, deeply distrustful of Japan, he wanted an arrangement like the Locarno Treaty, in which third powers guaranteed its enforcement. Wang Ching-wei agreed with him.[60] As expected, Chiang's opponents within the KMT took a different position. Hu Hanmin and the Southwest Political Council blasted the report as being pro-Japanese and harmful to China. A group of KMT central committee members, including Feng Yu-xiang and Li Lie-jun, also strongly denounced the report as unfair, ambiguous, and sacrificing China's sovereignty.[61]

Chinese public opinion varied on the Lytton Report. The *Dagongbao* considered the controversial proposal of an autonomous Manchuria acceptable so long as Japan withdrew her troops from occupied areas. Moreover, it also accepted the demilitarization in Manchuria. However, the dominant opinion was that the report was fair except for the creation of the autonomous region under a foreign council with China and Japan having basically the same influence: this was a clear compromise of China's sovereignty. Many disappointed critics also accused the League of Nations of being a power broker for imperialist countries, sacrificing China's sovereignty. Little wonder that the press considered the Lytton Report as legalizing Japan's aggression.[62]

In spite of its compromising nature, the Lytton Report did find supporters. Dr. Hu Shi, perhaps the most influential intellectual in China, saw no reason to oppose the plan of the autonomous government in Manchuria, because Nanking was too weak to control the region. In his view, a future federal form of government would be beneficial to China. Hu thought the report reflected the world's opinion of justice. Others from the *Independent Review* group also favored close relations with the League. For example, Ting

Wen-jiang worried that hostility to the League might drive away the friend-liness and sympathy of the powers. Jiang Ting-fu even urged the government to accept the Lytton Report in its entirety. One person compared the League to a mediator in a ransom case whose intentions and efforts should be appreciated. The standard argument of this line of thinking was that China could not afford to lose a friend, even one that was not powerful.[63] But those who were dissatisfied with the report clearly represented the dominant opinion in China. The government's efforts at influencing opinion failed because the gap between public expectations and the government's abilities to realize them was too large to be bridged.

"DISTANT WATER AND NEARBY FIRE": COLLAPSE AT TANGGU

It became clear by the time of the publication of the Lytton Report that the League was a totally impotent organization. Worse for the Chinese, the Japanese army continued to advance into the province of Rehe in late 1932. Once again, Zhang Xue-liang enraged the public by offering almost no resistance. The Japanese army actually occupied the capital city of Rehe with 128 men! This time, even conservative professors from the *Independent Review* favored resistance.[64]

By the beginning of 1933, Japanese forces had taken all of Rehe and were threatening to take the Peking-Tientsin area. Nanking could not lose any more territory and still maintain the legitimacy of the central government of China. Between March and May 1933, Chiang Kai-shek, for the first time since the Manchurian Incident, put up a fight in the well-known Great Wall battles. He even made a secret trip to Peking in late March. About 30 divisions of the Chinese army, 12 of which belonged to the central govern-ment, were thrown into battle. The scale and duration of the war surpassed that of the Shanghai fighting, and China suffered between 20,000 and 30,000 casualties. When the military situation worsened in May, Chiang ordered his generals to defend the Peking-Tientsin area to the last man.[65] The decision to fight also reflected Chiang's disillusionment with the League and the powers. Now that Chiang felt he could no longer rely on the powers to stop Japan, he had to show some determination on the battlefield to halt Japan's advance south of the Great Wall.

Late 1932 was also a time when Chiang was preparing to deal with Japan both militarily and diplomatically. On August 25, 1932, Chiang Kai-shek told Huang Fu that he would open direct negotiations with Japan if there was somebody to deal with and if there was some slight change in Japan's policy. He personally ordered the Chinese minister to Japan, Jiang Zuo-bin, to convey such a signal to the Japanese government.[66] This new posture came at a time when the official policy was to hold no bilateral negotiations. It may have been Nanking's secret diplomatic attempt to appeal to Japanese liberals, but the failure of the League and the powers to live up to Chinese expectations was the main factor in the demarche.

Given public emotions over the Japanese aggression and the political opposition, Chiang had to keep secret his new moves. The result was chaos and inconsistency. The Foreign Ministry continued the internationalist approach by firmly refusing to deal with Japan directly. Foreign Minister Luo Wen-gan ruled out any compromise in a public statement of March 19, 1933. When asked by the American minister, Nelson Johnson, about rumors that Chiang Kai-shek and Wang Ching-wei were willing to engage in direct negotiations with the Japanese, Luo flatly denied them, saying that he favored "nothing but stubborn and at least passive resistance."[67] In February and March, the Foreign Ministry even seriously considered breaking off diplomatic relations with Japan to show China's determined cooperation with the Western powers. It was also rumored in Nanking that Foreign Minister Luo's position was supported by Chiang's rival, the Southwest regime, and T. V. Soong, in order to frustrate the Wang-Chiang government. Such a strong stand by Luo was partly influenced by the Chinese diplomats at Geneva who hoped that their home government could strengthen their position at the League with a better military performance and a strong diplomatic action against Japan. Wellington Koo worried that any compromise or policy of nonresistance would cause 17 months of diplomatic efforts at the League of Nations to be irrevocably lost. Koo and others at Geneva even wished that China would declare war with Japan so that the League would be forced to adopt stronger measures such as economic sanctions. The loss of Rehe so frustrated them that they threatened to resign in protest against the lack of will to resist Japan.[68]

It may seem that China had won a diplomatic battle by adhering to the internationalist policy. After months of maneuvers and compromises, the League adopted the recommendations in the Lytton Report on February 24, 1933. They clearly stated that the Japanese military occupation of Manchuria was "incompatible with the legal principles which should govern the settlement of the dispute."[69] They also recommended negotiations under the auspices of the League. Japan cast the only dissenting vote and withdrew her membership from the League in March. Yet this seeming victory was undermined by secret contacts with Japan and by the heavy military losses along the Great Wall that forced Nanking to search desperately for an alternative. As Wang Ching-wei's protégé Chen Gong-bo admitted in April, the majority of government officials thought that direct negotiations were the only way out.[70]

The internationalist policy collapsed in April and May 1933 when China had to negotiate a settlement with Japan face to face. Huang Fu, who had influential Japanese friends, was named commissioner of civil affairs in North China in hopes that he could make a deal with the Japanese. Huang and other officials, such as Chen Yi, political vice minister of military affairs, and Zhang Qun discussed Sino-Japanese relations with Nemoto Hiroshi, Japanese military attaché, in Shanghai on April 19. On the same day in Peking, He Ying-qin summoned Jiang Meng-lin, president of Peking University, Hu Shi, Ding Wen-jiang, and General Yu Xue-zhong and explained to them the difficulties of the situation. As a result, Hu and Ding, who had been pushing for strong resistance, changed their minds. They all agreed to look for another way to save the Peking-Tientsin area from impending Japanese advances. They sent Jiang Meng-lin to approach the British minister, Miles Lampson, for mediation. Two days later, Chiang Kai-shek and Wang Ching-wei instructed Jiang Meng-lin that China was willing to enter into negotiations for a truce in North China, but not into any political discussions of Manchuria.[71]

The failure of the international approach was in many ways related to the attitudes of the concerned powers. The powers seemed to have lost interest and were unwilling to stick their necks out. Britain was reevaluating its Far Eastern policy and considering a possible understanding with Japan. In early May, Wang Ching-wei, through T. V. Soong, who was in Washington, appealed desperately to the United States for assistance or mediation. The response was "let aggression run its own course." As Stanley Hornbeck of the State Department put it, "The American government should avoid taking any initiative, for the present time at least, along the line apparently sought by the Chinese premier."[72] When President Roosevelt urged nonaggression among nations, Wang lost faith in the powers because moral sympathy could not prevent the loss of the Peking-Tientsin area. He warned Huang Fu not to place any hope in Roosevelt's moral gestures. "Distant water cannot extinguish a nearby fire," he cabled Huang, ". . . and before any Western policy could be backed up by the powers' military strength, China could not change the policy [of coming to terms with Japan]."[73]

The desire of the United States and Britain to avoid conflicts with Japan was fully shared by the Soviet Union. After the Japanese occupation of Manchuria, the Soviet Union grew uneasy about Japanese military intentions and prepared for a possible confrontation. It also advocated international sanctions against Japan at the League of Nations and at the same time tried to appease Japan by offering a nonaggression pact.

One of the sources of Soviet-Japanese conflict was the Chinese Eastern Railway (CER). Though originally built by Russia, it had been jointly owned and operated by China and the Soviet Union since 1924. By May 1933, when China was negotiating the Tanggu Truce, the Soviets were contemplating the sale of the railway in an obvious attempt to avoid conflict with Japan. The Soviet ownership of the railway was a hindrance to Japan, who regarded it as strategically vital to its military operations. Many Soviet employees of the CER were killed, wounded, or harassed, and CER properties were damaged. The Soviets not only moved some of the rolling stock into the Soviet Union, but also charged Japan with failing to pay 30 million Yuan for transporting its troops. Leo M. Karakhan, the Soviet deputy commissar for foreign affairs, was keenly aware of the explosive troubles with Japan and that the Japanese military were "for war with us" and sought "any causes for conflict, sharpening and inflating any sort of misunderstandings that arise between us in Manchuria." Under these circumstances the Soviet Union decided to sell the railroad, sacrificing commercial interests for security since the Soviet Far Eastern forces were not ready to take on the Kwantung Army. Therefore, the sale of the railway, in Karahkan's own words, "knocks the Japanese advocates of war from their position."[74]

The news of the Soviet intention to sell the CER dealt a heavy blow to the Chinese. The Chinese government had hoped that the Soviet ownership would create a more active policy to confront Japan. The Foreign Ministry protested many times from April to June through Ambassador Yan Hui-qing in order to prevent the Soviet sale of the CER. In spite of these protests, Soviet negotiations with Japan's puppet regime started anyway. The Soviet move was disappointing to China; as one high KMT official put it, the initial joy from resuming diplomatic relations with the Soviet Union had been turned into a nightmare.[75]

In late May, the Chinese leaders succumbed to Japanese demands. Huang Fu reported that Japan was going to take Peking and Tientsin. If that happened, the political situation in China would become explosive and the government would be shaken. To prevent that scenario, Nanking instructed him that everything was negotiable so long as it did not imply any recognition of the puppet regime and the cession of the four provinces in North China. The National Defense Council, composed of Wang, Chiang, and other high officials, decided to enter negotiations on the following grounds: first, diplomatically, the Anglo-American powers might be helpful to China but in the short term they could not remove the immediate threat to the Peking-Tientsin area; second, the military could not solve the life-and-death situation either (central government troops in Jiangxi province encircling the Communists could not be moved north, and other forces, such as those in Guangdong and Guangxi provinces, would not accept orders from the central government); third, the government was still short of financial resources, and the loss of Peking and Tientsin would result in the forfeiture of customs receipts, an important source of revenue. Therefore, Nanking decided to sue for truce at the front.[76]

The Chinese diplomats in Geneva objected to any agreement with Japan. Koo wired Nanking arguing that the Sino-Japanese conflict had become a test for the League Covenant and the Kellogg-Briand Pact. The last section of the report adopted by the League Assembly, Koo told his government, stipulated that no country was to take unilateral action with regard to the problem of Manzhouguo. If China concluded a truce, all prior League resolutions against Japan would lose their validity, and China would be discredited. Luo Wen-gan reassured Koo on April 26 that no direct negotiations with Japan were to take place, but the Foreign Ministry and diplomats were not in the inner circle of the KMT decision-making process and were thus not kept well-informed. Luo soon resigned in protest.[77]

On May 31 the Japanese military representative demanded at Tanggu that China sign the Japanese draft agreement without changing a word and within an hour and a half. Chinese delegates complied. According to the agreement, Chinese troops had to withdraw to south of the fighting area and Japanese troops returned to north of the Great Wall. The area was to be patrolled by those Chinese police friendly to Japan and amenable to its wishes.

In spite of its short-term failure, one should note that China's international approach to the Manchurian crisis marked the end of previous revolutionary diplomacy and the beginning of a policy to ally with the powers against Japan, which lasted for the next ten years.

3

Dilemma of Gradualism, 1933–1935

The collapse of the international approach to the Manchurian crisis caused a visible demarche in China's foreign policy. Disappointed with the powers and yet still anticipating an upcoming conflict between Japan and the powers (including the Soviets), the Nanking government pursued a gradualist strategy in order to gain time to establish control all over China. For that purpose, gradualists went out on a limb until the end of 1935 to stabilize Sino-Japanese relations.

The policy of the Chinese government for this period was generally referred to as appeasement. The term has the derogatory connotation of its postwar European definition, and it was something of a misnomer when applied to the Chinese context. Except perhaps in name, Nanking's policy, in its purposes and contexts, had little in common with that pursued by the British and the French. In Britain, for example, it was guided by an appreciation of German grievances and legitimate interests and supported by the pacifist public, which was horrified by World War I.[1] The Chinese situation was the opposite: the public demanded fighting. Unlike the British, who envisioned peace as the objective of the appeasement policy, the Chinese expected an eventual war with Japan. The Nanking government conceived appeasement as an expedient policy. As much as circumstances permitted, it was actively preparing—militarily and diplomatically—for an eventual conflict with Japan by maintaining strong and improving ties with the Powers, including the Soviet Union. Consequently, the term *appeasement,* if not qualified, does not reveal the full intention and implications of Nanking's policy as well as the word *gradualism.* Ironically, the Japanese military in China realized the meaning of gradualism and refused to buy Chiang's friendly overtures at face value even though the Chinese public did.

Eventually, even Chiang's most vehement opponents, such as Feng Yu-xiang, came to realize that Chiang did have a plan for resistance and was preparing the nation for war.[2]

THE GRADUALIST RATIONALE

The gradualists were never a cohesive political group. Political factions in the KMT were formed around personal ties rather than along ideological or political lines. Regardless of their personal affiliations, gradualists were people who shared similar views on China's foreign policy. First, they all believed that China was incapable of fighting Japan and that a premature war would result in defeat and complete Japanese domination of China. They also saw China's political unification and economic modernization as prerequisites for a war with Japan. Third, they viewed the international situation as temporarily unfavorable to China. Their conclusion was that for the survival of the nation, the government should appease Japan while eradicating military-regional rival regimes.

Chief advocates of such a policy were Premier Wang Ching-wei, Chiang Kai-shek, and Huang Fu. Wang had a small band of followers, the KMT Reorganization group, and Chiang controlled many factions, such as the CC Clique, the Whampoa Clique, and the Political Science faction, that were loyal to him and followed his policies. The Political Science faction was especially supportive of the gradualist policy. The main figures in this group, Huang Fu, Zhang Qun, and Yang Yong-tai, enjoyed intimate relations with Chiang and occupied most important positions in government. Huang was in charge of North China dealing with Japan, Zhang was the chairman of Hubei Province and later foreign minister, and Yang Yong-tai was the secretary-general of Chiang's headquarters.[3]

Besides politicians, many well-known intellectuals also believed in gradualism. Among them were Hu Shi and Jiang Ting-fu, who served as undersecretary of the Executive Yuan and ambassador to the Soviet Union in 1936 to 1937. Professor Jiang's views were quite representative. By 1933, he was convinced that postwar internationalism was being replaced by aggressive nationalism. The salvation for China lay in speedy political unification and economic reconstruction within the next five years. During this period, he advised Chiang Kai-shek, war with Japan should be postponed.[4] Zhang Zhong-fu, who served during the war on Chiang's foreign policy staff, estimated that China needed 20 to 30 years of economic reconstruction to build up enough strength to defeat Japan. The first step to achieving these developments was appeasement so as to eventually "drive Japan out." Hu Shi used the French loss of Alsace and Lorraine in 1871 to justify gradualism and was even willing to wait for 50 years to regain lost territories.[5]

Wang Ching-wei, premier and foreign minister, was a pessimistic gradualist. Wang was convinced that gradualism, though at a price, was the only practical policy to save China from destruction. To many people, the concession made at Tanggu could be justified only on the grounds of expediency, because the loss of Peking and Tientsin was imminent, but not as a long-term policy. Hu Shi told Wang Ching-wei that gradualism should not mean abandonment of close relations with the Western powers.[6] Disillusioned with the powers, Wang answered Hu that China could not rely upon the Western powers for the time being, since "we had appealed for assistance, but nobody came to our rescue." Unlike most Chinese, Wang did not entertain the notion that a future world war would save China. According to him, China was a resource-poor country and its economy was concentrated in the coastal regions. Once a war broke out and these regions were taken over by Japan, the vast Chinese army could hardly be supported when driven inland and would either become Japanese puppets or bandits. Whoever won the war against Japan, China, without economic and political reconstruction, was bound to be a victim, either Sovietized by Russia or partitioned by other powers. Wang's prescription for China's future was "striving to be a Belgium [meaning a neutral country], . . . and to prepare for eventualities one day and one thing at a time. But preparations need time and resources whether people like it or not." In military terms, Wang had no confidence in Chinese military capability and compared Chinese armaments to those of Japan as "arrows to machine guns." Consequently, "an isolated China could not deal with an isolated Japan."[7]

Unlike Wang, Chiang was not a pessimist and regarded appeasement as a policy for only three to five years, since he believed that within that period of time, "there will be new developments in the international situation and new changes in the enemy's country that will give our nation a ray of hope in our desperate condition." As mentioned in Chapter One, Chiang seriously expected a war between Japan and the powers to break out as early as 1936. During this period of respite, Chiang wrote in his diary, the Tanggu Truce would give China the time for reconstruction and preparation for war.[8] In assigning the handling of appeasement to Wang, Chiang could not only concentrate on military campaigns against the Communists and put pressure on his other opponents, but also disassociate himself from the unpopular policy.

THE SETBACK FOR INTERNATIONALISTS

The failure of the international society to support China following the Manchurian Incident undermined the position of the Chinese internationalists, whose policy was completely based on their faith in postwar security organizations such as the League of Nations and the Nine Power Treaty system. Between June and September 1933, a new foreign policy based on gradualist rationale came to dominate the Nanking government.

Chiang was directly behind this policy turnabout. On June 13, he consulted Zhang Qun and decided on a principle of double-edged diplomacy. Instead of openly identifying with the Western powers, China, on the one hand, would maintain "impartiality" between Japan and the Western powers, and on the other, would wait quietly for changes in both the international situation and Japanese domestic politics. It was during their meeting that Chiang decided formally to ask Wang Ching-wei to take over the portfolio of the foreign minister.[9]

Wang Ching-wei spelled out the new approach in his telegram of June 29, 1933, to Minister of Finance T. V. Soong, who was attending the World Economic Conference and meeting with members of the Chinese delegation to the League of Nations. It was composed of three parts: policies toward Japan, policies toward Europe and the U.S., and policies toward the Soviet Union. The new Japan policy refrained from demands such as severing of diplomatic relations and economic sanctions. China would watch which way the international wind blew before making any move. Moreover, if Japan showed any sign of returning Manchuria, China would express a willingness to establish new relations. Otherwise, the Manchurian case should be suspended for the time being. The Chinese government would not involve itself directly in a military confrontation with Japan.[10]

By contrast, China's attitude toward other powers, including the Soviet Union, underwent few changes. Obviously, the erstwhile internationalist approach gave way to a kind of quiet diplomacy toward Europe and America aimed at obtaining economic assistance. In Chiang's own words, "accommodation with Japan should serve as a smokescreen for the diplomacy (toward the powers)."[11] The same applied to China's Soviet policy. Despite protests over the sale of the CER, the Nanking government did not intend to estrange the Soviets. Wang Ching-wei stated explicitly that Sino-Soviet relations should not be permitted to deteriorate whatever the result of the Soviet railroad negotiations with the puppet regime of Manzhouguo. China also would continue to improve commercial relations with the Soviets. In addition, China would support the rapprochement between the Soviet Union and the United States. Hopes for Soviet-American cooperation in the Far East against Japan were widely shared. China feared that "Russia would finally drift into special relations with Japan unless the U.S. government gave her recognition."[12] It is doubtful whether China could play a role at all in linking the United States and the Soviet Union. Yet the fact that the Nanking regime made this its fundamental policy spoke volumes for China's foreign policy conceptions and expectations at this particular time.

The gradualist policy did not go unchallenged. Committed international-ists, such as T. V. Soong and Wellington Koo, now minister to France, vehemently opposed any attempt at appeasement and insisted on a close relationship with European-American powers to confront Japanese expan-sionism. Because of their Western education and pro-Western sentiments, they were loosely labeled as the European-American faction in Chinese politics.[13] They firmly believed that Japan's aggression in China was on a collision course with the Western powers and blamed the lukewarm moral support from the powers on "the passive policy" of the Nanking government. In their reaction to Wang's June 29 telegram, Soong, Yan Hui-qing, ambas-sador to the Soviet Union, Koo, and Guo Tai-qi, minister to Britain, held a conference in London and formulated a long, strongly worded response. They warned that "a passive policy vis-à-vis Japan would be too dangerous to pursue" and "would not only mean to the world at large a voluntary abandonment by China of the Four Eastern Provinces but might in fact lead to her dismemberment."[14]

They were strongly convinced that "another world conflagration might arise in the next five or ten years," probably between Japan and the Soviet Union or Japan and the United States. In anticipation of such an event, they demanded "an active policy of steady resistance against Japan and speedy preparation for the coming international crisis." Though they were realistic enough to rule out military confrontation with Japan at this stage, they had no doubt that the Anglo-American powers would win the second world war and therefore they advocated a policy of "economic resistance" in close cooperation with the powers. Not only could China cause damage to the Japanese economy by holding boycotts and by closing China's markets to Japan, the Western powers would also participate and lend active support. China ought to take the initiative in forming "a united economic front" with these powers.[15]

To realize his idea of active economic resistance and a united front, Soong conceived of a plan to obtain financial support for China's economic recon-struction. Immediately after he obtained a loan of $50 million to purchase American wheat and cotton in August 1933, he proposed to the American government the organization of a consultative committee with the participation of prominent foreign bankers and businessmen. This group would replace the existing international banking consortium and provide a means for China to borrow loans for various projects. The purpose of such a plan was, as Soong put it, to "force Japan out of the consortium." Half of the members of this new organization would be Chinese and there was to be no Japanese participation. The Japanese strongly objected to this scheme. In the face of Japan's opposition, the United States and Britain did not lend any support to Soong, and the plan was thus aborted. The main reason for the powers' rejection was that the exclusion of Japan was considered China's diplomatic scheme of playing the powers against Japan. No power at this moment was willing to provoke Japan.[16] The rejection from the powers rendered untenable the position of the internationalists in the Nanking government. One month later, Soong showed a greatly modified attitude regarding foreign policy in two meetings with Huang Fu, though he still believed that another world war was soon to come.[17]

Chiang Kai-shek considered this an opportune moment to unify the KMT and the government behind his gradualist foreign policy. On September 6, Chiang met with 13 top KMT leaders at his summer resort, Guling. T. V. Soong and Sun Ke, who was considered pro-Soviet and like Soong favored resistance to Japan by promoting strong ties with other countries, were present, but they were greatly outnumbered by the gradualists, Wang and his followers Tang You-ren and Zeng Zhong-ming, Yang Yong-tai, and other supporters of Chiang. At the Guling Conference, Chiang Kai-shek "repeatedly argued that after the Tanggu Truce, past mistakes ought to be corrected and a new policy toward Japan is needed." Soong and Sun did not raise any objections to such a policy reorientation.[18]

The fundamental principle adopted by the Guling Conference was a great victory for the gradualist strategy. It called for "Wei Qu Qiu Quan" (compromise in order to preserve the whole). The purpose of such a principle was to "win several years to achieve stability, solid foundation of the nation, and party unity." The conference decided that except for the cession of territories in Manchuria and Jehe and recognition of the puppet regime, Manzhouguo, China would deal with Japan in a flexible manner, avoid any activities provoking Japanese ill feelings, and give North China authorities (Huang Fu) more discretionary power in pursuing such a policy. The Guling Conference went a step further than the policy enunciated in Wang's June 29 telegram. Though it recognized that foreign aid from other Western powers was "an important element in rebuilding the nation," relations with these countries had to be conducted on the condition that Japan would not be offended.[19]

The Guling Conference marked a total defeat for the internationalists. As a result, T. V. Soong resigned his position as finance minister and vice premier in November 1933, ostensibly over a dispute with Chiang Kai-shek over military expenditures. The real reason for his resignation was Soong's opposition to the gradualist policy and the belief that Japan was not appeasable. In his conversation with the American consul in Nanking, he insisted that "it was the settled determination of Japan to reduce China to a condition of subordination to Japan" and that "Japan would never be satisfied with what she had already acquired."[20] For the next a few years, Soong did not associate himself with the gradualist policy. Soong's defeat was viewed by the public as a shift in the government policy, a shift from the West to the East.[21]

Soong's resignation upset Sun Ke and other internationalists. As president of the Legislative Yuan, Sun Ke used this organ of the government to attack Wang Ching-wei and Huang Fu and tried to bring Soong back into the government. Resentment over the appeasement policy also existed in the CPC of the KMT. The CPC passed a resolution forbidding negotiations with the Japanese by Huang Fu in the North.[22] Since the real power was in the hands of Chiang, who was behind the new policy and not on good terms with Soong anyway, none of these maneuvers were successful except in causing the gradualists embarrassment.

As Soong and others were contemplating ways to oppose Wang and Chiang's gradualist policy, other opponents took it upon themselves to resist Japan. Between May and August 1933, Feng Yu-xiang, a former warlord, formed the People's Anti-Japanese Allied Army in North China under the banner of fighting the Japanese. It is hard to judge Feng's motives for organizing this army. Pro-KMT historians consider it an outright rebellion against Nanking for the sake of personal power, whereas historians on mainland China attribute it to patriotism and disagreement with Nanking's appeasement policy. His biographer, James Sheriden, considers his motive a mixed one.[23] There was no question, however, that Feng formed an alliance with the Communists and allowed more than 300 CCP cadres to work in his army, several of whom were top military commanders.[24]

Like Soong, Feng also believed in the advent of a second world war but considered it an imperialist conflict to control colonial countries like China. Feng vehemently opposed the gradualist policy and advocated active resistance against Japan. In his book *China and the Second World War,* Feng argued that "we must firmly oppose any empty words of preparation and launch a war in a positive and active manner." In this book, Feng adopted the motto "my enemy's enemy is my friend" and pushed for alliances with the Soviet Union, Britain, and the United States. He was especially in favor of allying with the Soviet Union in political, economic, and military areas since it was a socialist country with no aggressive designs on China. He also viewed the United States as having no territorial ambitions and as being very friendly to China.[25]

Feng's organization of the People's Anti-Japanese Allied Army showed China's chronic symptom of military separatism and was definitely perceived to be a threat by Nanking on two grounds. First, it undermined Nanking's new policy by openly confronting Japan. The result would be more Japanese pressure on Nanking. Moreover, public opinion grew more discontented with appeasement and the entire gradualist approach, especially when Feng's forces captured the lost city of Duolun in Chahar Province. Second, perhaps more important for Chiang Kai-shek, his old rival Feng Yu-xiang once again controlled an independent army that could challenge Nanking's authority as it did in 1929 and 1930. This was a life-and-death matter for Chiang. Therefore, Nanking was determined to put down the People's Anti-Japanese Allied Army from the outset, and interestingly enough, even cooperated with the Japanese army in suppressing Feng's forces.[26]

If Feng's deviation forced Nanking to realize the necessity of its gradualist policy, the revolt of the 19th Route Army in late 1933 produced the same result. The Fujian rebellion renounced its allegiance to the KMT flag and vowed to overthrow the Nanking government. Leading the rebellion were the famous generals of the 19th Route Army, which had fought the Shanghai war in 1932. Among those who joined the new government was Chen You-ren, who was named foreign minister. The primary aim of the rebel government was to lead an anti-Chiang war, hoping that Chiang's other opponents would rally to their flag.[27]

The foreign policy of the Fujian regime pushed Chiang further toward accommodating the Japanese. It denounced Chiang's policy as being pro-Japanese and betraying the nation and yet, at the same time, it also aimed to abolish the vestiges of Western imperialism in China, such as extraterritoriality, and demanded complete tariff autonomy.[28] The program was on the surface a return to the pre-1931 anti-imperialism at a time when China's urgent problem was how to cope with Japanese aggression. Its anti-imperialism seemed like a propaganda ploy. The Fujian regime reportedly informed the Japanese specifically that their movement was strictly anti-Chiang Kai-shek and not anti-Japanese.[29]

Nanking therefore had reason to suspect that the Fujian rebels' anti-Western pronouncements were a friendly gesture to Japan. Huang Fu cabled Chiang Kai-shek expressing his suspicion that the Fujian regime pretended to be anti-Japanese but was in fact hand in glove with the Japanese. In another telegram, Huang informed Chiang that the Fujian rebels had sent envoys to Japan to obtain its understanding before setting up the government.[30] Nanking feared the possible Japanese connections of the rebels. Such fears forced the Nanking government to be more friendly to Japan so as to preempt support for the Fujian regime.

Chiang quickly suppressed these rebellions, and by the fall of 1934 he also succeeded, with the assistance of his German advisers, in defeating the Communists who were forced into the Long March. In order to finish off the Communists completely, Chiang, through Huang Fu in North China, begged Japan to assist Nanking with the job.[31] The cooperation between Chiang and Japan in putting down internal rebellions showed an important aspect of gradualism: to achieve internal stability at the expense of foreign policy.

APPEALS TO JAPAN

In addition to domestic difficulties, the unfavorable international atmosphere of appeasement also convinced Nanking of the exigency of its gradualist strategy. What characterized the Far East situation was a silent retreat by the powers that can best be seen in their reactions to the Amau Doctrine. On April 17, 1934, the Japanese foreign ministry spokesman, Eiji Amau, stated that Japan had a special mission to maintain peace and order in East Asia and opposed any financial and military assistance to China by foreign countries. This statement was accurately termed in China and elsewhere as "the Japanese Asian Monroe Doctrine," which boldly and openly challenged the Open Door Policy and the Nine Power Treaty system.

Reactions from Britain and the United States to the Amau Doctrine were weak at best. In his second statement on the Amau Doctrine, John Simon, the British foreign minister, conceded that Japan "had special rights recognized by the other powers and not shared by them."[32] When the Chinese minister to Britain inquired about the British attitude, the response was that "if the Chinese are dissatisfied with the Japanese declaration, they must say so directly to Tokyo." The Chinese government was especially dissatisfied with the British reply that the "special rights" meant the Japanese concessions and the railway zone in Manchuria. Even after Chiang Kai-shek threatened Britain with the possibility of leaning to either the Soviet Union or Japan, the British attitude still remained the same.[33]

British unwillingness to offend Japan was shared by the American government. Many State Department officials saw no reason for the United

States to stick out its neck over the Amau Statement. The State Department's aide-mémoire to Japan on April 29 declared that it would adhere to the Nine Power Treaty, but it was worded in such a way as not to be provocative. In a further effort to avoid any confrontation with Japan, Cordell Hull, the secretary of state, ordered the Far Eastern Division to review American policy toward China. The division recommended no further aid to China.[34] It became clear that no vigorous American position could be expected.

And yet the Chinese government had briefly expected strong reactions from Britain and the United States. Though shying away from confrontation with Japan, the Chinese government intended to push quietly for concerted action because it believed that the effect of the Amau Doctrine would link the powers with China "as victims of Japanese treaty violation." The Southwest clique also called upon the powers for the same action.[35] The subsequent disappointment lead many Chinese to interpret the promise of independence to the Philippines in March 1934 and the withdrawal of the American fleet from the Pacific to the Panama Canal in April 1934 as further proof that America was backing down under Japanese pressure.[36]

For China, the Amau Doctrine was nothing unusual. Since the Manchurian Incident, Japan had defied the League of Nations, ignored the Western powers and achieved a unique position in the Far East. This statement was merely a reflection of the status quo. For the sake of saving face, Wang Ching-wei's Foreign Ministry issued a mild statement on April 19. Though it declared that no country had the right to claim hegemony in East Asia, the statement did not strongly protest Japan's treatment of China as her colony; it merely explained that China's efforts to obtain foreign assistance were for reconstruction and for maintaining internal peace and order and that Japan need not worry about this.[37] Two days later, the only thing Chiang could do was to urge Wang to ask Chinese diplomats to maneuver the powers against the Amau Doctrine.[38]

Dissenting voices of protest were heard in and outside China. Wellington Koo issued a statement in Paris on April 20 denouncing the Amau Doctrine in very strong terms. He called it "a revelation of the Japanese tradition of aggression and expansion in East Asia, especially in China." T. V. Soong also refuted the Amau Doctrine and insisted that China should not give up cooperation with the powers because of Japanese opposition. A *Shenbao* editorial equated the Amau Doctrine with the infamous 21 demands of 1915. It warned the Chinese people to realize the grave danger of national annihilation.[39]

The Amau Doctrine further proved that in the face of Western inaction, the policy of gradualism was the only practical approach for the time being.

China had to deal with Japan face to face and make some concessions in order to limit Japanese demands. Indeed, Huang Fu's main task as commissioner for North China was to mitigate Japan's demands on a case-by-case basis. As Tang You-ren, vice foreign minister, put it, "by a process of wrangling and whittling, Huang . . . would make a small concession on what originally had been a large request, and the Japanese would go away feeling happy."[40] It is under such a general principle that Huang conducted his dealings with the Japanese.

The Japanese had been demanding the opening of railways and postal services between Manchuria and North China since 1933, and Nanking leaders had indicated willingness to meet these demands. Negotiations were held back partly because of the Fujian rebellion.[41] In early April 1934, the Japanese put more pressure on Nanking to settle the question of direct traffic between Manchuria and China. Wang Ching-wei arranged a secret meeting with the American consul in Nanking, Willys Peck, and asked him for advice. Both Peck and Ambassador Johnson declined to offer any opinion. On April 19, Huang sent a telegram to Wang Ching-wei reiterating the original decision to make a swift settlement of the postal and traffic matter.[42] When Huang Fu, Wang Ching-wei, and Chiang Kai-shek met in May at Chiang's headquarters in Jiangsi Province, they decided to give in to Japan's demands. Since direct traffic with the puppet Manzhouguo would be tantamount to recognition of its existence, their decision was to let a sort of international travel agency, not the government, handle the traffic problem.[43]

The postal and traffic questions caused considerable opposition from the anti-appeasement elements inside the government. While Huang, Wang, and Chiang still were conferring in Jiangsi, Sun Ke called a secret meeting in the Legislative Yuan to discuss diplomatic problems in North China. Huang was reprimanded for appeasement, and three resolutions were passed: first, that Huang should not be charged with responsibility over foreign relations; second, that China would not accept any mail with stamps of Manzhouguo; and third, that the Japanese demand for the opening of railway traffic should be refused.[44] So unpopular was Huang's dealings with Japan that on June 1, 1934, someone threw a bomb into his residence in an obvious attempt to assassinate him. However, Chiang stood firmly behind Huang. Under some compromised form, railways opened in July and the postal service, after several months of difficult negotiations and under heavy Japanese pressures, was restored between China and Manchuria by the end of the year. China had to accept Manchurian stamps that bore the name of Manzhouguo, and, for all practical purposes, this amounted to a de facto recognition.[45]

In 1934, Chiang Kai-shek took special pains to stabilize Sino-Japanese relations. He wrote an article entitled "Enemy or Friend?" in September but had it published in December 1934 in *Diplomatic Review* under the name of a legal scholar, Xu Dao-lin. The purpose of the article was to break the impasse in Sino-Japanese relations and to persuade the Japanese to cease aggressions in China. Fully aware of Japan's perceived threat from the Soviet Union and the U.S., Chiang advised Japan that she would have to befriend China if she intended to fight either of these two powers, because China, geographically standing either behind or beside Japan, could decide her fate in such a war by allying with the other powers. With its size, he continued, China could not be conquered; therefore, the only way Japan could solve her strategic problem was to be a good neighbor.[46]

Chiang also criticized the Chinese intransigence which in part led to the deplorable state of relations. To legitimize his argument, he quoted Dr. Sun Yat-sen's remark that "without Japan in East Asia, China would have been dismembered or jointly controlled by others," and that "if China severs relations with Japan, she can wipe out China within ten days." To further justify the concessions Nanking made after the Manchurian crisis, he utilized Lenin's concessions at Brest-Litovsk to support his argument that they were necessary in the short term.

Chiang Kai-shek deliberately distanced himself from the Western powers. For example, he refuted the view that another world war would save China from Japanese imperialism. According to Chiang's article, a destroyed Japan was not necessarily a blessing, and the Nine Power Treaty and the Open Door Policy were not guardians for China. Instead they were a means for imperialists to deal with their semicolonies, though on the surface they appeared to be instruments for protecting commercial interests and maintaining the power balance.[47]

Did Chiang truly want to give up playing other powers against Japan? The answer is obviously not. As mentioned before, Chiang Kai-shek had expected Japan's conflict with the powers all along and had thought that China could take advantage of such opportunities to gain independence. In March, only six months before his article "Enemy or Friend?" was written, Chiang told the Investigating and Planning Committee of his headquarters to prepare for world war. In the same month, Chiang voiced his opinion that the international situation was so tense that the following events were "enough to trigger this world war": the termination of the Naval Agreement among Britain, Japan, and the U.S.; Japan's withdrawal from the League of Nations; the American naval build-up; and the British fortification at Singapore. In July he stressed the same theme of Japan's inevitable conflicts with the powers and the Soviet Union in a speech to high-level army officers.[48] Such expectations clearly showed that Chiang was not entertaining any permanent Sino-Japanese cooperation. It was a friendly gesture aimed at disarming Japan's suspicion that Nanking intended to cooperate with the powers. It was also a reflection of his strategy, "Yi Heri Yanhu Waijiao" [using accommodation with Japan as a smokescreen for diplomacy (cooperation with the powers)].

Nanking and Tokyo seemed ready to begin a new relationship when Foreign Minister Hirota responded positively to Chiang's message in January 1935 in a speech to Parliament. Immediately after the Hirota speech, Wang Ching-wei responded with a speech in the Central Political Council of the KMT.[49] Accompanied by Huang Fu and Tang You-ren, Chiang had an interview with the Japanese minister to China and the military attaché. Chiang welcomed Hirota's speech as a turning point in Sino-Japanese relations, and he also used Japanese overtures of friendship to convince his critics that a peaceful solution to the Sino-Japanese crisis might be possible.[50] Chiang felt rather confident about this new gesture to Japan. In his diary, he wrote that after making his foreign policy views known to Chinese and Japanese reporters, people had shown some understanding, and most supported it. He felt that his move not only caused changes in Chinese foreign policy but also "influenced the West."[51] Although it is not entirely clear what Chiang meant by influencing the West, judging from the context, Chiang's appeasement was partially designed to make the Western powers feel uneasy about the prospect of a Sino-Japanese rapprochement and to spur the Soviet Union into a more active role in the Far East. In so doing, the powers might have to assist China for their own interests.[52]

To speed up the rapprochement, Chiang Kai-shek suggested in February that Dr. Wang Chong-hui, on his way to the World Court, visit Japanese high officials. The purpose was to ascertain "Japan's intentions."[53] In Tokyo, Wang Chong-hui met with Foreign Minister Hirota and was instructed by Chiang to stress China's willingness to negotiate a friendship treaty based on three principles: equality between the two nations, abolition of unequal treaties, and cessation of Japanese assistance to local governments in China. Though the most important issue—the Manchurian problem— was touched upon, it was no longer a precondition for improving relations, as insisted upon by China in mid-1933, and its solution could "wait for an opportune time." Though the relationship was warmed and diplomatic representation was later elevated to the ambassadorial level, Wang Chong-hui reported to Chiang Kai-shek that Japan still intended to control China militarily, economically, and even culturally, "to eradicate our nation."[54]

CHALLENGE TO GRADUALISM:
THE HE-UMETSU AGREEMENT

While Nanking and Tokyo were approaching each other, the Japanese military was actively pursuing a scheme for an independent North China. Japanese officers in the Kwantung Army and Tientsin Garrison had no faith in Chiang's professed accommodation with Japan. They regarded Chiang's recent gestures as "merely the temporary expedient" aimed at unification of China and thought that Chiang was "making a fool of Japan." If Chiang quelled the opposition in the Southwest and obtained economic aid from the Anglo-American powers, Nanking would be anti-Japanese again. Consequently, their policy was to promote an autonomous North China free from Nanking's control and to support the Southwest clique against Nanking.[55]

In May 1935 the assassination of two pro-Japanese journalists furnished an excuse for the Kwantung Army to put its scheme into action. The Japanese army presented a series of demands to the Chinese authorities in Peking, including the withdrawal from North China of Chiang's Central Army and the Third Gendarme Regiment; the disbanding of the Blueshirts, the KMT Hebei branch, and the political unit of the Peking Military Branch Council; and the termination of all anti-Japanese activities. In addition, the Japanese also demanded the dismissal of the chairman of Hebei Province, Yu Xue-zhong, a general of the Northeastern Army.

Not willing to jeopardize chances for his gradualist policy, by the end of May Chiang Kai-shek conceded to almost every Japanese demand except withdrawal of the Central Army (2nd and 25th divisions). On this key question, Chiang resisted. Since Nanking's power extended only to where Chiang's troops were, their removal would mean a complete loss of control by the central government. On June 9 he argued that "if the Central Army moved south, it is equivalent to abandoning Peking and Tientsin, and the entire North China." He pointed out to Wang Ching-wei that Japan had sent an emissary to the Southwest to encourage its independence and that in Inner Mongolia and East Chahar the Japanese were doing the same thing. "Their purpose was to overthrow the central government and to dismember China." Chiang warned Wang that the withdrawal of the Central Army from North China would create a bad precedent and also provide a pretext for the Southwest to start civil wars. It would cause people to lose confidence in the government and thus cause its downfall. Consequently, Chiang considered this "the most pivotal and important issue, and therefore, such a demand should be flatly refused."[56]

However, Chiang's position was not shared by Premier Wang Ching-wei and War Minister He Ying-qin, who was dealing with the Japanese in Peking.

Eager to avoid conflict at any price, Wang favored total compliance with the Japanese demands and wired Chiang in Chengdu on June 8 that "the Central Army in the Peking-Tientsin area should move south somewhat to avoid giving the Japanese military any excuses. If this was delayed two or three days, Japanese forces would clash with Chinese forces."[57] War Minister He supported Wang's position. He reported to Chiang Kai-shek that the Japanese army was seeking both to fight with the Central Army and to start war in the lower Yangtze River area at the same time. War Minister He further argued, "we are not prepared at all militarily and diplomatically. If war breaks out, Peking and Tientsin will be lost immediately. Collapse would also occur in the Nanking and Shanghai area." The forces in North China were not in a position to engage in war. Based on his estimate of the military situation, He agreed with Wang that the central government army should withdraw from Hebei in order to preserve the national strength for a protracted war against Japan in the future.[58]

The position of Wang and He encountered opposition in the National Defense Council on the morning of June 10. The majority wanted Chiang Kai-shek to make the final decision. But Wang had informed Chiang at the beginning of the crisis that he would take responsibility in emergency situations and, supported by He Ying-qin, Wang asserted his authority as premier in this case.[59] Chiang finally gave in to Wang and He's views. On June 10 He Ying-qin replied orally to Takahashi Tan, the Japanese Military attaché, that China would satisfy all Japanese demands, including the withdrawal of the Central Army from Hebei. Nanking simultaneously issued a government order forbidding all forms of anti-Japanese activities. But instructed by Chiang, He Ying-qin immediately refused to provide anything in writing.[60]

As the crisis mounted, He Ying-qin seemed to have lost his courage, deserting North China and returning to Nanking. He was the only central government official of sufficient rank and caliber in North China to deal with Japan. His desertion was not without precedent. Sensing the impending crisis, Huang Fu, the civil commissioner for North China, had deserted the region two months earlier. When Huang's resignation was refused several times, he said that sending him north was equivalent to Chinese emperors asking their officials to commit suicide. He also noticed that the allegedly pro-Japanese vice foreign minister, Tang You-ren, was preparing for his retirement, too. In the next few days, Chiang repeatedly urged him to go north, but he refused.[61] At this crucial moment, Nanking could not even find an official of high position and courage to face up to Japan in North China. Such cases of desertion indicated the gravity of the situation and, moreover, showed the complete demoralization within the Nanking government. In the words of John Pratt, a British expert in Chinese affairs, the Nanking government was at this moment "a collection of frightened individuals."

Like the Chinese, the British and the Americans were no less "frightened individuals." When the desperate Nanking government appealed for help, responses from Britain and the United States were characteristic of the global atmosphere of appeasement. After Nanking refused to sign any written agreement on the concessions, the Chinese ambassador to Britain, Guo Tai-chi, immediately presented a note to the British Foreign Office informing it of the grave situation in North China and requesting Britain to invoke the Nine Power Treaty, since the Japanese action clearly constituted a breach of that treaty. On June 15 Ambassador Clive of Britain was instructed merely to make inquiries of the situation in Tokyo and to point out that such demands as Japan's prior consent for Chinese official appointments were not in accord with the Nine Power Treaty. The Japanese Foreign Office denied any treaty violation and stated that the Japanese military "had indicated the advisability of only appointing officials friendly to Japan."[62] Few people would fail to understand what "advisability" meant in the North China context. The general policy of Britain was to make its concerns known but not to invoke the Nine Power Treaty and not to provoke Japan. Prime Minister Chamberlain made it very clear as early as May 7 that he would like to maintain good relations with Japan and that Britain could not contemplate war against Germany and Japan simultaneously.[63]

During the crisis, the American government did not even care to put up a show like the British. After being approached by the Chinese government, Nelson Johnson, American ambassador to China, like his colleague Grew in Tokyo, doubted "the value of inviting attention of the Japanese Foreign Office to the obvious contravention of the Nine Power Treaty."[64] William Phillips, the undersecretary of state, stated to the British ambassador his "determination not to pull the chestnuts out of the fire for them (the Chinese)."[65] The final decision of the State Department was not to get involved in the crisis. Such a do-nothing policy prompted the Chinese to complain that the American government "had shown a very cold attitude to China in these difficulties."[66]

With the powers indifferent to China's fate, the Nanking government faced no other alternative but to meet all Japanese demands in a written agreement. On July 6 Wang and He sent a letter under the name of He Ying-qin to General Umetsu, the Japanese commander in Tientsin, which came to be known as the He-Umetsu Agreement.

That potential foes of Japan generally remained aloof to China's difficulties may have prompted Nanking to request the help of the Germans. Sino-German relations had been quite congenial, with Germans supplying Nanking with weapons and military advisers and the Chinese in turn furnishing Germany with strategic raw materials. Though Germany was not a crucial factor in Chinese strategic calculations in the Far East, Nanking, after the He-Umetsu agreement, hoped to co-opt Germany into playing a role in Sino-Japanese relations because of Germany's credentials as Japan's anticommunist partner. Wang Ching-wei proposed to the Germans that they mediate Sino-Japanese tensions. In return, China would cooperate with Germany and Japan in anticommunism and in economic areas. For a while, Germans were attracted to, and were prepared to entertain, this idea, for it would benefit the overall German anti-Sovietism.[67] But like the Americans and the British, the Germans withdrew, as the North China crisis mounted again in December 1935, from playing any mediating role for the same fear of offending Japan. They did, however, assume such a role only three years later when both Japan and China desired mediation.

CHALLENGE TO GRADUALISM: NORTH CHINA AUTONOMY

After Japan obtained similar concessions in Chahar Province as in Hebei Province, Chiang became alarmed and seemed determined to put up some resistance. He reasoned that North China was practically lost and the appearance of a puppet regime was just a matter of time. Therefore, China had nothing more to lose by standing firm to any further Japanese demands.[68]

Though military confrontations with Japan were still regarded as a last resort, Nanking quietly made preparations for war. As early as 1933, a fortification plan was drawn up by the Military Affairs Commission for six cities in the lower Yangtze River valley. It considered 1936 as the year in which the second world war would break out, and ordered that, in the face of Japan's continuous designs on China, fortifications be ready by that year at a cost of 76 million Chinese yuan.[69] In addition, Chiang also ordered the construction of batteries and other military facilities along the Yangtze River in four provinces. Both before and after the He-Umetsu Agreement, Chiang ordered Liu Shi, chairman of Henan Province, to build a secret defense line along the Yellow River. All of these endeavors were to be completed with the same deadline: by 1936.[70]

Another important aspect of Chiang's preparations for war was Nanking's plan to control the western provinces, Guizhou and Sichuan, still under local warlords' control during this period, and develop these provinces economically and militarily as bases in a long, drawn-out war with Japan. A KMT central committee meeting had passed a resolution in January 1934 establishing "a military center for national defense in these regions not threatened by foreign forces." Fighting and chasing the Red Army offered Chiang a unique opportunity to move his Central Army into these provinces. By the time of the He-Umetsu Agreement, Chiang had established firm control of Guizhou Province and instituted in Sichuan a number of reforms in areas of currency and finance, abolishing the old warlord military districts and reducing the local armed forces, though Sichuan was still in the hands of the local warlords. During the North China crisis, Chiang especially urged his finance minister, H. H. Kung, to move more silver into Sichuan and to have a basic financial policy in the province.[71]

Despite Japan's challenge and Nanking's preparations for war, the gradualist strategy continued to dominate the Nanking government. At a secret meeting of high government officials in the autumn of 1935, Feng Yu-xiang demanded armed resistance against Japan. But Chiang brushed him aside angrily and said: "In my opinion, when we are not fully prepared to fight, it does not matter if the land north of the Yellow River is lost. We can get it back by taking advantage of international intervention."[72] Chiang's remarks truly reflected his belief that Japan's war with the powers over the control of China would erupt soon. Therefore, Chiang's emphasis was still on defeating domestic rivals and on military preparation.

To forestall any future crisis, Nanking renewed its efforts to negotiate the proposed friendship treaty and hinted at limited cooperation against communism. In July, under direct supervision of War Minister He, negotiations were conducted three times in Shanghai between Chen Yi, the governor of Fujian Province, and the Japanese military attaché in Nanking, Isogai Rensuke. The Chinese side proposed a peace treaty to replace the Shanghai Truce and the Tanggu Truce as a basis for a new relationship. Rensuke requested that Chiang Kai-shek visit Japan himself in order to show that he sincerely wanted to improve relations with Japan, a demand refused by Chen on the grounds that the domestic situation in China would not permit such a move. Chen also threw out the lure for military cooperation against the Comintern and for improvements in economic and cultural relations.[73] This channel was later dropped because the Chinese leaders did not trust low-level Japanese army officers and favored direct contact with Tokyo. They urged Jiang Zuo-bin, the Chinese ambassador to Japan, to return to his post immediately.

After consultation with Chiang Kai-shek in Sichuan in late August, Ambassador Jiang Zuo-bin returned to Tokyo and continued negotiations with Hirota. The new package approved by Chiang Kai-shek as basis for a friendship treaty contained three basic principles: 1) respect for each other's independence and relations on the basis of equality, including the abolition of the unequal treaties; 2) no sabotages of unity and security in each other's country; 3) peaceful solution for all problems and the abrogation of previous agreements such as the Shanghai Truce and the Tanggu Truce and restoration of pre-Manchurian Incident conditions. These items were clearly aimed at restricting the Japanese army in North China. In exchange, China was prepared to 1) stop all anti-Japanese activities; 2) put aside the Manchurian problem; 3) discuss economic cooperation based on mutual benefits; and 4) discuss military cooperation if economic cooperation proved successful.[74] After consulting with the military, Hirota raised three counterproposals, the Hirota Three Principles, which were agreed to by various army, navy, and foreign ministries at least two months earlier. First, China should give up the policy of playing the powers against Japan; second, China should recognize Manzhouguo, or at least respect the existence of Manzhouguo; and last, China and Japan should join in a common defense against communism. Recognition of Manzhouguo was the most thorny issue, for no Chinese government could accept such a demand. At the very most, China promised not to use other than peaceful means to solve the Manchuria problem. With both sides unwilling to give in, the negotiations ended in a stalemate.

In the meantime, the Japanese military in North China was engineering an independence movement. It had applied constant pressure on local governments to declare independence from Nanking. On November 18 Major General Doihara of the Kwantung Army presented an ultimatum to Song Zhe-yuan, commander of the 29th Army stationed in the Peking area, giving him two days to declare autonomy and threatening that otherwise Japanese forces would take action. Chiang immediately instructed Song not to give in and claimed that Doihara's action was not supported by the Japanese cabinet. The Japanese government "was afraid of arousing international complications and forbade the use of force."[75] Upon learning that Japan would not support the use of force to carry out the autonomy movement, Chiang felt confident and stood firmer against any attempt at autonomy. When he was informed of Song's negotiations with the Japanese, Chiang warned him that these were matters of negotiation between two national governments and that Song was exceeding his authority.[76] Simultaneously Chiang sent a telegram to Shang Zhen, chairman of Hebei Province, warning him not to join any autonomous movement. Chiang also showed his determination to take military action. "If Peking and Tientsin [meaning Song Zhe-yuan] acts independently and surrenders to the enemy, there won't be any possibility for the central government to allow it to happen." On November 20 Chiang ordered Song to stop all negotiations.[77] Chiang's firm stand worked. Song went into seclusion in Tientsin, avoiding the Japanese.

On the same day, Chiang also appeared intransigent in his interview with Ambassador Ariyoshi, who had just arrived in China. In an uncharacteristically direct style, he told the ambassador unambiguously that the so-called North China autonomy movement was entirely the work of the Japanese.[78] Chiang's stand showed that he began to have serious doubts about the gradualist approach. As he admitted in his diary a month earlier, he felt that "there is no longer any other way to deal with Japan except to resist forcefully."[79]

In the midst of this crisis, the KMT Fifth National Congress was in session. On the opening day of the Congress, Wang Ching-wei was shot and wounded. Zhang Qun took over the portfolio of foreign minister. This left Chiang completely in charge of foreign policy. In his speech on November 19, Chiang insisted that peace would not be abandoned until all hopes were exhausted and that sacrifice would not be easily decided upon until the last minute. Such a slogan only showed the appeasement side of Chiang's gradualism. However, Chiang began to talk about the limits of tolerance and the determination to sacrifice in the same speech.[80]

Chiang's talk of resistance was in part backed by his new military position. Shortly before the opening of the Congress, top military leaders including Chiang Kai-shek, the Young Marshall Zhang Xue-liang, Yan Xi-shan, He Ying-qin, and Wang Ching-wei had held a luncheon meeting together. Chiang told Wang that "from now on, we won't be bullied by Japan like in last June (referring to the He-Umetsu Agreement). Our troops will be gradually returning back [meaning some troops would be relieved from fighting the Communists]."[81] For all intents and purposes, the Chinese Communists had ceased to be a major military threat to the Nanking government. Therefore, Chiang wrote in his dairy that the major task for him in 1935 was suppressing the Communists, and for 1936 the main work was resisting Japan.[82] Indeed, from this point onward, Nanking was no longer willing to make substantial concessions to Japan, even though it would still maintain gestures of rapprochement.

The creation of the Political Council of Hebei and Chahar was a perfect example to show both gradualism and the new tendency to resist Japan under the unique circumstances of North China. With central government forces no longer in North China after the He-Umetsu Agreement, the five provinces, Hebei, Chahar, Shanxi, Shandong, and Suiyuan were genuinely semi-independent. But Nanking still aimed at maximizing its control through political maneuvers. He Ying-qin was again dispatched north to deal with both Song and the Japanese in Hebei and Chahar. When Song proved difficult in his negotiations with He and played the Japanese autonomy scheme to his own advantage, He Ying-qin and Chiang agreed to set up a Hebei-Chahar Political Council, and thus a de jure semi-independent regime came into being in mid-December 1935. It partially satisfied Song's desire for more power and partially placated the Japanese desire for autonomy without sacrificing Nanking's nominal authority. By creating this semi-independent regime, Nanking was not really making any substantial concessions; it was merely recognizing the status quo.[83]

CHALLENGE TO GRADUALISM: THE PROTESTS

Japan's drive for an independent North China gave rise to a resurgence of nationalism. In Peking two student demonstrations occurred, one on December 9, which gave name to the December 9 Movement, and the other on December 16. The famous December 9 Movement became a milestone in the Chinese student movement, which quickly spread to other cities. On December 18 student demonstrations also took place in Shanghai, Tientsin, Nanking, and other major cities in China.[84] In an effort to soothe student anger, Chiang invited them to Nanking to exchange views, but Peking students refused to go. To those who did come to Nanking, Chiang explained that the government was not afraid of fighting Japan, but that it was just a question of time and strength. He promised that he would not compromise on national sovereignty.[85]

The protests echoed a national consensus that gradualism had failed to check Japan's aggression. Support for the students came from all segments of society. Most significantly, even those conservative intellectuals such as Hu Shi, who had supported the government's gradualist policy, came to realize that such an approach was wishful thinking. Though not in favor of student emotionalism and violent confrontations with the government, they shared the students' opposition to the autonomy movement. On November 25 university chancellors in Peking and many famous intellectuals including Hu Shi and Jiang Ting-fu issued a declaration opposing the autonomy scheme and demanding that Nanking "maintain territorial and administrative integrity by our national strength."[86] The *Shenbao Monthly* quoted Hu Shi as saying that "plans of appeasement are all empty talk. . . . If we retreat an inch, others will advance a foot. Taking insults is endless; making concessions to preserve ourselves is impossible."[87] Because of their militant position, the *Independent Review* was temporarily closed. In

Shanghai, more than 300 intellectuals issued a declaration on December 12 calling on people to fight for national salvation. It sharply criticized the appeasement policy as trying "to discuss with the tiger to get its skin."[88]

Gradualism, with its emphasis on appeasement of Japan, was a direct response to unfavorable and unmanageable domestic and international conditions of the early 1930s. It aimed at gaining time to rebuild China's economic strength and political unity while awaiting conflicts between Japan and other powers to develop. Yet time was on Nanking's side, as the Japanese military was putting more pressure on North China and the patience of Chinese public was wearing thin.

4

Politics of Unity and Diplomacy, 1936–1937

By 1936 the emotional demand for resisting Japan dominated public opinion, and various power groups found themselves responding, willingly or not, to the outcry in different ways. The formation of the anti-Japanese united front in 1937 was a major development on the road to war with Japan. It has been credited either to the Comintern or the CCP, but this interpretation neglects the role played by the growing indigenous and spontaneous nationalism. It also neglects Chiang Kai-shek's response to nationalism. After all, it was Nanking that first approached the CCP for negotiations and that actively promoted a military alliance with the Soviet Union. The year 1936 was a year of delicate diplomacy marked by secret negotiations between Nanking and the CCP, the CCP and Zhang Xue-liang (and other local militarists), Nanking and Moscow, and Nanking and Tokyo. Chiang Kai-shek came very close to realizing his dream of unifying China.

THE SALVATIONIST CRUSADE

The Japanese scheme of an independent North China revived nationalist fervor, kindled a wave of protests throughout major Chinese cities, and aroused a sense of political responsibility among urban intellectuals. In spite of Nanking's prohibition of anti-Japanese activities, national salvation organizations mushroomed in the wake of the December 9 Movement. Salvation societies grew in almost every major city and formed a formidable political force. There were more than 30 such societies in North China alone. Finally in May 1936, a National Salvation Association (N.S.A.) was set up in

Shanghai as the central organization linking various salvation groups of different occupations and in different cities.[1]

One of the most important leaders of the N.S.A. was Zhang Nai-qi, a Shanghai banker who became a political activist. The loss of Manchuria and especially the January war in Shanghai motivated the banker to enter into political life. Zhang criticized Nanking's gradualist policy and preparations against Japan as empty talk. He not only demanded resistance against Japan but also saw termination of the civil war and alliance with the Soviet Union and other powers as prerequisites for national survival.[2]

Another leader of the national salvation movement was the writer Zou Tao-fen. Initially a follower of Sun Yat-sen's Three People's Doctrine, Zou became a Marxist after traveling to Europe, America, and Russia, adopting Lenin's doctrine that national liberation was part of the world's anti-imperialist struggle.[3] Since the Manchurian Incident, Zou had been attacking Nanking's nonresistance. Zou had close ties with underground Communists and was made a posthumous member of the CCP. *Mass Life Weekly,* a magazine he founded in November 1935, enjoyed a weekly circulation of 200,000.[4]

Du Chong-yuan, another well-known Salvationist, was a Northeastern entrepreneur. He had been head of the Shenyang Chamber of Commerce before the Manchurian Incident and enjoyed a close association with Zhang Xue-liang, commander of the Northeast Army. Dissatisfied with Nanking's nonresistance policy, Du had engaged in various resistance efforts after 1931. He formed a close relationship with Zou Tao-fen. As editor of *New Life Weekly* magazine, Du wrote in the summer of 1935 an article indirectly satirizing the Japanese emperor, and as a result, the magazine was shut down and Du was sent to prison. His imprisonment was mostly a show to appease Japan, and since he was a good friend of Shanghai garrison commander Cai Jin-jun, he actually enjoyed the freedom of meeting people and operating from prison to promote the Salvationist cause.[5]

Other leading Salvationists included many prominent people in Shanghai. They included Shen Jun-ru, a lawyer and political activist; Li Gong-pu and Wang Zao-shi, both professors; Shi Liang a prominent woman lawyer, and Sha Qian-li, a lawyer who later became a Communist. Also active in the salvation movement was the famous educator Tao Xing-zhi, who was a student of John Dewey. What these people had in common was their concern for national survival, which was threatened by Japan. The N.S.A. was open to everyone and its members included underground Communists, KMT members, Third Party members, National-Socialist elements, and so on.

Since both the Soviet Union and the Salvationists desired Chinese unity against Japan, the Comintern representatives, such as Pan Han-nian and Hu Yu-zhi, exerted some influence on the movement through Zou Tao-fen.[6]

The most representative and systematic demands of the salvation groups were contained in the "Preliminary Political Platform for Resisting Japan and Saving the Nation," adopted by the N.S.A. on June 1, 1936. The basic idea was to launch what it called a "national revolution" against Japanese imperialism. It urged internal unity among various social groups under the slogan "Resist Japan first." It opposed Chiang's drive for unification by force, and instead favored unification based on a democratically elected salvation government. Regarding the foreign powers, the platform considered the Western powers imperialists who nonetheless showed little likelihood of intervening in the Chinese revolution and who also feared Japan's complete domination of China. Therefore, China should obtain help from them or at least keep them neutral in Sino-Japanese conflicts. The Salvationists declared that the Soviet Union would be China's most reliable ally in war against Japan. As Zhang Nai-qi explained, such a position was taken not because they loved the Soviet Union but because it shared with China geopolitically the same threat from Japan.[7]

Opponents of Chiang Kai-shek regarded the Salvationists as their natural allies. The CCP sent its members to work within salvation groups all over the country. The anti-Chiang factions within the KMT also lent their support to the movement. Madame Sun Yat-sen was elected a member of the N.S.A.'s standing committee, and Feng Yu-xiang was among its most vehement supporters. The local power holders also maintained contact with the Salvationists. Generals Cai Ting-kai and Jiang Guang-nai, commanders of the 19th Route Army who fought Japan in 1932 and led the Fujian revolt, attended the first meeting of the N.S.A.[8]

The Salvationists' demand for resistance encouraged, quite unintentionally, regional militarists to oust Chiang from power. In June 1936 the Southwest militarists Chen Ji-tang and Li Zong-ren mobilized their forces and demanded that Nanking wage war against Japan. They also marched their troops into Hunan Province under the pretext of going up north to fight Japan. This move was considered by most Chinese as an excuse to overthrow Chiang Kai-shek. It backfired after the defections of General Yu Han-mo, his First Army, and the air force of the Southwest clique. Chiang quickly seized this opportunity to extend his control in the Southwest in the next few months. For all practical purposes, the Southwest ceased to be a challenge to Nanking, though Li Zong-ren's Guangxi Province remained outside Chiang's control.

During the revolt, the N.S.A. welcomed the Southwest's demand to fight the Japanese but opposed its move to start a civil war. It asked the Southwest "to pressure the central government to resistance, but to avoid confrontations with it." To prove their sincerity, the Salvationists refused the political offices offered to them by the revolting Southwest.[9] A representative, Yang Dong-chun, who was an underground Communist, was sent to the south to state the position of the Salvationists.[10] Zou Tao-fen, who was in Hong Kong in June, was invited to Canton by Chen Ji-tang. During their subsequent conversations, Zou objected to any war against Nanking and asked Chen not to start a civil war. He flatly refused Chen's bribe of 3,000 yuan. Zou's views reflected the Comintern's united front policy because a Comintern representative, Pan Han-nian, was working closely with him to promote the new policy.[11] The Soviet Union, for its own security interests, wished for a unified China under Nanking and shared the views of the Salvationists. It branded the revolt "a plot by the Japanese."[12] Thus the Salvationists and the Soviet Union both ended up as opponents of the Southwest move. By contrast, the CCP regarded the revolt as an excellent opportunity to exploit differences between Nanking and the Southwest. It praised the revolt as "the beginning of the broad united front to resist Japan."[13] The CCP's view of the revolt was actually discussed within the N.S.A., but it was rejected.[14]

The Southwest revolt under the slogan of fighting the Japanese did push Nanking closer toward confronting Japan. For example, on June 12, Nanking instructed Wellington Koo "to sound out the representatives of the principally interested powers at Geneva as to their reaction should the national government be forced by the action of Canton to go to war with Japan."[15] Three days later, Chiang Kai-shek told Leith Ross, a British financial expert assisting China with currency reform, that "a clash with Japan was inevitable and not far distant" and that he hoped Britain would consider an anti-Japanese cooperation among the Soviet Union, the United States, Britain, France, and China.[16] Throughout its negotiations with Nanking, the Southwest insisted on fighting Japan. In replying to the Southwest's motion at a KMT meeting, Chiang Kai-shek promised that Nanking would stand firm against Japan. More specifically, for the first time, he defined his "limit of tolerance" to be any violation of China's territorial integrity. He declared that "we will never tolerate any fait accompli of territorial violation. To put it plainly, if somebody forces us to sign a treaty recognizing the puppet country which violates our sovereignty, this is where we cannot tolerate and this is when we should make the sacrifice."[17] This was undoubtedly a big step forward that defined China's policy in clear-cut terms in the face of the North China autonomous movement. Even the Salvationists expressed their satisfaction.[18]

However, the Salvationist activities were at odds with the government policy. Chiang Kai-shek tried to silence the Salvationists by both co-optation and oppression. First, Nanking sent Liu Jian-qun, a leader of the Blue Shirt Society, and Zhang Dao-pan, KMT minister of information, to persuade Zou Tao-fen to follow the government's gradualist strategy of resistance. Chiang Kai-shek invited Zou for a talk at Nanking and offered him a high position in the government. These efforts to buy off Zou Tao-fen failed.[19] Wang Zao-shi, another radical Salvationist who was uncompromisingly against the appeasement policy, was named by Chiang Kai-shek as a member of the proposed People's Political Council in 1936.[20] Frustrated with their recalcitrance, Chiang arrested seven major leaders of the N.S.A. on November 11, 1936. These Salvationist leaders—Zou, Zhang, Shen Jun-ru, Sha Qian-li, Shi Liang, Wang Zao-shi, and Li Gong-pu—came to be known as the "Seven Gentlemen."

This arrest turned out to be a serious political blunder. It enraged public opinion and made seven instant heroes. A group of 109 intellectuals from Peking sent a telegram to Nanking demanding their release. Such well-known opponents of Chiang in the KMT as Li Zong-ren and Bai Chong-xi also publicly demanded their release. Feng Yu-xiang repeatedly pressured Chiang for the same purpose. Zhang Xue-liang, the commander of the Northeast Army who was driven by Japan out of Manchuria, also pleaded for the Seven Gentlemen. On several occasions he argued with Chiang about his policy of internal pacification first and reminded him that the cry for resistance had to be heeded. Chiang remained unmoved, believing that the Salvationists "were deeply poisoned by the leftist naïveté" and "were shaking people's confidence in government by propagandizing the popular front." He intended to use their imprisonment as an example to silence the growing discontent with the government policy.[21]

MAO: ANTI-CHIANG REGIONAL ALLIANCE

In the summer of 1935, the Comintern adopted a policy of "popular front," instructing Communists all over the world to work with capitalist governments against Fascists. In keeping with the Comintern's change of policy, Wang Ming, head of the CCP delegation to the Comintern, authored the August 1 Declaration for a united front against both Chiang and Japan, though it called for a national defense government and a united army. The establishment of this government was based on negotiations among various parties and groups, famous individuals, and local governments. The CCP was to obey resolutions and orders from this democratically organized coalition government.[22] Wang's anti-Chiang stance was in part due to his having optimistically estimated the strength of the Red Army to be 485,000 and that of Red guerrillas to be 995,000 and his total ignorance of the Communist defeats in Chiang's Fifth Encirclement Campaign. Not until the end of August did he learn of the bad news and begin to formulate a united front policy including Chiang Kai-shek.[23]

In November, the new Comintern policy, in line with the August 1 Declaration but not with Wang's later version of a united front including Chiang Kai-shek, was transmitted to China. Mao Ze-dong, who had just defeated his rivals and emerged as the actual leader of the CCP during the Long March, developed the CCP version of the united front around his homegrown strategy: formation of anti-Chiang alliances with regional warlords. The essence of this approach was to exploit differences in the KMT camp by utilizing nationalist sentiments to ensure the survival and growth of the Red Army.[24]

At the Wayaobao Politburo Conference in late December 1935 Mao continued to emphasize that the splits in the KMT camp were a result of Japanese aggression. In Mao's view, the KMT was nothing but a conglomerate of independent militarists whose conflicts Mao characterized as fights between "large and small dogs" and between "well-fed and ill-fed dogs." Mao's strategy was to exploit such conflicts and form alliances with those "small" and "ill-fed dogs" to fight Chiang. Mao spoke not only of Cai Ting-kai and Feng Yu-xiang as such "dogs" but also Han Fu-qu, warlord of Shandong, and warlords in Guangdong and Guangxi provinces (the Southwest Clique) who resented Nanking's control.[25] He confidently predicted that "splits will occur in the enemy camp when all China comes within the range of Japanese bombs." Mao was in essence using Japan's threat to China's survival to overthrow Chiang's government. Mao applied his strategy to the armies fighting the CCP, the 17th Route Army under Yang Hu-cheng, and Zhang Xue-liang's Northeast Army stationed in Shaanxi— the "ill-fed dogs" in Mao's terminology. The Northeast Army was especially a target for Mao's strategy since it was driven out of its home, Manchuria, and was nationalistic. Anti-Japanese propaganda would appeal to its officers and the rank and file. A series of secret contacts between the CCP and these two armies led to a historical meeting between Zhou En-lai, the second most important person in the CCP, and Zhang Xue-liang on April 9, 1936. They reached broad agreements of regional cooperation. A regional military alliance, called Northwest Trinity, of the 17th, the Northeast, and the Red armies, was formed in mid-1936.[26]

As Mao pursued his anti-Chiang alliances, the Comintern instructed the CCP, after telecommunications between Moscow and the CCP were restored in June, to support Chiang as leader of a united front against Japan. The Soviet Union at this time was actively engaged in negotiations with Nanking and desired, for its national interests, a strong and united China. And yet, Mao seemed only to pay lip service to the Comintern and persistently stuck to forging anti-Chiang alliances with other regional militarists.[27]

The Southwest revolt against Chiang provided an example of the sharp difference between Mao and the Comintern. Moscow condemned the revolt in *Izvestiia* as a "mask for controlling the national government." Mao's CCP took a totally opposite position. As early as the Wayaobao Conference, Li Zong-ren and the CCP had established secret relations, and the latter encouraged the former's anti-Chiang activities. When the revolt broke out in June 1936, Mao praised the Southwest revolt as "revolutionary and progressive," "a magnificent action worth celebrating," though there were inappropriate motives to enlarge its turfs. It also marked the beginning of the Anglo-American imperialists' active opposition to Japan (the CCP regarded the Southwest as representing the interests of Britain and the United States.) Mao promised that "we are prepared to give the Southwest all kinds of possible assistance, military or otherwise." The CCP Northern Bureau also called for signing an agreement with Li Zong-ren. Guangxi and the CCP exchanged representatives, and Yun Guang-ying, a CCP representative sent by Mao, held talks with Li Zong-ren and others facilitating the CCP-Southwest connections.[28]

As John Garver and other scholars have pointed out, Mao's strategy and the deviation from the Comintern line persisted all the way to August and early September 1936. Compromises with Zhang Xue-liang, pressures from the Comintern, and the increasingly tough Japan policy of Nanking all influenced the CCP's decision to adopt a policy of "forcing Chiang to resist Japan" and including him as a possible partner in the united front.[29]

The CCP was more flexible, however, in its attitudes toward the powers, and it not only dropped its anti-imperialist slogans but also began to accept the Comintern's position and the prevailing notion of the day, which was to support alliances with other imperialist nations against Japan, because such an attitude did not compromise the CCP's military position. In July 1936 Mao Ze-dong told Edgar Snow, an American reporter, that Japanese imperialism was the enemy of all nations who desired peace. These nations included Britain, the United States, France, Holland, and Belgium. The CCP now "considered them our friends and invited their cooperation."[30]

NANKING AND MOSCOW

Mao and other opponents of Nanking gained a propaganda edge over Chiang by advocating resistance. By contrast, Nanking, by virtue of being the central government of China, was forbidden to play the nationalist game without incurring the wrath of Japan. Therefore, Chiang had to shroud his plans to fight Japan in secrecy and thus lost the propaganda war politically. In actuality, Chiang could not remain totally indifferent to demands for resistance, even though he counted on the powers to challenge Japan in the near future.

Chiang's preparations for a possible war against Japan consisted of two aspects: an attempted alliance with the Soviet Union and negotiations with the CCP. Before 1935, Nanking was busy improving relations with Japan and feared that any overt pro-Soviet policy on its part would be counterproductive and would probably provoke the Japanese military even more. On November 18, 1934, Wang Ching-wei admitted to William Bullitt, the American ambassador to the Soviet Union who was passing through Nanking, that Japan "had threatened immediate military action should China move toward a rapprochement with the Soviet Union."[31]

However, Chiang Kai-shek did send feelers to Moscow to probe Soviet intentions as early as 1934. In his yearlong tour of Europe as head of the Chinese military delegation, Yang Jie, president of the Army Staff College, visited the Soviet Union in March 1934. The Soviet vice-commissar for foreign affairs, Sokolinkov, indicated to Yang that in the event of war with Japan, the Soviet Union would not only drive Japan out of Manchuria but also return it to China. Such a signal obviously aimed at changing Chiang's appeasement policy. The Soviet defense commissar, Voroshilov, also expressed the desire for Sino-Soivet cooperation. Yang Jie immediately wired this important information back to Nanking with his opinion that "the Soviet Russia was sincere in cooperation with us."[32]

Encouraged by the Soviet responses, Chiang Kai-shek, in October 1934, asked Jiang Ting-fu to further ascertain the possibility of a Sino-Soviet cooperation against Japan. In Jiang Ting-fu's meeting with the Soviet undersecretary of foreign affairs, Stomaniakov, the latter assured him that the Soviet Union would like to see a "powerful and united China under the rule of Chiang Kai-shek." The professor relayed Chiang Kai-shek's assurance that China would not join Japan in its attacks on the Soviet Union under any circumstances. On the contrary, under certain conditions, China would fight on the Soviet side.[33]

Chiang reinforced his new overtures to the Soviets in February 1935 by sending back to Moscow Ambassador Yan Hui-qing, a proponent of close Sino-Soviet ties. Yan informed the Russians that in case of war between the

Soviet Union and Japan, the former "could count on the armed support of China."[34] Chiang's new gestures reflected, to some extent, his calculations about a possible Soviet-Japanese conflict. Tensions and border incidents between the Soviet Union and Japan had risen dramatically by 1935 and an armed conflict seemed to be a real possibility.[35] Sending such signals to the Soviets could relieve the Soviet fear of Sino-Japanese cooperation and thus promote a strong Soviet policy toward Japan. In any case, Chiang's moves might have furnished part of the impetus for the popular front policy the Comintern adopted in the summer of 1935. But the Soviets were careful enough not to be manipulated to confront Japan.

However, these preliminary contacts were far from enough to offset the fears of Japan. This was why Chiang made it clear to the Soviets that he preferred these contacts to be made in "nondiplomatic channels" rather than in any open agreement like the proposed nonaggression treaty. In mid-1935, appealing for Soviet help would only anger Japan and furnish excuses for its military to detach North China. However, after the He-Umetsu Agreement, Chiang became alarmed because his gradualist scheme did not prevent Japan from menacing North China. He not only objected to the agreement, but also appeared determined to improve relations with the Soviet Union and to solve the CCP problem peacefully if possible.

Since late 1935, Chiang actively engaged in negotiations with the Soviet Union. On October 19, 1935, he invited Domitri Bogomolov, the Soviet ambassador, for talks. Chiang was interested in Soviet policy toward Japan and intimated that he would like to sign a substantive military agreement with the Soviets in the name of the commader in chief of the Chinese armed forces.[36] Chiang designated Chen Li-fu in charge of Sino-Soviet negotiations and possible contacts with the CCP. Chen, in his talks with Bogomolov, tried to ascertain the Soviet position in a possible Sino-Japanese war and also pressed for the conclusion of a military alliance.[37]

The purpose of Chiang's intended Sino-Soviet alliance was to "threaten the Japanese."[38] Eager to come to terms with the Soviet Union, Chiang proposed, in a meeting with Bogomolov on December 19, 1935, that the Sino-Soviet relations return to the golden age of cooperation of the early 1920s. Specifically, Chiang wanted to base the relations upon the Sun-Joffe Declaration of January 1923, which highlighted the Soviet support for the nationalist revolution and also acknowledged that communism was not applicable to China. Chiang's repeated emphasis on the Sun-Joffe Declaration as the basis for a new relationship showed his seriousness in reaching an accord. On the Far Eastern international situation, Chiang suggested close cooperation among the Soviet Union, Britain, and China.[39]

The problem of the Chinese Communists was a thorny issue. Knowing too well that the CCP was influenced by Moscow, Chiang attempted to ask Moscow to pressure the CCP to give up their armed struggle against Nanking. He told Bogomolov that he was not opposed to the existence of the Communist party and that the CCP, like other parties, had a right to express its opinion. But if overthrowing the government remained the CCP's political objective, he would have to suppress it.[40] While assuring Chiang of Russia's support for China's unification under Nanking, the Soviet ambassador declined to play any role and suggested that Chiang get in touch with the CCP directly.[41] On January 22, 1936, the Soviet ambassador held another talk with Chiang Kai-shek and H. H. Kung. Kung suggested that the CCP could retain its armed forces and obtain legal status if it recognized Nanking as the national government. Once again, the Soviets still refused to get involved in KMT-CCP negotiations.[42]

The most important question in these negotiations was the proposed military alliance, which was so important that Chiang decided to order Chen to meet Stalin in Moscow where final Soviet decisions could be made. Chen left China on Christmas Day and did go as far as Germany secretly, but then, while waiting in Berlin, he was ordered back. The new ambassador to Berlin, Cheng Tian-fang, who travelled with Chen, explained that Stalin did not give a go-ahead signal. Chen Li-fu later recalled that the news of the trip had probably leaked out and that Stalin was afraid of publicizing the negotiations for a China-Soviet military pact. On his way back via Moscow in early 1936, Chen was not granted a meeting with Stalin, and by that time Chiang had decided to conduct negotiations in Nanking rather than in Moscow.[43]

The Soviets responded cautiously to Chiang's proposal for a pact of mutual assistance and suspected that it was a device to bargain with Japan. "Chiang Kai-shek is still making concessions to Japanese imperialist demands," the Foreign Ministry's telegram to Bogomolov read. "Perhaps, such concessions under present circumstances were a result of flexibility in order to win more time until changes favorable to China would occur. It is possible that they may reach a peaceful solution with Japan and for such a purpose, they are negotiating with us."[44] Bogomolov was instructed to find out Chiang Kai-shek's real intentions before the Soviet Union could conclude any agreement with China.

In addition, the proposed terms of Chiang Kai-shek's mutual assistance pact seemed to have strengthened Soviet suspicions, since it would only incur duties on the part of the Soviet Union: for instance, if provinces such as Shanxi and Inner Mongolia were invaded by Japan, then both China and the Soviet Union would assist each other. Clearly, by 1936, Inner Mongolia had been infiltrated by Japan and Shanxi was threatened. Signing such an alliance at such a time would only embroil the Soviet Union in the Sino-Japanese conflict. To remove Soviet suspicions that the Sino-Soviet negotiations were only a bargaining device to obtain better terms with Japan, Chiang assured the Soviets that China could not refuse to negotiate with Japan if the latter so desired; however, if China and the Soviet Union reached an agreement of mutual assistance, any Sino-Japanese understanding would be discarded by Nanking.[45]

Foreign Minister Zhang Qun also negotiated with Bogomolov many times in early 1936, but these talks made little progress on key issues. In March the Soviets concluded a mutual assistance treaty with Outer Mongolia, which was under China's sovereignty though under Soviet de facto control for more than a decade. In spite of Nanking's protest against such a violation of China's sovereignty, Chiang Kai-shek saw positive aspects in the Soviet arrangement with Outer Mongolia. He considered it an indication of Soviet determination to resist Japan's expansion and noticed increasing skirmishes along the Outer Mongolia and Manchuria borders. Therefore, Chiang did not allow this event to influence the secret Sino-Soviet negotiations. Chiang and H. H. Kung still discussed possible arrangements for an anti-Japanese cooperation.[46]

To improve relations between Moscow and Nanking, Chiang Kai-shek in October chose Professor Jiang Ting-fu as ambassador to the Soviet Union. Before his appointment, Professor Jiang had worked as undersecretary in the Executive Yuan where he had had access to its president, Chiang Kai-shek. His credentials as a scholar of China's foreign relations who had visited Moscow in 1934 made him a qualified choice to establish close relations with the Soviet Union. Professor Jiang advised Chiang Kai-shek that China's antagonistic attitudes toward both the Soviet Union and the CCP were wrong. The Soviet Union was a new international force, and China would have to seek understanding and cooperation with her. Only when China and the Soviet Union had achieved close relations could Chiang undertake to eliminate the Chinese Communists.[47] Ambassador Jiang was not optimistic about a mutual assistance treaty and had counseled Chiang Kai-shek against any unrealistic expectations.[48]

Serious negotiations were resumed in the fall of 1936 when Japan put new pressures on China. The Soviets, in order to avoid involvement in Sino-Japanese conflicts, desired a nonaggression pact rather than a mutual assistance pact. The Soviets did promise aid to China in case of war. Litvinov, Soviet foreign minister, even suggested to Wellington Koo that he was eager to discuss "concrete measures of cooperation."[49] Obviously, a nonaggression pact at this point would only be provocative to Japan and would not be advantageous to China. Therefore, Foreign Minister Zhang Qun pressed for a pact of mutual assistance. Bogomolov considered it difficult at that stage and instead suggested a commercial treaty as the first step in improving relations. Zhang then offered the Soviet ambassador a choice: either the Soviets accepted a treaty of "friendship, trade, and navigation" or balanced trade between the two countries. Bogomolov objected to the political connotation of the word "friendship" as intended by Zhang to mean alliance and also refused to consider the problem of trade imbalances between China and the Soviet Union.[50] The problem of Soviet penetration of Sinjiang by supporting Sheng Shi-cai was also raised by Zhang Qun. This proved to be another barrier preventing the two sides from reaching any agreement. It appeared that Nanking wanted nothing short of an ironclad mutual assistance alliance with the Soviet Union, because it was the only way Chiang could lock in the Soviet commitment in case of a Sino-Japanese conflict.[51]

Chiang reckoned that the Soviets at this time also needed China, since the German-Japanese Anti-Comintern Pact presented the Soviet Union with a dangerous possibility of fighting against two big powers with no certainty of support from either Britain or the United States. Chiang expected either Germany or Japan to attack the Soviet Union soon.[52] The Soviet rush to conclude defense treaties with France and Czechoslovakia and the initiation of the popular front strategy all revealed the fear of a global anti-Soviet war. Though China was not of great military value to the Soviets, her vast resources could be used against the Soviet Union if China sided with Japan. Yet throughout these negotiations, Stalin refused to commit the Soviet Union to anything, while still preventing China from joining Japan by keeping open the possibility of coming to an agreement.

NANKING AND THE CCP

As part of his effort to improve relations with the Soviet Union, Chiang also took the initiative to negotiate with the CCP. He sent Deng Wen-yi, his trusted aide and then military attaché in Moscow since the spring of 1935, back to Moscow to establish contacts with Chinese Communists. Deng returned to Moscow in early 1936 and held private talks with Wang Ming and raised the issue of direct negotiations between the CCP and the KMT. Wang suggested the negotiations be undertaken with the Communist leaders inside China.[53] Besides the motive to improve relations with the Soviet Union, Chiang's initiatives were also in part due to the weakened position of the CCP after its devastating defeats. As Chiang saw it, the CCP was no longer in a good bargaining position.

Inside China, Nanking actively sought contacts with the CCP. Zeng Yang-pu, an important member of Chen Li-fu's CC Clique and later mayor of Canton, was instructed to open channels with the CCP. He explained to Chen Xiao-qin, an old acquaintance of Zhou En-lai acting as an intermediary, that Chiang had changed his policy of unity by force to unity by peace and that Chiang was preparing for a war against Japan. Zeng and the intermediary agreed to a preliminary three-point understanding: first, KMT-CCP cooperation against Japan, signaling national unity; second, reorganization of the Red Army and the Soviet government; and third, union with the CCP to further the alliance with the Soviet Union and obtain foreign aid for China. By June contacts were established through many channels. In negotiations throughout 1936, the CCP essentially demanded the cessation of the civil war and launching of resistance war against Japan. In May, Nanking proposed that the Red Army be moved to the border region between Suiyuan-Chahar and Outer Mongolia. Mao regarded it as a malicious scheme to "create a Russo-Japanese war." [54]

Before the Southwest revolt, Nanking's conditions were fairly lenient in that both the Red Army, in a reorganized form, and the Communist government were allowed to exist in a specific area if the CCP recognized Nanking's authority. The CCP would also be granted legal status and be allowed to participate in government. Under Comintern pressure, Mao and Zhou En-lai decided in August to drop the anti-Chiang slogans and to promote the formation of a united front in earnest.[55] Zhou En-lai wrote Chen Li-fu expressing the CCP's hope for a united front and his readiness to negotiate personally with a high-level KMT representative. On November 13, the CCP accepted the KMT's previous conditions and instructed its representative, Pan Han-nian, to make an agreement with Chen Li-fu.[56]

However, Chen's position became hardened on November 19 and he put forward several harsh conditions. Chen insisted that the CCP abolish its government and army, retaining only 3,000 troops, and that the rest of the troops be reorganized or disbanded by the government. These conditions were tantamount to demanding surrender and were rejected out of hand by the CCP.[57] Apparently, Chiang Kai-shek treated the CCP as another defeated warlord army.

For fear of destroying army morale while fighting Communist troops and of provoking hostile reactions from Japan, Chiang had to keep these negotiations secret. But the whole nation was moving toward demanding KMT-CCP cooperation, including the Northeastern Army under Zhang Xue-liang.

Consequently, for all his efforts at creating an alliance with the Soviet Union and his efforts to reach a settlement with the CCP, Chiang's public image still remained an obstacle to national unity.

DEADLOCK IN SINO-JAPANESE NEGOTIATIONS

Chiang's abandonment of the gradualist policy was fully reflected in negotiations with Japan in 1936. Chiang became quite confident and assertive. Underlying Chiang's confidence was an optimistic analysis of Japan's difficulties. At a KMT conference in July 1936, Zhang Qun stated that Japan's position had been weakened due to a number of factors. First of all, China's stand on the North China crisis forced Japan to change its policy. Secondly, the February 26 military rebellion in Japan threw Japan's house into disarray. Third, the Soviet Union became hostile to Japan, as evidenced in several dozen border incidents. The Soviets, in Zhang's view, were abandoning their appeasement policy. Fourth, the tense economic competition between Japan and the Anglo-American powers forced Japan to look to China for markets in order to maintain economic growth. Thus Japan had to be friendly toward China. Lastly, Japan had been diplomatically isolated since withdrawing from both the League of Nations and the London Naval Conference.[58] Based on such estimates of Japan's domestic and international difficulties, it was little wonder that the Chinese gained a certain degree of confidence. This also partially explained why Chiang Kai-shek openly declared his limit of tolerance of Japan's aggression at the same conference Zhang Qun presented the above analysis. Even Chiang's enemy, Feng Yu-xiang, became convinced that Chiang Kai-shek was farsighted and was determined to fight Japan.[59]

While Nanking was aiming at diplomatic maneuvers with Japan, popular anti-Japanese feelings were growing in the country. In late August and early September, many incidents occurred in which several Japanese were killed in Shanghai, Sichuan, Guangdong, and other places. There were indications that Nanking, fearful of Tokyo's retaliation, was preparing for war. Troop movements and military preparations of both China and Japan were reported in the Shanghai area.[60]

Seizing upon the anti-Japanese incidents as an opportunity to pressure Nanking, Ambassador Kawagoe Shigeru wanted to discuss broad issues between the two countries. Between September and December Zhang Qun held seven talks with Kawagoe. The ambassador demanded an agreement for joint defense against communism with the obvious anti-Soviet intent.

The area of such cooperation was to include three provinces in North China along the line from Shanhaiguan, Rehe to Yanmenguan in Shanxi. Zhang refused this kind of agreement on grounds that the "people's inclination toward alliance with the Soviet Union and the Communists is on the rise, and such cooperation will cause suspicions." Zhang only agreed to anti-communist cooperation north of the line from Shanhaiguan to Baotou, where, as Kawagoe correctly put it, "there is no need for such cooperation." As a price for this kind of cooperation, Zhang was instructed by Chiang Kai-shek to counterdemand that Japan disband its puppet forces and governments in eastern Hebei, eastern Suiyuan, and northern Chahar, and that the Shanghai Truce and the Tanggu Truce be abolished. These "minimum conditions" were hardly negotiating positions; they were designed to resist any Japanese advance. When Kawagoe threatened to disclose these secret negotiations on November 10, Zhang replied: "That is fine. If your side discloses these talks, we will do the same."[61]

In contrast to Chiang's promise to Moscow that China would support the Soviet in a possible Russo-Japanese war, no such promise was ever given to Japan. Zhang, widely suspected to be pro-Japanese, only agreed "to consider benevolent neutrality if Japan so desired."[62]

The issue of an independent North China was raised by Japan, but under a different name. Kawagoe openly demanded on September 23 that North China's five provinces be a buffer zone between Nanking and Japan in which China was supposed to have only "suzerain rights."[63] Zhang Qun refused to discuss the North China problem and considered Japan's activities as encroachments on China's sovereignty. To the demands for suppression of the Communists and employment of foreign advisers, Zhang insisted that these were the business of China and would be considered in due time. These could not be presented as demands, and nobody should dictate policies to Nanking.[64] Frustrated with Zhang, Kawagoe asked for direct talks with Chiang Kai-shek.

Chiang received the Japanese ambassador on October 8, 1936, and expressed complete confidence in his foreign minister, insisting that respect for China's sovereignty and administrative integrity should govern Sino-Japanese negotiations.[65] In spite of his amiable manner, Chiang was even firmer than his foreign minister. To back up his tough diplomatic stand, Chiang Kai-shek ordered his war minister and other high military leaders to be prepared for war, especially in the areas of Nanking, Shanghai, and Wuhan, in case diplomacy failed. In September he had believed that war was almost unavoidable and would begin if Japan occupied Hainan Island or Beihai in Guangdong Province. By late October, Chiang judged that Japan would not dare to start war and yet he still insisted on military preparedness.[66] Other Japanese demands included direct air traffic between Shanghai and Fukuoka, employment of Japanese advisers, abolition of anti-Japanese activities, and so on, but Chiang Kai-shek overruled Zhang Qun's suggestion that China ought to agree to some minor demands, such as direct Shanghai-Fukuoka air traffic, and ordered Zhang to not to make concessions on any issue.[67]

Chinese diplomats in Europe were opposed to any concession to Japan and pushed for a firm position. Calling the Japanese threats "more extensive than the Twenty-One Demands," they contacted the powers and urged them to intervene. Later in November, Ambassador Koo wired a long telegram to Zhang Qun urging the government to change the fundamental foreign policy and to actively form close relations with the Soviet Union, Britain, France, and the United States in opposition to Japan, Germany, and Italy. There were even suggestions that China unilaterally declare the Shanghai and Tanggu truce agreements null and void.[68]

Public opinion was once again inflamed; the Chinese would not tolerate any more concessions. In Peking 104 university professors addressed a letter to the Nanking government on October 13, stating that they did not wish to see "our government abandon its promise about 'the limit of tolerance' for aggression and therefore lose its legitimate position of leadership." Nanking's diplomacy was not trusted by intellectuals because of its past record of yielding to Japan's wishes. Therefore, these professors in Peking demanded open diplomacy and claimed that everything that was going on ought to be published. They also urged Nanking to militarily aid Suiyuan Province in crushing pro-Japanese forces and to stop smuggling by force.[69] As John Leighton Stuart, a sharp observer and president of Yanjing University in Peking, reminded Chiang Kai-shek, "the most prevalent Chinese popular sentiment advocates resistance to Japan on the ground that yielding would be more disastrous than even unsuccessful resistance."[70]

In November Sino-Japanese negotiations were terminated by China due to fighting in Suiyuan. Under Chiang's orders, Fu Zuo-yi, chairman of the province, repelled pro-Japanese forces in Suiyuan and occupied the enemy headquarters in Bailingmiao. When Chiang ordered the attack, he did not believe Japan was ready for a military showdown, and he told Fu's patron, Yan Xi-shan, "not to worry about diplomatic repercussions." Intransigent attitudes on both sides and the fighting in Suiyuan not only served as a rallying point for public opinion but made further constructive negotiations impossible.[71]

The impasse forebode disasters in the minds of experts in Sino-Japanese relations. Huang Fu, architect of the appeasement policy and an expert in

Japanese affairs, died on December 6, 1936. On his deathbed, Huang predicted: "Unless it [Japan] desists from its activities in North China and its support of the bogus regime of Manzhouguo, rapprochement between the two oriental countries will be impossible." Similarly, Zhou Kai-qing, a well-known scholar, also lost confidence in diplomacy even before the Zhang-Kawagoe talks and concluded: "There is only one way to solve the Sino-Japanese problem; that is to meet in the battlefield."[72]

THE SIAN INCIDENT

At Sian, Zhang Xue-liang captured Chiang and forced him to abandon the anticommunist campaigns. It was a triumph for the Salvationists that directly benefited the CCP. Though undeniably influenced by the CCP, Zhang's action was a typical response to the crisis of his time. By all accounts, Zhang was a Salvationist.[73]

Zhang Xue-liang by 1934 was a loyal follower of Chiang Kai-shek. He came back from touring Europe a Fascist, believing that Germany and Italy furnished models for the regeneration of China. He not only worshipped Chiang as supreme leader of the nation but also truly believed in Chiang's internal pacification first policy. Zhang's faith in gradualism began to erode when Nanking made concessions to Japan in the He-Umetsu Agreement. The 51st Army that withdrew from Hebei was his. In the eyes of the entire nation he had lost Manchuria, and now his troops were retreating under Japanese pressure and losing North China. This proved too much for Zhang's already guilt-ridden conscience.[74] Zhang went through a complete change by the end of 1935 when a massive student movement against Japan's attempt to control North China took place. He became convinced that fighting the Communists would be detrimental both to his army and to the nation.

The Salvationist Du Chong-yuan exerted a special influence on Zhang. While attending the KMT's Fifth Congress in November 1935, Zhang lost another division in battles with the Red Army. As a militarist, he knew by instinct that the loss of troops would diminish his power, which in fact had dwindled from his prime in the late 1920s and early 1930s. This concern for his own future and for the national crisis drove him on a secret trip to visit Du Chong-yuan in his Shanghai prison. Seizing upon this opportunity, Du criticized his Fascist ideas and his support for Chiang's policies. Then he advised Zhang that he should cooperate with the CCP, work closely with Yang Hu-cheng, the commander of 17th Route Army stationed in Sian, and improve relations with the Soviet Union via Sheng Shi-cai, a native of Manchuria who was in control of the Xingjiang region and who was cooperating with the Soviet Union. Zhang expressed his acceptance of the plan.[75]

Though in favor of unity, Zhang did not agree to the CCP's anti-Chiang policy. After he established contacts with the Communists early in 1936, he stated clearly during his first negotiation with the CCP representatives that he was opposed to the CCP's policy of fighting both Chiang Kai-shek and the Japanese. The united front, he insisted, must include Chiang.[76] Zhang further explained his opinion about the united front in April when he had a direct talk with Zhou En-lai in Yanan. Chiang was the biggest power holder in China, Zhang argued, and therefore, a united front without him would be inconceivable. But Zhou En-lai still stuck to the CCP's position that Chiang was a virtual imperialist lackey in China, and that there was no basis for cooperation with him. Zhang seriously disagreed and argued that Chiang did have plans to resist Japan, but only insisted on eliminating the Communists first. On the key question of whether or not to include Chiang in the united front, the two sides had sharp differences. Zhou promised that he would report to the CCP center and "seriously consider" Zhang's position. It appeared that Zhang's opinion played a role in the CCP's open telegram of May 5 to Nanking calling for a common effort to resist Japan.[77] Such a change was partly due to Zhang's possession of 200,000 troops, a big persuading factor indeed.

In foreign relations, Zhang also accepted the analysis of the Salvationists. During his visit to Du Chong-yuan, Du advised Zhang specifically that the Soviet Union was the only anti-imperialist power and the only reliable supporter of China. Britain and the United States, for the sake of their own interests, could also be China's allies.[78] Zhang fully concurred. In his Yanan talks with Zhou En-lai, one of the agreements was to approach the Soviet Union by sending a representative. In July 1936 Zhang arranged a secret meeting with the Soviet ambassador, Bogomolov, in Shanghai. He pointed out to the ambassador that China's resistance efforts were related to the security of the Soviet Union and that the two countries shared a common enemy. Then he tried to persuade the ambassador to the view that it was difficult for China or the Soviet Union to meet with the Japanese menace individually; the two countries should form a military alliance. Zhang was extremely anxious to commit the Soviet ambassador to his alliance proposal, but the response from the latter was of course noncommittal, and Bogomolov only expressed the hope that China could be united.[79]

With Zhang Xue-liang getting close to the CCP, his differences with Chiang Kai-shek widened. One episode may help to illustrate. Zhang

Xue-liang set up an officers' training academy that served as the center for his new approach. In October 1936, Chiang Kai-shek spoke to the academy about the necessity of eliminating the Communists. To counter Chiang's influence, Miao Jian-qiu, an assistant to Zhang, spoke the next day to the same group:

> To unite to resist Japan is the only absolutely correct policy of salvation; to suppress Communists and to fight civil war is the absolutely ridiculous policy of killing the nation. Yesterday, somebody [Chiang] . . . wanted us to become slaves to another country, to fight Communists and to kill ourselves and not to resist Japan, not to recover the Northeast. He is farting! Now our Northeast has been occupied, and we have become homeless. If we Northeasterners had any manly courage, we shouldn't have let him walk out. We should have let him crawl out![80]

Miao's attack on Chiang expressed the general feeling of the Northeastern Army officers. It foreshadowed the mutiny two months later. In September Zhang Xue-liang frankly reminded Chiang of the explosive anti-Japanese sentiments of these young officers.[81]

When Zhang's moral suasion was ignored, he, together with Yang Hu-cheng, resorted to military suasion and kidnapped Chiang Kai-shek on December 12, 1936, when the latter came to organize the last battle against the CCP. The rebels at Sian demanded that their captive stop the civil war, release the salvation leaders and all political prisoners, and change the government policy completely.[82] These demands reflected the national opinion that foreign aggression had to be dealt with by a united front of all political groups.

Confronted with such an unprecedented crisis, the Nanking government immediately contacted the Soviet Union, suspecting that the CCP was involved in the kidnapping of Chiang Kai-shek. H. H. Kung, in charge of the Executive Yuan now, summoned the Soviet chargé d'affaires and told him that if Chiang was killed, then China would be forced to ally with Japan against the Soviet Union.[83] At the same time, the Chinese ambassador to Moscow, Jiang Ting-fu, also urged the Soviet foreign minister, Litvinov, repeatedly to work to release Chiang.[84] In Nanking, Chen Li-fu got in touch with his negotiating partner, Pan Han-nian, and allowed him to use the KMT government shortwave telegraph equipment to send two cables to the Comintern requesting assistance in attaining the release of Chiang Kai-shek. Chen's request was granted.[85]

Actually, the Soviet Union needed no lobbying; it had wished for a unified China under Chiang since 1934. The Soviet attitude toward the Sian Incident was negative from the beginning. It was too obvious that without Chiang, China would be plunged deeper into civil war, and it was in the Soviet interest to keep a strong and centralized China. Litvinov expressed his sympathy for the Nanking government, and the Soviet newspapers called Zhang's action "opportunistic" and "a blow to the emerging popular front in China."[86] On December 16 the Comintern also sent a telegram to the CCP instructing the latter to work for a peaceful solution of the Sian Incident.

The CCP at first was elated by Chiang's capture and publicly demanded Chiang's trial. After he arrived in Sian on December 17, Zhou En-lai realized that Chiang was "neither Nicholas the Second nor Napoleon," who at the time of their arrests did not have any military forces, and that the capture of Chiang did not mean the defeat of his army. Zhou feared that the Trinity forces were no match for Chiang's Central Army whose new commander, War Minister He Ying-qin, was eager to attack Sian. At the same time, Chiang was showing some signs of compromise. Zhou then accepted Zhang Xue-liang's idea that Chiang could be persuaded to stop the civil war and that he should be supported as the leader of China in a resistance war. The CCP agreed to Zhou's recommendation that Chiang's safety should be guaranteed in order to stop Nanking's attacking forces and to split the Nanking regime. It was realized that their captive was too valuable to be done away with.[87]

Paradoxically, nationalism caused the kidnapping of Chiang at Sian and also elevated him to undisputed national leader. His captor, Zhang, and his enemies, the CCP, the Salvationists, and the Soviet Union, all wanted to preserve his life. The National Salvation Association, though its leaders were still in prison at the time of the Sian Incident, publicly declared that Zhang Xue-liang and Yang Hu-cheng should restore Chiang Kai-shek's freedom.[88] Chiang's old enemy Feng Yu-xiang made tremendous efforts to secure his safety. He cabled Zhang Xue-liang, defending Chiang as "having made political and military progress [toward resistance] and . . . having ended appeasement diplomatically." Feng even volunteered to go to Sian as a hostage in exchange for Chiang's release.[89] Upon hearing of Chiang's release, Feng recorded in his diary: "Everyone is elated. Some jumped; some clapped hands; and some laughed and shouted. Somebody said that it was all right now and China would be saved."[90]

The fact that Chiang's enemies worked for his safety testified to a sudden and painful awakening: however unpopular he might be, Chiang Kai-shek was the indispensable leader of China and a symbol of national unity. He commanded the most military forces and prestige, and without him China would undoubtedly fall back into the period of warlords. To a large extent, the Soviet Union's and the CCP's stands during the Sian Incident were based on the same line of thinking, though motivated by self-interests. The American ambassador to China accurately observed the mood of the Chinese:

> "It was not so much the popularity which the generalissimo as an individual may have enjoyed that brought the country as a whole suddenly to his support, but the feeling that the forces in favor of unity had won a victory."[91]

The Sian Incident was somewhat ironic. Chiang was kidnapped for not resisting Japan and for not negotiating with the CCP when in fact Chiang had been preparing to fight Japan and been actively talking with the CCP. However, after the Sian Incident, not only was his image transformed from that of a villain to a hero, but also Chiang's military position actually improved vis-à-vis his opponents. The Northwest Trinity was quickly dissolved; with the Northeast Army dispersed all over the country and with the detention of Zhang Xue-liang, Chiang seemed to have removed another barrier to unification and to be in a better position to deal with any recalcitrant regional military regime.

PRELUDE TO WAR?

After the Sian Incident, the CCP and the KMT continued to bargain with each other over terms of the united front. Chiang Kai-shek initially insisted on tough terms in the KMT-CCP negotiations. His ceiling for the size of the Red Army was only 3,000 troops at first, but it increased to 15,000 in mid-February.[92] Zhou En-lai, who was negotiating with the KMT officials in Sian, refused to accept these limits. Moreover, the CCP would not accept any infiltration into its troops by Nanking officers. At one point, Mao Ze-dong told Zhang Chong, the KMT negotiator, that if Nanking insisted on terms of surrender, the CCP would have to fight. Finally, two months before the Marco Polo Bridge Incident, the two sides reached a tentative agreement by which the CCP would retain control of all its armed forces, though obeying orders from Nanking. The final details were being hammered out when the fighting at the Marco Polo Bridge broke out.[93]

The emerging unity in China seemed to have soothed Sino-Soviet relations. The Soviet Union took an initiative to secure a stable Far Eastern environment. Bogomolov proposed to the new Chinese foreign minister, Wang Chong-hui, that China undertake to call for a Far Eastern Conference to discuss a mutual assistance pact. The conference was to include Japan,

China, the Soviet Union, the United States, Britain, and other concerned Pacific powers. Apparently, the proposal was aimed at more American and British involvement in the Far East to check Japan. The Soviets figured that China was in a better position to call upon the powers than was the Soviet Union. Contingent upon China's acceptance of this proposal, the Soviet Union would sign a nonaggression pact as a second step, whether or not Japan or the other powers agreed to such a Pacific conference. As a third step, China and the Soviet Union would sign a pact of mutual assistance. Bogomolov explained to the Chinese foreign minister that if Japan refused to participate, then the blame for breaking the Far Eastern peace would fall on Japan. Coupled with his proposal, Bogomolov also promised the Chinese government that the Soviet Union would grant China a credit of 50 million Yuan to purchase Russian arms.[94]

Ambassador Jiang Ting-fu took Bogomolov's proposal seriously and urged Nanking to consider it.[95] And yet Foreign Minister Wang somehow remained dubious about the Soviet proposal. While promising careful consideration, he procrastinated on the discussion of the proposal until it was too late to discuss in July 1937. The Soviet ambassador interpreted Nanking's decision to slow down negotiations as reflecting its policy of giving priority to Sino-Japanese relations and having less interest in the Soviet offer.[96] But Wang apparently did not object to the Soviet-proposed Pacific conference. In fact, China would have most welcomed such a multinational security arrangement. In March 1937, Chiang Kai-shek told American Ambassador Johnson that the time was not far off when an international conference of the powers interested in the Far East should be held. Johnson inferred that Chiang was contemplating such a conference.[97] Therefore, Wang Chong-hui's response to the Soviet proposal did not reflect China's position on the merit of the conference per se, but rather Wang's worry that the powers might not participate in the conference. Taking the initiative also might give the impression that China followed the Soviet Union closely and thus invite more pressure from Japan. Bogomolov's new proposal did not offer any assurance that a mutual assistance treaty would be signed.

Before the outbreak of the Sino-Japanese War, Japan seemed to have relaxed its aggressive policy on China. There was much talk about economic cooperation between China and Japan. A Japanese economic delegation was sent to China in March 1937. Despite these temporary signs of peace, fundamental differences between the two remained. Nanking insisted on solving political problems before considering any economic cooperation.[98]

In essence, China's lack of willingness to compromise reflected the national demand for unity against Japan, a movement symbolized by the Salvationists and culminating in the Sian Incident. China was also encouraged by the increasingly close relations with the Soviet Union. There seemed to have existed a false sense of diplomatic strength, and Nanking no longer pursued its previous gradualist policy.

5

To War or Not to War, 1937–1938

In August 1937, Chiang Kai-shek decided to fight a war with Japan. One of the important clues to understanding China's decisions on war and peace might be found in its prewar beliefs about the inevitable conflicts between Japan and the Soviet-Anglo-American powers. Since wartime emotions prevented the acceptance of a humiliating peace, these beliefs formed perhaps the basis of confidence for Chiang Kai-shek and the prowar elements. While he also kept the door open for a peace settlement with Japan under acceptable terms, Chiang continued to fight and placed much emphasis on diplomatic efforts, expecting international intervention by the Soviets, the British, or the Americans. On the other hand, a small minority led by Wang Ching-wei viewed such beliefs as puerile and self-deceiving and entertained no illusions that the powers would pull the chestnuts out of the fire for China. They eventually collaborated with the Japanese. In retrospect, the year 1938 was the most crucial battleground for two different views on international relations and for the decision on war and peace that set the tone for foreign policy for the years ahead.

OPTING FOR WAR

Tensions between the 29th Army and Japanese troops stationed in the Peking area had been rising in the few months prior to July 1937. On July 7 and 8, 1937, Chinese and Japanese troops clashed near the Marco Polo Bridge, and in spite of several cease-fire agreements, fighting was not effectively contained. The Japanese took this opportunity to raise their demands and insisted on July 11 that the Hebei-Chahar government ban all anti-Japanese activities.[1] Nanking's reaction to the fighting was swift and uncompromising, unlike in previous years. Two days after the fighting erupted, Chiang ordered four divisions to immediately reinforce the 29th Army in Hebei, with more troops to follow. The movement of Chiang's Central Army into North China invalidated the He-Umetsu Agreement. Chiang reportedly had remarked: "What He-Umetsu Agreement! I have torn it to pieces." Anticipating a full-scale conflict, Chiang even ordered a draft of a declaration of war. [2]

In the meantime, Chiang Kai-shek tried to keep Song Zhe-yuan, commander of the 29th Army, in line with Nanking. The initial reaction from Song was conciliatory, and he negotiated with the Japanese army for a peaceful settlement. To some extent, Song feared the entry of Chiang's Central Army into his territory as much as he feared the Japanese, and he objected to Chiang's army movements until late July. Though Chiang showed delicate diplomacy in dealing with Song, he warned Song on July 13 that the Marco Polo Bridge Incident could not be solved peacefully, no matter what concessions China made. He also showed his determination to prevent Japan's plan to set up another puppet regime in North China. Whether peace or war, Song would have to act in line with Nanking, which would not tolerate any local concession to Japan without its approval.[3]

In spite of these strong measures, Nanking was not really ready for war. Xu Yong-chang, secretary of the Military Affairs Commission, explained on July 14 that China was not fully prepared yet and could not be sure of victory if war broke out. Therefore, if Japan really intended not to spread hostilities, China should seize the opportunity and make a compromise.[4] According to Sun Ke's conversation with Bogomolov on July 13, officials in Nanking worried about a large-scale war with Japan. Though Chiang was getting ready for Japan's saber rattling, he was by no means ruling out the possibility of the conflict being localized. He repeatedly indicated to Tokyo that Nanking would stop troop movements if Japan agreed to follow suit. Sun disagreed with Chiang's opinion that the clashes could be brought under control locally. [5]

The Japanese notion of localization precluded any participation of the central government by insisting on dealing with Song's regime alone. This attempt to get around Nanking was totally unacceptable to Chiang. Even though Song Zhe-yuan reached an agreement with his Japanese counterpart in Peking on July 17 and offered apologies, Nanking refused to recognize the arrangement. By doing so, Chiang asserted Nanking's authority over North China against both Japan and Song Zhe-yuan.

Diplomatically, Chiang also took steps to restrict the Japanese army in North China. After conferring with both Wang Ching-wei and Foreign

Minister Wang Chong-hui at Guling, Chiang Kai-shek ordered the foreign minister to return immediately to Nanking and to contact the Japanese embassy, demanding that both sides stop all military movements. Since the Japanese desired a local solution of the crisis in order to obtain concessions from Song Zhe-yuan, they were not willing to deal with Nanking. On July 11 Chiang ordered the Chinese ambassador to Japan to return to Tokyo immediately to express the hope that the Japanese government would be able to stop any new militarist ventures in North China.[6]

Realizing that the chances of his proposals being accepted by the Japanese were minimal, Chiang asked Britain, France, and the United States to mediate the Sino-Japanese conflict. On July 13 Chinese ambassadors in major Western capitals were instructed to contact various governments. Both Britain and the United States urged constraint on Tokyo.[7] But the American government considered it unadvisable to mediate the Sino-Japanese conflict. A week later, in spite of the fact that the United States did agree to the second British plan to ask for suspension of all troop movements, Tokyo did not respond with enthusiasm.[8]

After his proposal to stop troop movement was rejected by Tokyo on July 17, Chiang Kai-shek made a speech to national leaders from all walks of life at Lushan, reiterating the early pronouncement that if pushed to the limit of endurance, "we will certainly make sacrifices and we will have to resist." Chiang then presented four conditions for peace. First, China's sovereignty must be respected. Second, the government in Hebei-Chahar should not be changed illegally. Third, the officials appointed by the central government, such as Song Zhe-yuan, were not subject to others' approval. Finally, there should be no limit as to the movement of the 29th Army.[9] The firm tone in these conditions was self-evident. No further retreat was possible for him given the inflamed public opinion and pressures from other political groups. As Chiang wrote in his diary two days later, "since I have made a public determination to fight, I can only go forward and should not go back on my word."[10]

There appeared to be little chance of a peaceful solution to the ongoing clash in North China, but Chiang's patience was not exhausted. From July 21 to 26, he had interviews with ambassadors from Britain, France, Germany, and the United States, asking them to put pressure on Japan. In his interview with American ambassador Nelson Johnson, Chiang said that Nanking had withdrawn its opposition to a local settlement of the Marco Polo Bridge Incident, but would not accept the anticipated Japanese demands for de facto recognition of Manzhouguo, for joint cooperation against communism on a national scale, and for withdrawal of the central government army from

Hebei. According to Chiang, the only way to avert war was through joint action of the United States and Britain, "making it crystal clear to Japan that if it does not want war with China then it must not attempt to force China to make further concessions."[11]

By the end of the month, any slight hope of a local settlement was gone when the Japanese troops attacked Peking and Tientsin. On July 29 Peking was taken by Japanese troops; Tientsin fell the next day. Chiang Kai-shek, on the evening of July 29, made a press statement that finally put to rest the possibility of a Sino-Japanese agreement and commenced the eight-year war. "This is the last moment for us," Chiang said. "How can we regard Peking and Tientsin as local problems and allow the Japanese army to butcher us or make puppet regimes?"[12]

Chiang's decision for war was in essence a gamble based on his long-held views on international power politics in the Far East. As early as 1933 in a military conference, Chiang argued that "if we can resist for three or five years, I predict that there will be new international developments [meaning opposition to Japan] and new changes in the enemy country, too. Therefore, there is a ray of hope for our nation to survive."[13] Chiang's General Staff's War Plan A for 1937 anticipated that a Sino-Japanese war would probably trigger either a war between Japan and the Soviet Union or between Japan and the United States. Then the main forces of the Japanese army would have to face the Soviets or the United States navy and consequently, "only part of its armed forces will deal with us." In this world-war situation, according to Plan A, Japan could spare at the very most between 30 to 40 divisions in offensive and under 20 divisions for defensive operations in China.[14] Of course in this scenario, Japan would eventually be defeated by a combination of powers, and what China had to do was to hold out at the beginning of the war. Another scenario in War Plan A was a bilateral war between China and Japan in which Japan would only use 12 to 14 divisions. Then the Chinese army, with at least a million capable combat troops, would be able to resist Japan for a while.

Little wonder that when the war came, Chiang had some confidence and showed an uncompromising attitude. At a luncheon meeting on July 31, he was confident that China could hold out for six months.[15] And in August, Chiang remarked that the "Peking and Tientsin area is in the powers' sphere of influence, a place of their common interests. None of the concerned powers will tolerate Japan's hegemony!"[16] Chiang pinned much of his hope on the Soviets. In his speech to the Supreme National Defense Council on September 1, Chiang asserted that Soviet Russia would eventually enter the war against Japan.[17] Without this perceived involvement of the powers,

Chiang would probably not have made the decision to fight, since a war with Japan would only weaken his position vis-à-vis his rivals, such as the CCP and the Southwest.

MISCONCEIVED CAMPAIGN AT SHANGHAI

After defeats in North China, Chiang decided to take offensive in Shanghai, aiming to eliminate the Japanese forces from the city. When the fighting broke out on August 13, Nanking organized a High Command under Chiang, and the whole country was fully mobilized for war. Shanghai was one of the five war zones, and Chiang concentrated 400,000 to 500,000 well-equipped troops of his Central Army for its defense. Chiang ordered General Zhang Zhi-zhong on August 16 to launch an all-out offensive and to "wipe out the enemy army in one stroke." Four days later another order from the High Command called for smashing "the enemy's landing along our coastal lines as well as its base in Shanghai."[18]

The Chinese government's offensive in Shanghai contradicted the myth that Chiang Kai-shek's strategy of war was "trading space for time," that is, exhausting the enemy by making use of China's vast space and retreating in order to preserve fighting forces. Chiang Kai-shek, though anticipating the war to be a protracted one, still intended to defend the lower Yangtze River valley to the best of China's ability, and there was no trace of "trading space for time" at the first stage of the war. Instead, there was struggling for space.

The purpose behind this struggling for space, as spelled out in the High Command's orders, was to "consolidate the capital and the economic resource bases."[19] The city's importance for the central government was enormous. It was the largest and most industrialized city in China. Shanghai and other cities in the lower Yangtze River valley were centers of China's urban economy. Through its financial and political apparatus, the KMT government had a tight grip over this area. The KMT government derived 85 percent of its revenue from manufacturing and trade sectors.[20] Consequently, the area provided the financial base for Chiang's government and enabled him to own a superior army and to wield power over other recalcitrant warlords. Territorially, this was also the core base for Chiang. Therefore, the loss of this area to the Japanese would have a catastrophic effect on the authority of the Nanking government.

The economic rationale behind this campaign was realistic, but there seemed to be another equally important reason: diplomatic miscalculations.

Since Shanghai was vested with foreign interests, it was believed that the powers would not permit such a great city to become a battlefield. According to Li Zong-ren, commander of the Fifth War Zone, Chiang was convinced that Shanghai was an international city, with large European and American interests and investments, and if China could triumph over the enemy there, the West's traditional deprecating attitude toward the Chinese people might be altered. The importance of Western interests might also lead to mediation on the part of the European powers and the United States, or even to their armed intervention.[21]

The powers did react to the fighting in Shanghai with more concern but without any intention of fighting China's war. They refused Chiang Kai-shek's request that the powers serve as guarantors of the peace terms and proposed the withdrawal of both Japanese and Chinese troops from the Shanghai area. The British later came close to undertaking the mediation, agreeing to do so if other powers would join them, but such a feeble attempt was denied any chance when Japan simply killed the plan.[22] The Shanghai campaign lasted three months and ended in disaster for the Chinese. When Shanghai fell, Nationalist troops seemed to lose morale, and the defense of Nanking lasted only five days.

If expecting foreign intervention was part of the reason for launching the attack on the Japanese army, it became the only desperate hope, after military defeats, to maintain morale. Apparently, Chiang was disappointed by the absence of the anticipated support from the powers. Yet Chiang still expected some kind of international help. Even on December 6, when the Brussels Conference failed to show any result and when he was withdrawing from Nanking, Chiang told Li Zong-ren and other major military leaders that "in a month, the international situation will certainly undergo great changes and China's dangerous situation will be reversed."[23] Right after the American warship *Panay* was sunk by the Japanese air force, Chiang hoped that Chinese resistance would trigger a conflict between Japan and the Anglo-American powers. According to him, "the powers would not automatically join the war unless Japan challenges them; so long as we continue to fight, Japan will challenge the powers."[24] As we will see later, this was Chiang's consistent view throughout the 1930s.

AT THE BRUSSELS CONFERENCE

China's appeals to the League of Nations and subsequently to the Nine Power Treaty Conference at Brussels revealed both Chinese expectations and difficulties. Right after the fighting in Shanghai began, H. H. Kung, who had been touring major European countries and the United States, urged the government to ask for economic sanctions at the forthcoming League of

Nations meeting in September and to ask the United States to convene a Pacific conference of Nine Power Treaty signatories so that the powers would have no excuse to be bystanders in the ongoing war. Kung intended to force the powers to act, for he was fully aware that the British "were afraid of any undertakings before they were ready" and that President Roosevelt of the United States even considered the recognition of the Japanese puppet regime in Manchuria a matter of time. [25]

The National Defense Council, which replaced the KMT Central Political Council as the highest decision-making authority, passed a formal resolution setting the principle for the League approach. Though it demanded military as well as economic sanctions, Nanking did not expect any material aid from the League, but rather aimed at winning the support of international public opinion as a step toward that end. "The sympathy of public opinion oftentimes has unthinkable force in international war, for example, during the Russo-Japanese war, the Anglo-American public opinion was sympathetic to Japan and as a result, Japan got economic assistance and defeated Russia."[26]

Evidently, the problem for China was not the lack of sympathy, but rather how to translate it into material support. The major League members, such as Britain and France, discouraged China from appealing under article 17 of the League Covenant because if Japan refused the invitation to the conference, the League would be obligated to invoke article 16, which stipulated sanctions.[27] Under pressure, the Chinese delegates lowered their demands to a minimum, namely, to declare Japan an aggressor.[28] Even such a minimal request was opposed by the French and the British because, as Koo put it, "once Japan was declared an aggressor, Paris and London will be forced into a predicament and must consider the problem of sanctions."[29]

Japan's bombing of the Chinese capital, Nanking, and Canton in September provided China with a good opportunity to win more sympathy. Kung and other Chinese delegates pushed hard for an embargo on petroleum and other war materials against Japan.[30] Chiang Kai-shek even played on the British fear of the Soviet expansion in China by threatening that if the League refused to help China, he would turn to the Soviet Union.[31] President Roosevelt's "Quarantine Speech" of October 5 also made the League more responsive to China's case. The next day, the League passed a resolution, which, though not meeting the Chinese demands, criticized Japan for her violations of treaty obligations. It also asked its member nations to avoid any action that would weaken China or increase China's difficulties and to extend aid to China individually.[32]

The Chinese leaders realized that "no individual member state would like to apply sanctions alone lest other countries would take away markets in the sanctioned nation." Chiang Kai-shek pushed for a joint sanction of oil, iron, and steel either in the form of concerted action among major powers or parallel action between the League powers and the United States. He instructed the Foreign Ministry to make "the prevention of sale of oil, iron, and steel" its "most important task."[33] Lacking determination to resolve the Sino-Japanese conflict, the League of Nations referred it to a special conference to be convened at Brussels. Its participants were to be the signatories of the Nine Power Treaty and the concerned powers in the Pacific. Japan and Germany declined the invitation to participate.

Knowing well that the conference would not be successful, the Foreign Ministry instructed the Chinese delegates to "make Japan responsible for the failure" by adopting a soft and conciliatory attitude there. As laid out in the government instructions, China's objectives were, first, to obtain sanctions against Japan once the conference failed and, second, to urge Anglo-American powers to support and encourage the Soviet Union to fight Japan by force.[34]

Neither of these Chinese expectations were warranted by the attitudes of the powers, who had no intention of bringing pressures to bear on Japan. The British prime minister opposed sanctions and declared even before the conference was convened that "we are here to make peace, not to extend the conflict." In spite of an active attitude by Norman Davis, the American delegate, President Roosevelt encouraged other powers to consider sanctions but never committed the United States to any action.[35] It seemed that Britain, France, the United States, and the Soviet Union all agreed to the necessity of concerted action to check Japan, but no country took any initiative. Though Norman Davis did propose sanctions after the second Japanese refusal to participate in the conference, he failed to obtain backing from his own government.

The collapse in the battlefield undermined China's efforts at the conference table. In late October, the Chinese troops suffered huge losses on the Shanghai front and the overall military situation deteriorated to such an extent that China considered a temporary truce. On October 26 the National Defense Council favored such a truce because "at present our troops have been used up and the new conscripts are untrained and their fighting ability is poor." Fifty percent of arms and other supplies had been used up. By early November, the Japanese army had advanced to and occupied Taiyuan, the capital of Yan Xi-shan's Shanxi Province, the Shanghai front had collapsed, and the Chinese army was in chaotic retreat, exposing Nanking to attacks. So far, 240,000 troops had been sacrificed in the battle of Shanghai, most of them Chiang's best-trained and best-equipped divisions.[36]

In mid-November Ambassador Koo received eight urgent telegrams in a day from H. H. Kung, who had returned to China in October, directing him to work for a cease-fire. Afraid of public opinion at home, Kung wanted the powers to initiate such negotiations. Since Germany had offered to mediate the Sino-Japanese conflict, Kung emphasized strongly the desirability of joint mediation by the Anglo-Americans and the Germans. As he saw it, this was the most effective way to effect a cease-fire. Kung further indicated that "China will not make things difficult for the friendly countries and will not refuse reasonable solutions." The mediation could follow the precedent of settlement of the Shandong question at the Washington Conference, provided that the powers were present. China would also agree to any truce proposal and mediation within the Nine Power Treaty framework.[37]

Neither sanctions nor joint mediation by Germany and the Anglo-American powers appeared feasible. In fact, the powers simply adjourned the conference on November 24. The fact that nobody even bothered to resume the conference was very symbolic of its failure. The Chinese reaction was self-conceitedly bitter. One editorial writer for *Eastern Miscellany* reminded Britain, the United States, and the Soviet Union, that "If Japanese aggression in China succeeds, will the powers be able to sleep quietly?"[38]

REACTION TO BRUSSELS: THE GERMAN MEDIATION

The failure of the Brussels Conference and the collapse at the front forced Chiang Kai-shek to consider the German offer of mediation. On November 24 Chiang admitted privately that he had to accept the German mediation in order to slow down the Japanese military advance.[39] Chiang Kai-shek and other Chinese leaders were keenly aware of Germany's incentive to see the Sino-Japanese War end. China was Germany's third largest trading partner outside Europe and the total trade value stood at 262.7 million Reichsmarks. More than 70 German military advisers had been modernizing Chiang's army and directing military campaigns when the war broke out.[40] Germany however, did not want to alienate Japan, its anti-Soviet partner, either. Japan's war in China would diminish its deterrent value not only against the Soviet Union but also against England and France. Germany therefore tried to be an honest broker to end the Sino-Japanese conflict. Gan Jie-hou, a longtime diplomatic adviser to Li Zong-ren who was now on Chiang's foreign policy staff, openly stated that Germany was actually against Japanese aggression in China. He believed that Germany would not like Japan wasting resources on China. In addition, China was one of the major markets crucial to the German economy.[41] Even the Communist leaders Wang Ming and Zhou En-lai acknowledged that Germany had a conflict of interest with Japan in the Orient and that "we cannot blindly exclude her [from alliances]," although they opposed any mediation by Germany as a vehicle for peace with Japan.[42]

High-level contacts with Germans had been made as early as July 26, 1937 when Chiang Kai-shek asked the German ambassador to mediate the Sino-Japanese conflict. Right before the Shanghai war, Wang Ching-wei actually probed the possibility of Germany acting as a go-between. In late August, to the dismay of the Germans, China concluded a nonaggression pact with her arch foe, the Soviet Union. This seemed to have provided an impetus for the Germans to find a solution to the Far Eastern crisis. In early November Oskar Trautmann, German ambassador to China, transmitted to Chiang Kai-shek and H. H. Kung in Nanking the Japanese terms for peace, urging the Chinese to reach an agreement with Japan. Chiang Kai-shek rejected the Japanese terms outright and insisted on restoration of the status quo ante as a precondition for discussion.[43]

When it became clear that the Anglo-American powers would do nothing, Chiang met Trautmann again on December 1 and conceded that the Japanese terms he had brought a month earlier could serve as a basis for negotiations.[44] Chiang convened a meeting of military leaders in Nanking to discuss the Japanese terms. Most leaders agreed to accept mediation, including Bai Chong-xi, who had been fiercely anti-Japanese.[45] In his meeting with Trautmann on December 3, Chiang requested that Germany be present throughout the negotiations. Chiang also stated that Chinese sovereignty and administrative integrity in North China should be guaranteed. However, Chiang insisted that China's treaties with a third country should not be a subject of the negotiations, a clear reference to the nonaggression pact with the Soviet Union. To slow down Japanese military advances, Chiang insisted that a truce be arranged before any negotiations.[46]

Chiang was careful not to let the negotiations jeopardize Sino-Soviet relations by keeping Stalin well informed of the German mediation. By informing Stalin, Chiang could also increase his bargaining position with the Soviets and force them to take more positive actions in supporting China. Stalin called Chiang's bluff and stated that the Soviet Union did not object to peace efforts. "If Japan withdraws her troops from North and Central China and restores the status quo ante, China should not refuse negotiations," Stalin advised, knowing fully well that Japan would not permit such generous terms.[47]

In the same fashion, China was also in consultation with other powers, pushing for active involvements. Kung notified American ambassador Johnson of the mediation. When asked what China's reaction would be, Kung, in an obvious attempt to sound out America's position, replied promptly that "this would depend on the attitude of the American government toward the Sino-Japanese conflict." After arguing that China was fighting the war for democratic nations, Kung requested that the powers, led by the United States, issue "preliminary mobilization orders to their fleets or afford China assistance in money or war materials."[48] This kind of plea for joint military demonstrations was made repeatedly by Wellington Koo in Paris and in Brussels.

China's negotiating position was further undermined by the fall of Nanking, the capital of China. Bolstered by its new victories, Japan quickly changed its peace terms. The Chinese precondition that a truce be declared before negotiations could start was formally rejected by Japan. Moreover, it added new terms, such as cooperation with Manzhouguo and Japan in anticommunism, and reparations for Japan's war expenses.[49] Ambassador Trautmann, who relayed the Japanese terms on December 26 to Kung and Madame Chiang, urged acceptance. As noted by Chiang Kai-shek, the majority of Chinese officials were in favor of peace now, and at the National Defense Council on December 27, some even advocated acceptance of the revised Japanese terms.[50]

The Chinese government did not reject these harsh terms outright, though Zhang Jia-ao, minister of communications, informed Trautmann that the terms were intended to turn China into a second Manzhouguo. It immediately notified the major powers, including the Soviet Union, about these added terms and solicited their responses. Chiang Kai-shek informed the Soviet Union that these terms could not even be considered.[51] The United States was informed by Chiang's adviser, William Henry Donald, also on December 28. President Roosevelt, the man who wanted to quarantine aggressors, supposedly told Chinese Ambassador Wang Zheng-ting that the Japanese terms were "very lenient."[52]

The reactions of these major powers further caused Chiang to reverse his earlier position and to consider the harsh peace terms. The Foreign Ministry instructed its representative in Tokyo that the government was studying the Japanese proposal.[53] But the Chinese government procrastinated on the matter until January 16, 1938, when the Konoe government declared that it would not deal with Chiang's government and thus spared Chiang the difficulty of having to make a decision on whether to accept a peace settlement.[54]

CONFLICTING VIEWS ON WAR AND PEACE

The Sino-Japanese War crystallized political divisions within Chinese government and society on the question of peace and war. Throughout this period, there
were heated debates between the war faction and the peace faction. Their debates,
which had a profound impact on government decisions, centered around two
issues: China's ability to withhold Japan's military power, and whether the
powers would support China or even intervene.

The peace advocates had existed from the very beginning of the war.
Wang Ching-wei adopted a defeatist and pessimistic outlook and opposed a
confrontation with Japan. He asked the military leaders at the Lushan
Conference of late July 1937 that he be given five more years to reconstruct
the country and to prepare for a war. In high-official circles, a so-called Low
Key Club was informally organized, with members including Zhou Fuo-hai,
Chiang Kai-shek's aide de camp and director of the Department of Information; Tao Xi-sheng, a Peking professor and an old member of Wang Ching-
wei's Reorganization faction; Gao Zong-wu, head of the Asian Bureau of
the Foreign Ministry; and Hu Shi, who also attended these meetings and
advocated peace.[55] These peace advocates had shared two fundamental
convictions: China would be defeated in a war with Japan, and it was possible
to work with the Konoe cabinet for a peaceful settlement.

Hu Shi, who also joined the nation's leading intellectuals at the Lushan
Conference to deliberate on war and peace, shared the sentiment that China
could not win a war with Japan. He supported Gao Zong-wu and other peace
advocates in their last try at reversing the impending disaster. Upon Hu's
recommendation, Gao was received by both Wang Ching-wei and Chiang
Kai-shek on July 30. After the meeting, Hu and Gao were encouraged to
think that they were "working on a miracle," meaning the difficult work of
peace. The fighting in Shanghai practically sealed any chance of conciliation.
Zhou, Tao, and Hu Shi decided to lie low for three months and then start the
peace process again. In early September, however, Hu gave up hope for a
diplomatic settlement when he was sent abroad on a diplomatic mission. Hu
concluded in his diary that "peace was a hundred times more difficult than
war."[56] He advised Wang Ching-wei, Tao Xi-sheng, and Gao to give up the
idea of peace and to support the war effort.

Diametrically opposed to the defeatist outlook was the argument that
China would survive the war and emerge victorious eventually. This was
based on the commonly accepted strategy of protracted warfare. Japan
desired a quick victory because of its shortage of manpower and its economy,
whereas China, with her vast countryside, preferred a long, protracted war.

Major military leaders, such as Chiang Kai-shek, Yan Xi-shan, Chief of Staff Bai Chong-xi, and military strategist Jiang Bai-li all emphasized such a strategy. "Trading space for time" came to be adopted as a standard slogan in 1938. This theory was later explained by Mao Ze-dong in his famous tract, *Protracted Warfare.* Bai Chong-xi summarized the book as "accumulating small victories into big ones; trading space for time." The Military Affairs Commission even ordered officers all over the country to study the book, which was regarded as the guiding principle for the war.[57]

The reasons for the Communists to advocate a protracted war could have been many, but the main one was that the war provided them with an opportunity to breathe and survive. Advocating war was a good political strategy in terms of promoting patriotic emotions as well as their own interests. The Shanghai fighting in August quickly brought the CCP-KMT negotiations to a conclusion, and by agreement the former pledged to abandon its policies of armed struggle as well as its Sovietization and land confiscation. It also pledged to place the Red Army, now to be called the 8th Route Army, under the command of the national government. In return Chiang legalized the CCP and ended the long struggle between the two adversaries. Despite the cooperative veneer, Chiang was fully aware of the CCP's potential for expansion. The fear that the Communists would take advantage of the war and grow was precisely one of the arguments of the peace advocates. Zhou Fuo-hai wrote in his diary on October 6 that "the war was fought not for China but for Russia; not for the KMT but for the CCP."[58]

The proponents and opponents of war derived much of their arguments from their perceptions of international politics. The Communists and other opponents of peace generally adopted the two-camp theory, dividing the world into a Fascist block and a peace block. The Fascist challenge to the existing world order and peace would inevitably cause war between the two camps. In February 1938, Zhou En-lai wrote: "The ambitions of these few aggressor nations will never be satisfied. They will start the second world war without thinking. . . . There is no hope of compromise with them." Those who advocated the war argued that Britain, France, the Soviet Union, and the United States were also getting closer to one another. China therefore should cooperate closely with the peace camp and get economic and military aid from these countries.[59]

This two-camp theory of the world was branded by the advocates of peace as puerile. They considered the world a much more complex place and felt that there were no stable and unchanging alliances. Tao Xi-sheng, while acknowledging that there was such a division of the world into two camps, pointed out that after the aggressor countries had destroyed the international collective security system, the grouping of world powers would undoubtedly undergo a complete change. "The present international camps are based on temporary interests," Tao argued, "and not on their permanent interests. Changes in their interests would cause changes in international alliances." Tao concluded that China's foreign policy should be based on joining neither camp.[60] Moreover, Tao felt that the international situation had definitely changed for the worse. In January 1938, he wrote that Britain had approached Germany and Italy for compromises, and the Soviet Union had become isolated. The collective security system had been completely destroyed. Though these situations had changed, Tao continued, China's unilateral war with Japan remained unchanged. Other peace advocates simply denied the validity of the two-camp theory.[61]

The proresistance people in general held that the Soviet Union was China's best and most reliable friend. After all, the Soviet Union was the only country giving China massive amounts of military aid, including advisers and pilots. Obviously, it shared with China the Japanese threat. According to U.S. military intelligence reports, the general consensus in China favored close cooperation with the Soviet Union.[62] For a brief moment, there was the high expectation that the Soviet Union would enter the war on China's side. For example, Feng Yu-xiang truly believed Stalin's promise that the Soviet Union would join the war if China could hold out until the spring of 1938, and he repeatedly urged Chiang Kai-shek to join the Franco-Soviet alliance.[63] This turned out to be a dream. Wang Ching-wei ridiculed such trust in the Soviet Union as a gamble. In January Tao publicly called this expectation an illusion.[64] As Tao later recalled in 1964, he never for a moment succumbed to the popular notion that the Soviet Union would enter the war because he was convinced from reading the accounts of the Soviet purge trials in the spring of 1937 that the Soviets would avoid fighting a two-front war.[65] Unlike most people, he argued that there was no inevitable cause of war between the Soviets and the Japanese. Nor was there any reason for the Soviet Union to invite enemies by taking part in any war.[66]

Similarly, there was a diversity of attitudes toward the capitalist powers. Despite the failure at Brussels and the powers' unwillingness to aid China, most Chinese stubbornly held on to the belief that Britain and the United States would not permit the Japanese a free hand in Asia. One leftist author claimed that British investment in Central and South China amounted to 2.5 billion pounds and that Britain controlled China's customs. Besides, Hong Kong held a close security relationship with Guangdong Province. The Americans, he argued, were young imperialists full of vitality and expansionist needs. U.S. trade with China had already become the largest in terms of Chinese imports, and, he continued, China's vast markets, people, and unlimited resources offered the United States a good opportunity. In the views of Jin Zhong-hua, another leftist writer, and Hu Qiu-yuan, secretary of the National Defense Council, they were waiting for the best opportunity to strike at Japan. "Once the time is ripe, they will act immediately." Their temporary concessions to Japan were only a kind of diplomatic strategy and Japan's conflict with the powers, "an international storm," as Hu termed it, was coming soon.[67]

To the pessimists, the failure of the League of Nations and the Brussels Conference was self-explanatory. Zhou Fuo-hai distrusted Anglo-Americans, who in his view would compromise with Japan if given assurances by the Japanese that the markets in Central and South China would remain open. Zhou argued that China should not only have zero expectations about Anglo-American powers but should also be aware that she might be victimized by their policies.[68] Having lost faith in the collective security system, Tao Xi-sheng declared in early 1938 that the Anglo-American powers would not cooperate with Russia as most Chinese wished. Apparently, the pessimistic argument would lead to the conclusion that since the powers would not come to China's rescue, resistance would cause more disaster, and a settlement with Japan would prevent further loss of territory and total defeat. On the other hand, the optimistic argument was used to justify the continuation of war, since the powers would sooner or later join China in a total war or at least assist China's cause.

CHIANG, WANG, AND PEACE

Where did Chiang Kai-shek stand on this question of war and peace? His private thoughts in early 1938 suggested that Chiang still continued to hope for an eventual intervention by the powers while keeping the door open for a peace settlement with Japan under acceptable terms. In January he acknowledged that the powers were still not ready to act, yet at the same time he believed that President Roosevelt of the United States had already realized the danger of aggression and had prepared to strengthen the American forces. "So long as we hold out the resistance, the international situation will definitely change and Japan will ultimately be defeated." [69] The same idea was echoed in a speech Chiang delivered to high army officers. He rationalized that the powers failed to intervene because the opportune moment had not come yet. According to him, once persistent Chinese resistance exposed Japan's vulnerability, the powers would attack

Japan without any hesitation.[70] Undoubtedly his speech was to boost morale, but the consistency of his views both in public and in private did point to deeply held beliefs.

In spite of Chiang's beliefs, he faced an urgent dilemma. To fight with Japan would diminish his power vis-à-vis local power holders, since his power base and source of revenue was in the lower Yangtze River valley, now under Japan's control. Moreover, the loss of 20 percent of the central government troops in defense of Shanghai and Nanking, and a further loss of two-thirds by the end of 1938, drastically reduced Chiang's power. The removal of the government inland made Chiang more vulnerable and receptive to the wishes of other provincial military leaders. Besides, the CCP, in addition to the provincial warlords, might grow to threaten his rule. But a failure to fight Japan would not be tolerated by the public and would therefore strengthen Chiang's rivals. Chiang's government was hard-pressed for a viable strategy that would guarantee its survival as the central government of China. While the powers still remained inactive, dealing with Japan was a dangerous but practical option.

Chiang's ambivalent attitude explained why the peace advocates dared to engage in peace activities. Right after the Shanghai war broke out, Zhou Fuo-hai, Tao Xi-sheng, and Gao Zong-wu began to probe peace. Their efforts were carried on even after Konoe's statement closed the diplomatic channels in mid-January 1938. Under orders from Chiang Kai-shek and Wang Ching-wei, a government propaganda agency, the Institute of Art and Literature, was created with the exclusive purpose "first to create an independent theory to oppose Communist influence and then to create public opinion to enable the government either to fight or to reach a peace settlement."[71] Zhou and Tao controlled this propaganda organ, and they maneuvered Chiang Kai-shek to approve of Gao Zong-wu's trip to Hong Kong to "gather intelligence," that is, to open possible channels of communication with Japan. In Hong Kong, Gao set up the Institute of Japanese Studies, a branch of the Institute of Art and Literature, and made contacts with the Japanese.[72]

Chiang Kai-shek, after hearing the report about the mission, showed interest in this newly opened channel. He instructed Gao as to the terms under which a cease-fire might be arranged. He would accept nothing less than Japan's recognition of China's sovereignty south of the Great Wall. As for Inner Mongolia and Manchuria, negotiations could be held at a later date.[73] Receiving no response to this proposal, Chiang limited Gao's activities in Hong Kong to gathering intelligence only.

Wang Ching-wei's position within the government was at its nadir at that time. Since his cooperation with Chiang, he had been head of the KMT party and the government. Chiang was in charge of the Military Affairs Commission, though Chiang in fact controlled the Nanking government. The war situation had greatly elevated the status of Chiang Kai-shek. He was not only chairman of the National Defense Council but also was elected in April head of the KMT party with the title of *Zongcai*. Wang was only given second place in the party. This change hurt the vainglorious Wang greatly. His face showed much embarrassment when he gave his acceptance speech to the congress.[74] It was a moment of humiliation for a man who had followed Sun Yat-sen from the beginning and who was the oldest remaining founder of the KMT. For a while, Wang kept his discomfiture under control and continued to work with Chiang. He refused attempts by the Italian ambassador and pro-Japanese elements in China to separate him from Chiang and to lead the peace movement.[75] At the same time, he tried about ten times to persuade Chiang that the war should be stopped. Chiang rejected his views point blank.

However, Chiang's rejection of Wang's request for peace negotiations was related in part to the power struggle between the two men. To allow Wang to take the initiative for peace negotiations would destroy Chiang's standing within the government should a peace settlement become a reality and would totally discredit Chiang's decision for war. Evidence suggests that Chiang was also considering alternatives. Zhang Qun, a close follower of Chiang, sent a telegram to Ugaki Kasushige when he became foreign minister of Japan in June congratulating him on his appointment and suggesting peace negotiations with Wang Ching-wei as representative. Ugaki suggested that H. H. Kung come to Japan, since he did not have the label of "pro-Japanese" like Wang or Zhang.[76] These schemes failed partly because of unacceptable Japanese terms that included, among other things, the resignation of Chiang Kai-shek. Since July 1938, Konoe preferred to deal with Wang Ching-wei at the suggestion of Gao Zong-wu, who took a secret trip to Japan. Gao also had the task of persuading Wang to split with Chiang and take up the peace work. Perhaps wishing to boost his position, Wang Ching-wei handed over to Chiang the report that contained the Japanese demand for Chiang's resignation. Chiang became furious and vowed to cut off relations with Gao, who at this time dared not return to China and stayed on in Hong Kong.[77]

Japan's demand for Chiang's resignation was a factor in Chiang's hardening his determination to continue the war. For all Chiang's fury, however, contacts with Japan continued under the control of his brother in law, Kung. Kung was premier and enjoyed extremely intimate relations with Chiang. Actually, since the spring of 1938, Kung had been in contact with a certain

Kayano, who was an old friend of Sun Yat-sen. In June Kung sent his personal secretary, Qiao Pu-san, to Hong Kong to negotiate with the Japanese consul. After that, informal talks were held in Shanghai and Hong Kong. Kung insisted on the withdrawal of Japan's condition that Chiang Kai-shek resign. These talks in Hong Kong were without any quick result and stopped when Wang Ching-wei defected in December 1938.[78]

In addition to the factor of power, Chiang differed with Wang and other peace advocates in a crucial aspect: the terms of peace. Wang and those like-minded were ready to accept harsh peace terms in a Brest-Litovskian fashion, whereas Chiang insisted on the restoration of the status quo ante. In August, Chiang and He Ying-qin authorized Xiao Zhen-ying, a general of the 29th Army who had Japanese friends and who was then in Hong Kong, to negotiate with Japan. The terms Chiang offered for negotiation included restoration of prewar status quo and Japanese withdrawal from China within a year. In addition, Japan was to recognize China's sovereignty; the two countries were to undertake a joint defense against communism; and there were to be no reparations. According to Xiao, Chiang did not mention the fate of Inner Mongolia and Manchuria for fear that it would ruin the negotiations.[79] The newly published KMT documents lend support to these personal recollections. In two instructions to Xiao, Chiang insisted on a truce and restoration of status quo ante as preconditions to any agreement, economic or military, between China and Japan. Chiang admitted that he never sealed any road to peace and instructed Premier Kung that if Konoe was sincere in talking peace, Kung could meet him.[80] Xiao's negotiations came to a stop when Wuhan fell in late October.

Most important, Chiang and Wang differed on the question of the powers' attitude toward the Sino-Japanese War. While Chiang believed in eventual Soviet and Anglo-American intervention, Wang and his followers did not. In July, for example, Foreign Minister Wang Chong-hui approached both American and British ambassadors and requested good offices, and in early October, Chiang even wrote a letter asking President Roosevelt to "initiate a move for the peace of the Far East." Chiang's personal secretary, Chen Bu-lei, explained to Ambassador Hu Chiang's belief that mediation would have some chance of success if the United States took the lead.[81] Chiang's July request for mediation was considered impractical by Wang Ching-wei and Zhou Fuo-hai because they believed the United States would not take up such a role. Even if it did, Zhou was afraid that it was like "a distant water that cannot extinguish the nearby fire." The loss of Wuhan and Canton probably deepened their skepticism about Britain and the United States and pushed them further to seek peace.[82]

WAR OVER PEACE

Following Chiang's rejection of Gao Zong-wu's report, Zhou Fuo-hai and Tao Xi-sheng rallied around Wang Ching-wei, the man preferred by Japan to head the Chinese government. Wang was fully aware of this and began to involve himself in negotiations with Japan behind Chiang's back.

The most crucial moment for the decision on war or peace came in October when Wuhan and Canton fell into Japanese hands. The effect of these defeats on Chinese morale was devastating. Even Chen Li-fu, who had played such a crucial role in forming the Sino-Soviet de facto alliance at this time, was reported to be in favor of peace.[83] The fateful month of October witnessed a fierce battle between the resistance and peace factions, which finally resulted in Wang's defection.

Perhaps for the first time, Wang openly and unabashedly spoke for peace. On October 1 he told a Rueters reporter that "if Japan put forward a peace plan that does not hamper China's national survival, we should accept it as a basis for discussion."[84] Wang was the speaker of the wartime People's Political Council (PPC), a kind of parliament created at the beginning of the war. Its members included Communists, KMT officials, and some famous intellectuals. It was a perfect place for public opinion to be expressed or manipulated.[85] As head of this parliament and second in command of government, Wang's open call for peace indicated that the schism between the peace and war factions could no longer be contained.

Wang's public talk of peace was strongly condemned by the war faction. The KMT left, Madame Sun Yat-sen, Madame Liao Zhong-kai, Chen You-ren, and Xu Qian, a former minister of justice, addressed a letter to Chiang Kai-shek and other government leaders demanding that "these peace traffickers be dealt with."[86] Clearly they wanted to put more pressure on Chiang by making their statement public so that a government-sanctioned peace move could be forestalled.

In the meantime, the second PPC, which was convened in Chongqing, became an antipeace arena. The Communist analysis of the KMT characterized Chiang not as pro-Japanese but as representing the interests of British and American imperialism. Thus Chiang had, according to their line of reasoning, both tendencies to compromise with and to resist Japan. Therefore, they continued their strategy of making Chiang Kai-shek's image into that of national resistance and national supreme leader so that Chiang would not and could not openly support the peace movement. They led 73 councillors of the PPC to pass a resolution supporting Chiang's war efforts. The resolution artfully accused the enemy and traitors of spreading rumors about China's willingness to compromise and to surrender.[87]

Many non-Communist members of the Council also attacked the peace faction. Zhang Yi-lin and 40 members moved that the government issue decrees to affirm its determination to resist for the sake of national morale. The most violent blow to Speaker Wang Ching-wei was a bombshell fired from abroad by an absent councillor, Chen Jia-geng, a wealthy and influential overseas Chinese passionately supporting the war of resistance. He sent a "telegram motion" containing only 11 words: "Public officials who talk about peace should be punished as traitors." Chen's proposal was aimed at Wang Ching-wei. When it was passed, Wang read the resolution to the Council with his face pale and uneasy.[88]

The peace advocates were no match for overwhelming public opinion. Wang and Tao tried to influence the course of the PPC in vain. The Council passed all the resolutions favored by the resistance people.[89] Tao Xi-sheng attributed the defeat of the peace faction at the second PPC to the Communists, "who destroyed the feelings between Chiang and Wang."[90] Undoubtedly, this conference was a victory for the Communists and the resistance group. This kind of public opinion indeed limited government options regarding war and peace. As the British ambassador put it, government leaders such as Chiang and Wang lived in "a glass house" and had to formulate policies with this factor in mind.

Certain venerable and influential KMT militarists also did their utmost to expose potential peace moves so as to forestall what they considered capitulation. After Wuhan and Canton fell, General Li Lie-jun, a major military leader from the days of the Nationalist revolution in the early 1920s who did not have much power but had enough prestige to oppose Chiang, plotted with Feng Yu-xiang and another one of Chiang's old enemies, General Li Ji-shen. Suspecting that Chiang, Wang Ching-wei, and He Ying-qin might take advantage of the situation and negotiate with Japan, they decided that if that happened, they would organize their own army in North, South, and Central China, respectively, and continue the war in cooperation with the Communists. Feng Yu-xiang was sent to see Chiang Kai-shek right after the loss of Wuhan to prevent the latter from capitulating.[91]

While China was deliberating on war or peace, the Konoe government issued a statement on November 3 calling for a new order in East Asia. Konoe promised generous terms, including renunciation of Japan's claims to reparations and its extraterritorial rights in China. Moreover, the relations between China and Japan were to be placed on equal footing. On paper, Konoe's statement looked very attractive, as it indicated a reversal of his statement of January 16. Greatly encouraged by this statement, Wang and his followers quickly started actual negotiations with Japan in Shanghai. In December, Wang answered the Japanese call and left Chongqing for Hanoi, confident that he would gather a large following. Quite unexpectedly, even his most trusted follower, Chen Gong-bo, opposed his defection, though Chen, out of personal loyalty, joined Wang anyway. Wang's former supporter, Gu Meng-yu, and his military supporter, General Zhang Fa-kui, refused to go. The provincial warlord Long Yun in Yunnan also failed to throw his support to Wang's cause. In the end, only Wang, Zhou Fuo-hai, Gao, Tao, and a few personal friends joined the peace movement.[92] Wang's defection put to rest the debate on war and peace. Wang and his followers were branded as traitors and the peace movement became synonymous with treason.

At this crucial juncture, the United States joined the Soviet Union to aid China with a loan of $25 million, with the condition that Chiang Kai-shek continue resistance. The American loan of December 1938, as Ambassador Hu Shi observed, "greatly helped Chiang Kai-shek to gain the decision for continued and intensified resistance."[93] Indeed, bolstered by the American aid, Chiang was determined to continue the war. Moreover, Chiang viewed American aid as proof that the Chinese resistance did cause the powers to act and that his long-held beliefs were right. Therefore, Chiang wrote in his diary that he would count on diplomacy to "promote unity of Britain and the United States and provoke international intervention so as to abort the enemy's ambition of establishing hegemony in East Asia."[94] This meant that Chiang would more vigorously pursue alliances with the Soviet Union and the Anglo-American powers. In a speech at a KMT conference, Chiang openly declared the policy of allying with the non-Fascist powers and severing ties with Germany and Italy. According to Sun Ke, "Everybody became elated upon hearing Chiang's speech."[95] Dumping Germany and Italy from China's list of friendly nations was quite significant. In public it signaled the decline of the German approach, which was seen as a channel of compromise with Japan.

While it is true that secret peace probes continued beyond 1938, these activities were designed to achieve different purposes, such as delaying Japanese recognition of Wang Ching-wei's regime, delaying Japanese military advances, or bargaining with the Soviet Union, and later with the United States, for more support. Pressures from public opinion and domestic politics aside, Chiang had little to gain personally from a Japan-sponsored Chiang-Wang government. If anything, Chiang would have lost his dominant position. Internationally, the Anglo-American powers became more active in

1939 as Japan moved into Southeast Asia, and, from a Chinese perspective, Japan was one step closer to an inevitable conflict with the powers. Consequently, there was much less incentive than in 1938 for Chiang to truly entertain a peace settlement with Japan.

6

The Soviet Union:
An Ally in Distrust, 1937–1940

The outbreak of the Sino-Japanese War in July 1937 forced China to secure foreign alliances. In geopolitical and strategic terms, the Soviet Union and China shared a stake in Japanese expansion and consequently both found it convenient and beneficial to cooperate. These parallel interests formed a foundation for the de facto Sino-Soviet alliance in the first two years of the war. This relationship was the single most significant factor in sustaining the belief in the inevitable conflict between Japan and the powers (including the Soviet Union) and thus in keeping China in the war.

In this partnership of convenience, the ultimate Chinese objective was to bring about Soviet military intervention against Japan, a goal many Chinese believed to be attainable. The procurement of arms was obviously the immediate objective, since no other country was willing to extend substantial aid. For the Soviets, military aid was merely a security insurance premium. The Nazi-Soviet pact dealt a serious blow to the "inevitable conflict" thesis and the outbreak of war in Europe raised the specter of Soviet appeasement of Japan. In the final analysis, mutual suspicions and the European war prevented the Sino-Soviet relationship from developing into a full-fledged alliance.

BARGAINING OF THE NONAGGRESSION PACT

The Marco Polo Bridge Incident accelerated the previous Sino-Soviet negotiations and drew both sides toward rapid accommodation. On the morning of July 8 at Lushan, Chiang Kai-shek discussed the Soviet policy with

Foreign Minister Wang Chong-hui and Sun Ke, the proponent of Sino-Soviet alliance. In Chiang's view, if the Marco Polo Bridge Incident developed into a full-scale war, Soviet military supplies and a Sino-Soviet pact of mutual assistance would be most crucial.[1] Sun and Wang were ordered to resume talks with Bogomolov immediately and to ask for the mutual assistance pact the Soviet ambassador had proposed three months earlier. But the latter acknowledged that the circumstances had changed, and he was only willing discuss a nonaggression pact.[2]

The same effort was made in Moscow. In an interview with Litvinov, Ambassador Jiang Ting-fu inquired about Soviet aid in a war with Japan. Litvinov expressed his dissatisfaction with China's previous refusal to consider the Soviet proposal for a Pacific conference of the powers as a step in establishing a closer alliance between the Soviet Union and China. Jiang Ting-fu reported to Nanking, "It is obvious from the Soviet attitude that . . . Soviet actual aid to us cannot be counted on."[3] Ambassador Jiang repeated his opinion in a number of telegrams to Nanking. Such an estimate of the Soviet Union was clearly a mistake. If there was any power who would assist China, it was the Soviet Union. Now that Chiang Kai-shek was standing firm against Japan, the Soviets had every reason to cheer him on. Litvinov's lukewarm attitude only indicated a cautious policy to see whether Chiang would really commit himself to resistance or whether this would turn out to be another episode in concession-making.

In July, China was in a difficult negotiating position. To win Soviet support of either military intervention or material aid, China would have to demonstrate a determination to resist Japan; yet such a demonstration would escalate the war, which they had little hope of winning, and would make China dependent on the Soviet Union. In such a situation, Chiang initially tried to play it both ways. While he was still hoping for a peaceful settlement with Japan, he pressed the Soviet Union for material assistance and for a military alliance if possible. He requested a credit of 150 million Chinese yuan for the purchase of military supplies. On July 19, Chiang instructed Chen Li-fu to see Bogomolov about an increased amount of 200 million yuan. Chen tried to convince Bogomolov that after conquering China, Japan's next target would be the Soviet Union. Chen argued that only close cooperation between China and the Soviet Union could reduce Japan's threat.[4]

Distrustful of Nanking, the Soviets were not persuaded. The signing of the proposed pact would immediately involve the Soviet Union in the ongoing conflict. Bogomolov, suspecting that Chiang might compromise with Japan, recommended to Moscow that Chiang's request for military credit be granted only up to 150 million Chinese yuan. As a condition for this loan, China should sign a nonaggression pact and guarantee that the weapons would not be used against the Soviet Union.[5] In his subsequent talks with Chen Li-fu and Wang Chong-hui, Bogomolov was troubled by the ongoing negotiations between Song Zhe-yuan and the Japanese in the north. Wang reassured him that whatever the result of the negotiations, China and Japan were already on an inevitable collision course and that it was impossible for China to accept the Japanese Pan-Asianism. Following such assurances, Chen Li-fu reiterated China's wish to begin negotiations for a pact of mutual assistance.[6]

After intense negotiations, it appeared by the end of July that material assistance would be the most China could get from the Soviets at this time. On July 26 Zhang Qun, now secretary general of the KMT National Defense Council, indicated to Bogomolov that Chiang Kai-shek would like to conclude an agreement on military aid first without any reference to a pact of mutual assistance.[7] Chiang Kai-shek, like most Chinese, was very disappointed in the Soviet refusal to conclude a pact of mutual assistance. He asked the French ambassador to tell the Soviets that if the Soviet Union remained indifferent, China would do the same when the Soviet Union became a victim of aggression.[8]

Official Soviet reply to Chiang's requests came on July 31—not surprisingly, two days after Chiang had made the unequivocal speech on resistance. Bogomolov informed Chiang that the Soviet Union considered the possibility of a pact of mutual assistance remote, but would grant China military aid in the amount of 100 million Chinese yuan for the purchase of, among other things, 200 planes and 200 tanks. Moreover, the Soviet Union would send a small military delegation to Nanking to assist China and train Chinese pilots and tank operators.[9]

On the Chinese side, suspicions also abounded. Chiang wrote in his diary that the Soviet Union might use this nonaggression pact to pressure Japan for the same kind of agreement.[10] However, Chiang had almost no choice but to accept the Soviet offer and the attached condition. The domestic demand for strong resistance, the Japanese occupation of Peking and Tientsin, and the lukewarm attitude of the Western powers all weakened Chiang's bargaining position vis-à-vis the Soviet Union. By the time the Shanghai fighting broke out in mid-August, China became fully mobilized for war. Under such circumstances, China's dependence on Soviet assistance was almost imperative. Chiang Kai-shek quickly conceded to the Soviet demand for a nonaggression pact as a condition for military aid.[11] With the pact signed on August 21, Chiang Kai-shek lost his political advantage of playing the Soviets against Japan.

THE ILLUSION OF SOVIET MILITARY INTERVENTION

The Chinese public hailed the nonaggression pact as a step toward a pact of mutual assistance and a prelude to a Pacific collective security system that the United States and Britain might join later.[12] The hopes and predictions for Soviet military intervention against Japan became almost a political fashion in the latter half of 1937.

In September, under the cover of investigating Soviet industry, China sent a delegation to the Soviet Union to carry out the agreement on military aid. The delegation was headed by General Yang Jie, an undersecretary in Chiang's General Staff who remained in the Soviet Union for the next two years, and Zhang Chong, a member of the KMT central committee. In the negotiations, Yang presented the Soviets with a long shopping list that included, among other things, 350 airplanes, 82 tanks, and other military equipment, plus technical personnel.[13] By mid-October, the Soviets had delivered 400 planes and other military supplies, and the credit of 100 million Chinese yuan had already been exceeded.[14]

Expectations for the Soviet entry into the war, however, remained the biggest illusion the Chinese government and general public harbored for the new Sino-Soviet relationship. Chiang Kai-shek was influenced by this illusion and even predicted that the Soviets would take part in the war in three months.[15] In September, the Foreign Ministry instructed Ambassador Jiang Ting-fu to ascertain Soviet policy with regard to positive military actions against Japan.[16]

Such Chinese hopes were partly encouraged by Bogomolov. Before the war, Bogomolov reportedly made assurances to the Chinese that the Soviet Union would offer armed support to China in case of war.[17] The effect of such encouragement from the Soviet ambassador was still felt among high-official circles after it became clear that the Soviet Union was not prepared to enter the war at all. For example, the chief of staff of the Military Affairs Commission, General He Yao-zu, considered a pact of mutual assistance possible. In September General He urged Chiang to take active steps to promote such a relationship and to remove Soviet suspicions that the Chinese government might compromise with Japan.[18]

The strong Soviet support for China in international conferences, in contrast to the Western powers, might have encouraged Chinese optimism regarding Soviet intervention. In September 1937, Litvinov supported China at the League of Nations. Koo, who had a very good working relationship with Litvinov, felt satisfied with the Soviet Union's sympathetic and cooperative attitude. During a subsequent meeting at the League,

Litvinov fulfilled his pledge of support, calling for collective resistance against aggressors in both Europe and Asia. Wellington Koo in his memoir lauded this speech as "wonderful from the Chinese standpoint."[19] China and the Soviet Union also cooperated closely at the Brussels conference. After learning that Japan had refused to participate in the Brussels conference in late October, Chiang Kai-shek worried about the compromising inclinations of the Anglo-American powers. He told Ambassador Jiang in Moscow that China would refuse any compromise plan by the powers that was harmful to China. Fearful of being isolated, China counted heavily on Soviet help.[20] The Soviets had nothing to fear from strong actions by the League such as economic sanctions against Japan. Soviet exports to Japan, for instance, had already dwindled from 13 million yen in 1937 to only 0.7 million yen in 1938.[21] Politically, the Soviet Union had been attacking Japanese aggression in China from the very beginning, and the Soviet position at the League added nothing more to the already hostile Russo-Japanese relations.

The Soviet Union also deliberately encouraged the Chinese illusion of Soviet military intervention in the Sino-Japanese conflict. Stalin received the Chinese representatives General Yang and Zhang Chong on November 11. Stalin offered an interesting excuse for not intervening. He said both the wealthy Japanese companies, such as Mitsubishi, and the Japanese peasants opposed the militarists' aggression in China; therefore, a Soviet declaration of war on Japan would help unify the Japanese nation behind the militarists. In addition, Stalin continued, a Soviet war against Japan would cost China half of the world's sympathy because of anti-Soviet feelings all over the world. However, to keep up the Chinese hope, Stalin never closed the door on military intervention. He promised that if the war turned unfavorable to China or the situation became desperate, the Soviet Union would go to war against Japan. As a compensation for not entering the war, Stalin offered to build heavy war industries for China. These included factories producing airplanes and cannons and an oil refinery in Xinjiang.[22] Six days later, Voroshilov repeated Stalin's promise that if the war came to the worst for China, the Soviet Union would certainly intervene militarily and would never be a bystander.[23]

Chiang Kai-shek immediately grasped this slight indication of Soviet military intervention and pleaded to Stalin that with the imminent collapse of Nanking and the failure of the Brussels conference, China had already reached the desperate point Stalin mentioned in his talks with Yang and Zhang. The time had come. However, Stalin found another precondition for Soviet military intervention. Knowing too well that the powers would not unite against Japan, Stalin told Chiang that if the signatories of the Nine Power Treaty or its major members agreed to form a common front against Japanese aggression, the Soviet Union would no doubt declare war on Japan, and only in this way could the Soviet action be justified in world opinion.[24]

Nanking fell and Stalin did nothing. Yang Jie, who was naively optimistic about eventual Soviet entry into the war, still took Stalin's promise at face value. He suggested to Chiang Kai-shek that in order to persuade the Soviet Union to join the war, China must make the Anglo-American powers support the Soviet Union and guarantee its European security. Or China should move closer to the Soviet Union so as to provoke a Japanese attack on the latter, thereby forcing the Soviets into war. Yang's naivete and misjudgment were quite indicative of the epidemic of illusion in China. Psychologically, in a situation as difficult as the Chinese were in, anything that glittered was gold.[25]

Needless to say, Chiang equally desired the cooperation of the major powers in the Far East as a formidable deterrent to Japan's aggression. The British distrust of Russia and the unwillingness of the United States to get involved were obviously undesirable. Both Chiang and Zhang Qun urged Britain to act jointly with the Soviet Union and asked for Anglo-American assurances to protect the Soviet Union from a "stab in the back" in Europe. At one point, Chiang expressed dissatisfaction at British inaction and reminded them that if China had joined the Japanese efforts to drive out the Anglo-American powers, there would have been no war with Japan.[26]

Unlike Yang and many others, Jiang Ting-fu maintained a cool head and continued to be very critical of both the Russians and Yang Jie. While the hope for Soviet intervention was running high, Ambassador Jiang reported that such expectations were unrealistic. When inquiring about Soviet help to China beyond material assistance once the United States made a move, Jiang Ting-fu was told in no uncertain terms that "we never used such a formula," meaning there was no connection between Soviet policy and that of other countries.[27] However correct, Jiang's judgment was politically unpopular. At a National Defense Council meeting, Sun Ke attacked Jiang and charged him with having misunderstood Soviet intentions. The ambassador was recalled in December because of domestic dissatisfaction with his views on the Soviet Union and with his performance. Ironically, he was even blamed for the failure of Soviet entry into the war.[28]

Despite some disappointment, many Chinese still entertained the notion of an eventual Soviet intervention in the spring of 1938. Some regarded economic and political cooperation between the two countries as a "historical certainty," not just a possibility.[29] Many Chinese began to rationalize the failure of the Soviets to enter the war. Gan Jie-hou, a believer in Soviet intervention who was now working on Chiang Kai-shek's foreign policy staff, explained that the Soviet Union faced enemies like Germany and that it could not take any action without cooperating with the Anglo-American powers and without establishing a self-sufficient military region in Siberia. These conditions were not met from July 1937 to early 1938. Gan believed that the Soviet Union would be in a better position in mid-1938 to consider strong measures in the Far East.[30]

Evidently, the vague Soviet assurances that they would enter the war once the Chinese resistance came near collapse were purely intended to keep China in war. The Soviets always suspected that Chiang was still pursuing a peace settlement as an alternative. When Chiang informed him of the German mediation of December 1937 to bargain for more active Soviet involvement, Stalin called his bluff and "ordered a cessation of activity by their aviators and had halted other plans for military assistance pending the outcome" of the German mediation.[31]

SUN KE'S MISSIONS

By the end of 1937, China had lost major coastal cities, including Shanghai and Nanking. In the meantime, it became increasingly dependent on one source of support: the Soviet Union. The temporary loan of 100 million yuan was quickly exhausted, and the next question was how to secure more assistance to prevent a collapse of the resistance. It was militarily imperative and politically crucial for Chiang to obtain more Soviet aid and even direct military intervention, and for that purpose he sent Sun Ke, in January 1938, to Moscow to improve ties between the two countries.

Being the son of Sun Yat-sen, Sun Ke was a unique individual and known for his pro-Soviet views. Since the Manchurian Incident, he had constantly urged close relations with the Soviet Union. He was head of the Sino-Soviet Cultural Association that was set up in 1936. Sun not only viewed the Soviet Union as a true friend but also as one that shared with China a common interest in opposing Japan. In October 1937, Sun urged Chiang Kai-shek to adopt a genuine pro-Soviet policy by cutting ties with the Fascist powers, Germany and Italy, and thus showing complete solidarity with the Soviets.[32] As the president of the Legislative Yuan, Sun was the first high-ranking KMT official to visit Moscow since the KMT broke relations with the Soviet Union in 1927. Sun was endowed with full authority and the mission was considered so important that during his three weeks' stay in Moscow, he did not even telegraph the Chinese government for fear that the message might be decoded.[33]

Sun's mission was to persuade the Soviets to enter the war and to grant more aid to China. For long-term strategic reasons, Sun wanted to build up mutual trust by placating the Soviet Union and by getting rid of its suspicion that China would make peace with Japan at her expense. Sun thought that to show Chinese resolve for a defensive-offensive alliance was best the means to assure the Soviets. In addition, Sun was planning to promote cooperation between the democratic powers and the Soviet Union. He seemed confident that the Soviets would welcome and respond to his initiatives.[34]

Upon his arrival in Moscow on January 21, 1938, Sun immediately made it clear to the Soviets that China wished Soviet-Chinese cooperation to be established on a permanent basis.[35] After talking with Stalin, Sun reported to Chiang Kai-shek on February 7 that Stalin treated him "as a revolutionary comrade and talked in an extremely frank and confidential manner."[36] The Chinese chargé d'affaires also told his American counterpart in Moscow that Sun's mission had created mutual trust between the two countries.[37]

This "mutual trust" was not translated into any progress on the question of Soviet military intervention. Sun reported to Chiang that "the Soviet Union will support us all the way to victory. But immediate military intervention will have to wait for a better international situation. If, for instance, the League of Nations decides to penalize Japan, or at least, Britain, France, and the United States agree to act in accordance with the Soviet Union, the Soviets will take military actions against Japan."[38] Litvinov told Sun specifically that Washington was the key and China should do whatever it could to influence American public opinion.[39] Though Sun Ke appeared optimistic about bilateral relations as a whole, he was not pleased with the "political arrangement," meaning the Soviet refusal to enter the Sino-Japanese War.[40]

While Sun was absent from Moscow, Japan launched an offensive to capture Xuzhou, the strategic communications center in eastern China. Chiang appealed to the Soviets in March for a Soviet assault on Japanese forces in Manchuria to relieve pressure on Xuzhou.[41] In May, Sun was ordered back to Moscow because of disputes between Yang Jie and Voroshilov over the disorganized situation of Soviet aid and China's inability to pay cash. Sun was instructed to ask the Soviet government to at least prevent the transfer of Japanese troops to Xuzhou by concentrating Soviet forces in the border areas. Once again the Soviets refused to take any action.[42]

China at this time was unable to pay cash for the arms purchased from the Soviet Union. In May this seemed to be a major problem. Chiang had to personally appeal to Stalin and Voroshilov for more shipments of planes and other weapons and apologize for the inability to pay for the goods previously delivered because of the war situation. Stalin and Voroshilov suggested payments in such Chinese products as tea, wool, tin, antimony, and other goods and promised that airplanes would be shipped out immediately.[43]

Sun Ke took up the matter of a second loan directly with Stalin, who, unlike his subordinates, seemed to be very generous. He suggested that the first loan be extended to $50 million, which was about 200 million Chinese yuan, twice the original amount. Moreover, the Soviet Union would lend China another $50 million to cover future purchases of war materials. Sun, in view of the vast need for military weapons, requested that the second loan be increased to $100 million. Stalin promised to float a third loan if the second became exhausted.[44] Sun was very satisfied with Stalin's offer and considered the Soviet loan worth more than twice its value if measured by arms delivered because the Soviet arms were at least twice as cheap as those in the international market. Sun also deemed it strategically vital that the Soviets deployed 75 divisions in Siberia, two-fifths of their entire force.[45]

In the summer of 1938, Japan commenced its drive to Wuhan, the last industrial center still in China's hands, and threatened Canton, the major transportation link to China's army. Chiang once again pressured for Soviet military intervention. On June 14, Chiang met with the Soviet ambassador, Lugants Orelski, and suggested that as the Japanese troops concentrated in inland China, it was "the best moment" for the Soviet Union to enter the war. Chiang never failed to use China's low morale and collapse of the resistance as a bargaining chip and argued that "if the Soviet Union enters into a secret military cooperation with China, then China's army will rise in spirit."[46]

The Soviet-Japanese tensions provided the Chinese with an excellent opportunity to revive fantasies about a Russo-Japanese war and a long-sought-for Sino-Soviet military pact. A border war between Japan and the Soviet Union erupted in Zhanggufeng, a group of hills west of Lake Khasan near the junction of the borders of Manchuria, Korea, and the Soviet Union between July 31 and August 10, 1938. Heavy casualties were inflicted on both sides.[47] Most Chinese hoped the conflict would become a large-scale war.[48] At a high-level dinner meeting, Zhang Ji-luan, chief editor of *Dagongbao,* advised Chiang Kai-shek that the Zhanggufeng Incident was the beginning of war between the Soviet Union and Japan. Others present agreed. Indeed many Chinese were elated to hear the news and some even predicted that the government would be able to move back to Nanking in 1939. According to his memoir, Jiang Ting-fu was the only person present who considered the conflict a local skirmish that would not result in a war.[49]

Chiang Kai-shek seemed to have demonstrated a keen interest in the incident and repeatedly instructed Ambassador Yang Jie to inquire about the Soviet policy over the Zhanggufeng dispute. Chiang attributed the inaction of Japanese forces in China to this conflict and expected the Soviets to keep up their pressure on Japan so that the latter would not be able to transfer more troops from Manchuria to the Wuhan campaign.[50] Chiang's premier, H. H. Kung, was convinced that "the incident will definitely spread out" [Shi Jiang Kuo Da].[51] Kung hoped very much that the Zhanggufeng fighting would turn into a major war and did his best to promote such an outcome. On July 30, Kung had a long talk with the Soviet chargé d'affaires expressing China's support for the Soviet Union. He tried to convince the Soviets that "the basic target of Japanese aggression is the Soviet Union. . . . A military solution is a better way. Japan has been weakened by the war in China. The combined forces of the USSR and China could crush Japan's military power." Kung also assured the Soviet official that there was no need to fear Germany since Blomburg, the German defense minister, had told him personally in 1937 that Germany would not be ready for war in two or three years. Nor should the Soviet Union fear hostility from the democratic powers for attacking Japan because they were all on China's side.[52]

The Chinese government also tried to prevent a peaceful solution of the conflict. Kung sent many telegrams to Ambassador Koo urging him to stop any attempt by France, the Soviet ally in Europe, to pressure the Soviet Union for conciliation, since France naturally preferred a strong Soviet Russia in Europe checking Germany rather than fighting Japan. Kung told Koo that France should support the Soviet Union in order for her to join forces with China and deal Japan a deadly blow.[53] Upon hearing the rumor that France was going to persuade the Soviet Union to make concessions to Japan, Chiang Kai-shek immediately cabled Koo on August 6, ordering him "to do everything possible to make France actively support the Soviet Union's expansion eastward."[54]

On August 4 Chiang Kai-shek ordered Sun, who was then in France, to proceed to Moscow. Obviously, Chiang sensed that the Zhanggufeng fighting provided a good opportunity to induce the Soviet Union into an alliance. He wanted the Soviet Union to know that the Chinese government was committed to Sino-Soviet cooperation against Japan, regardless of the Soviet readiness.[55]

Sun Ke, who had not been satisfied with Chiang's expedient approach to Sino-Soviet relations, took this opportunity to press Chiang Kai-shek for a more comprehensive Soviet policy. He reminded Chiang that the Soviets doubted Chiang's determination to carry on the resistance and suspected his inclination to respond to Japanese peace overtures. In fact, the Soviets were outspoken about the peace advocates around Chiang Kai-shek. Litvinov told Koo in Geneva two months earlier that peace advocates were traitors and ought to be shot.[56] Sun asked Chiang Kai-shek to make cooperation with the Soviet Union a permanent policy "without any time limit." Sun wanted China "to coordinate its political, military, and diplomatic policies" with the Soviets. Second, Sun indirectly assailed Chiang's dictatorship by demanding democracy at home and a federalist system of government like that of the Soviet Union or the British Commonwealth. Third, he asked for economic reforms, such as land equalization and the development of industry. Sun told Chiang that the Soviets, though silent publicly, suspected that "we have the dangerous tendency toward fascism after the war is over. Therefore, we should take steps to remove their suspicions so that future cooperation could be ascertained." The Soviets were apprehensive of the alleged unfair treatment of the Communist forces in China, Sun continued.[57]

In essence, Sun was demanding a return to the type of full Sino-Soviet cooperation of the early 1920s. Sun insisted that his trip to Moscow was contingent upon Chiang Kai-shek's acceptance of his proposal. He flew back to Wuhan in August to hammer things out with Chiang.[58] Chiang flatly refused Sun's demands to tie China's future completely with the Soviet Union and to give up links with Anglo-American powers.[59] By August 15, three days after the Soviet Union and Japan signed a truce, Chiang realized that this border conflict had failed to trigger a major war.[60]

The League of Nations in late September seemed to give Chiang another chance for hope. Owing to Wellington Koo's diplomatic maneuvers, the League passed nonbinding resolutions on September 30, 1938, recommending sanctions. However, it was up to individual governments to decide whether to apply them. For Chiang, the League resolutions for sanctions met the condition Stalin outlined to Sun, i.e., Soviet intervention depended on the League of Nations sanctions against Japan. As soon as he heard about the League decisions, Chiang met with the Soviet ambassador and asked about Soviet preparations to carry out the military sanctions as specified in Article 16 of the League Covenant. More important, Chiang considered this an opportunity to ask the Soviets to conclude the mutual assistance treaty. Chiang cabled Yang Jie the next day, instructing him to ask Stalin to fulfill his promise to take military action. Chiang reminded the Soviet leaders that China's own forces had been exhausted and morale was deteriorating.[61] With Japanese troops just about to attack Wuhan and Canton, the situation was indeed fatal for China. Chiang was not alone in praying for Soviet action in the wake of the League of Nations resolutions. One Chinese commentator asserted that Soviet military intervention at this time was well justified by international justice and morality and would get rid of the Fascist threat to the Soviet Union as well as help China. "We demand that the Soviet Union change its foreign policy quickly and this is the only chance."[62]

The Soviets responded negatively to the Chinese demand. On October 9 Litvinov cabled Ambassador Orelski, who met Chiang on the same day, that "the proposed pact of mutual assistance between the USSR and China would only be used by the powers for isolation on grounds of Bolshevization of China."[63] Four days later, Litvinov explained to Yang Jie that when Article 16 was passed at the League, Britain, France, and other countries disliked it, and Poland, Belgium, and Sweden still opposed it. Therefore, the Soviet Union considered individual action inappropriate, but would continue the policy of material support. As for the conclusion of the mutual assistance treaty, Yang was told, the Soviet Union would "consider it." The matter was thus tabled in spite of repeated urgings from Sun and Kung in October.[64]

HOPES FOR THE BIG POWERS'
ANTI-JAPANESE COOPERATION

By the end of 1938, Chinese politics had become more crystallized than before. The defection by Wang Ching-wei was good news for the pro-Soviet elements. Sun Ke cabled Ambassador Yang Jie from Chongqing, informing him that "Sino-Soviet relations are getting better and better. After Wang left, our diplomatic line became more crystallized and more secure."[65] Very quickly, the Chinese government found itself in need of another loan from the Soviet Union in order to carry on the war. Once again Sun, the key negotiator, was sent as envoy to Moscow on April 7, 1939.

At this time, the Chinese government had high hopes for promoting Far Eastern cooperation among China, the Soviet Union, Britain, and France. Japan's occupation of the Hainan Islands at the beginning of 1939 seriously threatened French Indochina and British Southeast Asia and thus created another favorable condition for a common front of these countries, especially for direct Sino-British military cooperation. Chiang ordered Yang Jie to talk with the British chiefs of staff and propose a comprehensive plan of military cooperation in the Far East according to which China would provide manpower and the Anglo-French military would supply air and naval forces. The British, who paid most of their attention to Europe, were not in the least receptive to Chiang's idea. The only encouragement the chiefs of staff gave Yang was to suggest the possibility that Britain might accept Chiang's proposal for sending British volunteers to China.[66] Not discouraged by the British response, Chiang Kai-shek continued to think that the Anglo-French difficulties in Europe and the increasing Japanese threat to their interests in the Far East still made Chinese-Western military cooperation possible. He desired to participate in the ongoing Anglo-French talks regarding Japan's threat to Southeast Asia so as to form a regional coalition.[67] In March, Guo Tai-qi, the Chinese ambassador to Britain, and Wellington Koo were instructed to put forward essentially the same proposal adding that the Soviet Union should be invited to join the Anglo-French-Chinese military cooperation and that the United States should be encouraged to take parallel action. The British foreign minister, Halifax, believed that China wanted to draw Britain into war with Japan and considered China's offer of little value.[68]

One encouraging sign to the Chinese was that after April Britain had finally shown a friendly attitude toward the Soviet Union, and the two began exchanging views on European cooperation. The subsequent negotiations between the Soviet Union and the Anglo-French powers till the signing of the Nazi-Soviet pact of nonaggression were considered an occasion for a broader Far Eastern cooperation, and the Chinese thought they might be able to achieve what they had failed to achieve at the League of Nations the previous September: close cooperation among China, Russia, Britain, and France. Chiang Kai-shek instructed Sun to ask the Soviet Union to raise the Far Eastern question in negotiations with the Anglo-French powers. On April 25 Chiang expressed to Stalin China's willingness to "participate in the unity of the anti-aggression front and join the common efforts of democratic nations for justice, so that the European and Far Eastern problems can be solved by the same principle."[69]

As the Soviet and Anglo-French negotiations were getting under way, Litvinov was replaced by Molotov. Litvinov was seen as an advocate of collective security, and his departure was generally viewed as a change of policy. Certainly Chiang Kai-shek had plenty of reasons to be worried. For one thing, Sun had been in Moscow for two weeks, and Stalin had not yet granted him an interview. "This must be related to their China policy," Chiang told Sun, "otherwise, he would not have delayed seeing you for such a long time."[70] Though Sun was reassured on May 8 that the change of personnel would not affect Soviet foreign policy, Chinese leaders remained as deeply worried as ever.

When Sun finally met Stalin, Voroshilov, and Molotov on May 13, the Soviet leaders denied any change in Soviet foreign policy. On the question of a loan, Stalin agreed to grant China $150 million. As Sun later recalled, Stalin appeared very generous as usual. The details of the loan agreement were negotiated between Sun and Anastas Mikoyan, Soviet commissar of trade. The third loan was to be used between July 1, 1939, and July 1, 1941, at an interest rate of 3 percent.[71] By now, the Soviet Union had granted China a total of $250 million, by far the largest amount China had received from a power.

Regarding China's proposal for a Far Eastern collective security arrangement, the Soviet leaders promised their consent, but like before, passed the ball to Britain, France, and the United States. Nor were the Soviets willing to argue China's case with Britain and France. The Soviets were distrustful of the two European powers and informed Sun Ke that Britain and France only wanted Soviet assistance in the European anti-Fascist alliance, not vice versa. Therefore, the ongoing negotiations had not produced any agreement.[72]

In June, Chiang and some of his foreign policy advisers, such as Zhong Zhong-fu, believed it was possible for Britain and Russia to form an alliance that would push Japan into the Fascist camp.[73] Obviously, the Chinese were in the dark, knowing nothing about the ongoing secret negotiations between Germany and the Soviet Union and innocently believing the Soviet's sincerity in negotiating with Anglo-French powers as the only approach. As late as August, Chiang was still urging Stalin to take the lead in forming a world antiaggression peace bloc.[74] After hearing that the Far Eastern question was brought up in the British-Soviet negotiations, Chiang instructed Sun to ask for possible Chinese participation in, or at least observation of, the negotiations.[75] But the Soviet government denied the report that the British-Soviet negotiations included the Far East. Sun Ke reported to Chiang that under the circumstances, it was unnecessary to raise the question of Chinese participation.[76]

JITTERS AFTER THE NAZI-SOVIET PACT

The Nazi-Soviet pact came as a shock and dealt a heavy blow to the idea of "two-camp" diplomacy. The expected lineup of the world peace camp of the Soviet Union, Britain, France, and the United States versus the aggressor states of Germany, Italy, and Japan was shown to be flawed and fallacious. "The two-camp diplomacy," one commentator wrote, "was made bankrupt by the Soviet-Germany rapprochement, and we should wake up from our long dream about the two-camp world."[77] Another called the Nazi-Soviet pact "a revival of fifteenth century Machiavellianism." It was a good example for sentimentalists to learn the lesson that in international politics, "there are only interests and no sentiments." [78] Naturally, the CCP, the chief advocate of the "two camp" theory before and defender of the Nazi-Soviet pact, now was ridiculed in the press. [79]

The Soviet secret dealings did provoke an atmosphere of fear and uncertainty in government circles. If the Soviets purchased security by allying with its sworn enemy, Germany, why couldn't it do the same with Japan? This was enough, Chiang Kai-shek thought, to make every country afraid. [80] Worried about its devastating effects on Britain, which might retreat from the Far East or possibly make a deal with Japan, Chiang Kai-shek moved quickly to prevent possible damages. He instructed Ambassador Guo to do everything he could to prevent a revival of Anglo-Japanese negotiations and the possibility of an alliance between the two powers. He pointed out that the British should be reminded that the Soviet interest in the Far East was identical to that of the British. Consequently, any Anglo-Japanese rapprochement would weaken the Soviet stand against Japan and in the end hurt the British more than anybody else. [81] The Chinese ambassador to France, Wellington Koo, who was an embodiment of Chinese wishful thinking, considered the Soviet demarche more harmful to Japan and still clung to the dead scheme of Sino-Soviet-Anglo-French cooperation against Japan in the Far East. He urged Chiang to persuade the Soviet Union to take military action by, for example, increasing forces along the Manchurian border and to persuade the United States to send its fleet to the western Pacific. Chiang endorsed Koo's idea in late August. [82]

Chiang Kai-shek faced tough choices. The outbreak of the European war not only divided the Anglo-French and the Russians into two opposing camps, but also would leave Japan a free hand in the Far East, thus raising the specter of possible appeasements of Japan by both the Soviet Union and Britain. Therefore, Chiang tried to prevent Japan from reconciling with and joining the Anglo-French side, and he also tried to prevent a possible Soviet-Japanese rapprochement. The best policy, Chiang wrote on September 2, was for China to formally join the British side so that Japan could not join and so that Japan might oppose Britain. Even if Japan joined the British side, the Sino-Japanese conflict would be solved without loss of sovereignty. [83]

On both September 2 and 4, Chiang insisted at top-level meetings that China declare war on Germany so as to prevent any Anglo-Japanese rapprochement. Such a drastic position was opposed by Zhang Qun, H. H. Kung, Wang Chong-hui, and Zhu Jia-hua, who worried about a Soviet cutoff of aid and preferred a wait-and-see attitude. On September 5 Chiang was finally persuaded not to declare war but he still decided to show support for the Anglo-French powers through the League of Nations and by recalling the

Chinese ambassador from Berlin. In another meeting on September 8, the prevailing opinion was that China express no official position regarding the European war.[84] On September 12 Chiang Kai-shek personally drafted instructions to Quo Tai-qi, ambassador to Britain, informing him of the government's decision not to formally join the war on the British side. However, Chiang let the British know that China would offer manpower and material support and, moreover, China was still interested in reaching a secret military agreement in the Far East.[85]

Many Chinese were fully aware that the Nazi-Soviet pact dealt a blow to the Japanese anticommunist diplomacy. Shao Yu-lin, a Foreign Ministry official, wrote that the Soviet Union "aimed at breaking Japan's plot to join the Axis alliance by concluding the pact with Germany. The past anti-Comintern agreement has been destroyed." He predicted that the Soviet Union, now free of threat in Europe, would not only have no possibility of compromise with Japan but would also probably step up its assistance to China.[86]

One of the factors allowing the Chinese to see a silver lining was the Soviet-Japanese armed conflict in Nomonhan from May to September. The fighting had incurred Japanese casualties of 17,000 and had kept alive the Chinese belief that their hostilities would lead to an eventual Soviet war against Japan rather than any rapprochement. Following the Nazi-Soviet pact, however, instead of continuing, as Koo and other Chinese had imagined, the conflict ended in a truce agreement by mid-September.[87]

The Nomonhan Truce and the Soviet invasion of Poland meant the reeducation of Sun Ke. Sun was at first sympathetic to the Soviet apprehension of the capitalist powers, blaming the Nazi-German pact on the British and French. The Soviets, he told Chiang, had known that a European war was in the making, and in order not to be drawn into such a conflict, they had rushed to conclude the pact with Germany. As for the Soviet Far Eastern policy, Sun thought that the Soviets would still continue to assist China against Japanese aggression. Unlike Wellington Koo, who wanted China to side with the British and French, Sun advised Chiang Kai-shek against taking the Anglo-French side in the European war unless they gave China large amounts of weapons and a guarantee that they would not compromise with Japan.[88]

By now Sun had given up any expectation of Soviet entry into the war against Japan and informed Chiang that "it is impossible to ask the Soviets to join the [Sino-Japanese] war out of generosity."[89] Sun's disillusionment was in part caused by the Soviet invasion of Poland on September 15. Prior to that, Sun still had some faith in the peaceful and socialist Soviet diplomacy. Just one day before the Soviet invasion, Sun refused to believe that there might be a secret military agreement between the Soviet Union and Germany to divide up Poland, something he considered absolutely impossible.[90] The Soviet invasion was a slap in Sun's face. This blatant act of aggression seriously damaged the Soviet image as a friend of the weak and the victim of aggression. It dawned on Sun Ke that the Soviet Union was no different from other powers. He reversed himself and admitted to Chiang on September 18 that "the Soviet invasion of Poland . . . is in fact to assist Germany and to wipe out Poland. It has reversed its traditional policy of defending its territory only. It is unavoidable that the Soviet Union might get involved in the European war. As a result, it will have to compromise with Japan in the Far East."[91] It is significant that even the most pro-Soviet leader in China admitted the imminent possibility of Soviet compromise with Japan. Sun left Moscow soon despite Chiang's request that he stay on. The education of Sun Ke symbolized the declining position of the pro-Soviet faction, which was never able to be influential again within the KMT.

At the time of the Nomonhan Truce, Chiang Kai-shek feared the possibility of a Soviet-Japanese rapprochement. Rumors abounded in September that Japan and the Soviet Union were secretly negotiating a nonaggression pact, with Germany acting as an intermediary. The Chinese government ordered its ambassadors abroad in early September to gather information to that effect.[92] In fact, Chiang Kai-shek believed these rumors and asserted that "after the signing of the (Nomonhan) truce, there will definitely be a conclusion of a nonaggression pact between Russia and Japan." After Ambassador Yang and Zhang Chong made the Chinese concerns known to Soviet officials, Moscow denied that any such negotiations were going on.[93] In his telegram of September 18, Sun Ke had informed Chiang of the Soviet assurances that the Soviet Union would continue to aid China and that, though it was seeking a nonaggression pact with Japan, Japan had not proposed such a treaty to the Soviet Union.[94] The rumors of a Soviet-Japanese nonaggression pact led some to speculate that they might cut a deal to carve up China like Stalin and Hitler had done with Poland. Jiang Ting-fu, former ambassador to the Soviet Union and now undersecretary of the Executive Yuan, firmly held such views and was extremely pessimistic about the future. He further believed that the Soviet Union would form a four-power bloc with Germany, Italy, and Japan against Britain and would force China to join this bloc. Jiang told James McHugh, U.S. assistant naval attaché, that only the American support could prevent such a situation.[95]

These rumors seemed to be confirmed by some Soviet policy pronouncements. On October 31 Molotov gave a speech to the Soviet Congress showing friendly attitudes to Germany and hostile attitudes to the democratic powers.

Chiang Kai-shek read it as a clear signal to reach compromises with Japan.[96] Chiang tried personally to persuade the Soviets to desist from embarking on a road to a Soviet-Japanese understanding. On November 8 Chiang had a lengthy talk with the Soviet ambassador to China, Alexander Paniushkin, and reminded him that the Chinese people were very sensitive to the rumor that the Soviet Union would cooperate with Germany and Japan to carve up China. He also strongly objected to the alleged commercial treaty negotiations between the Soviet Union and Japan. Chiang argued that if the Soviet Union proceeded to sign such a commercial treaty, it would nullify American efforts to economically isolate Japan and would discourage the recent active American attitude indicated by the termination of the 1911 commercial treaty with Japan and by Ambassador Joseph Grew's speech in Tokyo opposing the Japanese "New Order in East Asia."[97]

It was clear that China's Soviet policy, which had aimed at Soviet military intervention, had gone bankrupt by the end of 1939. The illusions of many Chinese, including Chiang Kai-shek, about Soviet military action against Japan had been completely shattered. There was a visible change from a positive diplomacy to a preventative one that aimed at forestalling any Soviet-Japanese collusion. Moreover, China could no longer take Soviet aid for granted. Weng Wen-hao, the economic minister, expressed the opinion of many when he told Ambassador Hu Shi that "it is hard to predict if the Soviet Union would continue to help our war efforts."[98] As a consequence, a major shift in China's overall foreign policy took place. Chiang Kai-shek began to move his diplomatic emphasis from Moscow to Washington, since the United States became the only power that could effectively promote his idea of a Pacific anti-Japanese coalition. As Minister of Information Wang Shi-jie, put it, Chiang Kai-shek now "regarded Anglo-American friendship as above anything else."[99]

THE DECLINE: FROM SOVIET-FINNISH WAR
TO SOVIET-JAPANESE NEUTRALITY

To keep the Soviets from appeasing Japan, Chiang Kai-shek named General He Yao-zu, chief of staff of the Military Affairs Commission who was already in Moscow, as his personal representative to Stalin. General He was to discuss further political and economic cooperation and to obtain the last shipments of military supplies. This last purchase list was the fourth, which had been presented as early as June 1939.[100] But the Soviets had slowed down the process of military procurement, perhaps as a gesture toward improving

Soviet-Japanese relations. This might be related to Soviet anger at China's lack of support in the League of Nations over the Soviet invasion of Finland. When the Finns took their case to the League, China faced a tough choice between obligations to the League principle and close military connection with the Soviet Union. This dilemma could be seen in Dai Ji-tao's letter to Chen Bu-lei, Chiang Kai-shek's civilian chief of staff: "We are put in a great predicament between moral obligations and self-interests. After carefully brooding over it for several days, I still could not think of a way to deal with the situation."[101]

The Chinese officials were divided on this issue. Wang Shi-jie desired to abstain from voting at the League to avoid the dilemma but worried that such a policy might anger world public opinion, especially that in the United States. Feng Yu-xiang had no such worries. He was in favor of supporting the Soviets. War Minister He Ying-qin also argued at the National Defense Council that China should not vote against the Soviet Union for fear that the latter might cut off aid. Feng and He's arguments were opposed by Dai Ji-tao and others. By December 9 Chiang informed the United States via Ambassador Hu that if China voted against the Soviet Union, the Soviets would probably reach compromises with Japan.[102] In the end, China abstained when the League Council expelled the Soviet Union.

The Soviets regarded China's abstention as an indication that China had sided with Britain and France. Molotov called such an act "helping the British and the French in attacking the Soviet Union." He also complained that Chinese public opinion did not show any support for the Soviets either. Just as War Minister He had feared, Molotov warned Ambassador Yang that future aid to China depended on Chinese attitudes.[103] When General He was finally received by Molotov on January 10 and 12, 1940, Molotov demanded that China openly express sympathy with the Soviet Union over the Finnish War and refused to discuss aid unless he received a satisfactory answer. He also flatly rejected China's idea of Soviet-American cooperation in the Pacific as out of the question. Chiang Kai-shek pleaded ignorance about the League incident in an interview with Ambassador Paniushkin.[104]

Chiang and other leaders suspected that the Soviets were using the League issue as a pretext to distance themselves from China so as to pave the way for a Soviet-Japanese rapprochement. Soviet coldness toward China, General He estimated, was primarily for carrying on negotiations with Japan; the Soviets wanted to know if China was going to join the British and American anti-Soviet policy. He Yao-zu proposed that China reassure the Soviets that it would never join any anti-Soviet bloc. Without expressing such a position, the problem of military supplies would never be solved.[105] Just as He feared,

Voroshilov received him on January 20, 1940, but tabled his shopping list, which was within the amount of the third loan of $150 million, for 200 planes and other supplies.[106]

The Soviet refusal to continue providing military supplies not only caused serious concern, but also irritated Chiang Kai-shek, who summoned General Chuikov, head of Soviet military advisers in China. Chiang refuted Molotov's accusation that China failed to be supportive regarding the whole Finnish affair.[107] Chiang was so bitter that he instructed his envoy in Moscow not to beg the Soviets for military supplies and, if the Soviets still ignored Chinese initiatives, to leave Moscow the next month.[108] General He remained in spite of the humiliating fact that for seven months (September 1939 to April 1940) Chiang's personal representative was never received by Stalin.

The halt of Soviet supplies and the strained relations forced Chongqing to send a new ambassador to Moscow after Ambassador Yang Jie returned to China in January 1940. Shao Li-zi was chosen for the post.[109] Shao was on the left of the KMT political spectrum and, among other things, vice president of the Sino-Soviet Cultural Association. Shao hoped that China could reestablish its strategic relations with the Soviet Union. Before leaving Chongqing, he had suggested to Chiang that China propose to support the Soviet Union in opposing the menace of the Fascist powers, Germany, Italy, and Japan. However, impressed with the German success, Chiang Kai-shek thought that the Soviet Union would have to face the more powerful Germany and would not be able to play a stronger role in the Far East.[110] Shao's arrival in Moscow in early June did not avert the downward trend in Sino-Soviet relations, although the Soviets showed much hospitality to the new ambassador and even promised to do their best to resupply China with airplanes and other materials.[111]

When the Axis pact was signed in September, Shao again took the occasion to press Chiang to regain Soviet goodwill by showing solidarity. "Soviet-German relations are in fact hostile though on the surface very close," Shao suggested, "and this proves that Soviet-Japanese relations are not going to be good either. We, Britain, and the United States should take this opportunity to improve relations with the Soviet Union either separately or collectively."[112] Chiang paid lip service to Shao's suggestion. He thought that Stalin had a hand in forming the Axis bloc to promote wars among imperialist countries. Even though Chiang welcomed the Axis pact as a definite turning point in effecting a Japanese-American conflict, he still refused to identify with any bloc of powers before the Soviet attitude was made clear. For this reason, Chiang cabled Stalin on September 29 to inquire about the Soviet policy in light of the new development and to express his willingness to coordinate China's policy accordingly.[113]

In reply, Stalin avoided Chiang's suggestion for coordinating Sino-Soviet policies. He told Chiang that the Axis pact broke the basis of Anglo-American neutrality to Japan and this would be beneficial to China. As for the rumored Soviet-Japanese nonaggression pact, Stalin denied any knowledge of it. The overall tone of Stalin's letter was quite encouraging, especially in light of the recent troubles.[114] Chiang was quick to respond and instructed Ambassador Shao to raise the question of military supplies. For a little while, relations improved somewhat, and military aid was resumed in December, when 300 truckloads of matériel reached Hami in Xinjiang.[115] The Soviet decision to resume aid to China might well have been caused by the rising Soviet-German tensions in late 1940 but Chiang Kai-shek attributed this change in Soviet policy to China's refusal of Japanese peace overtures and its determined resistance.[116]

As the vicissitudes of Soviet-Chinese relations took their turns, the relations between the CCP and the KMT deteriorated. Rapidly expanding Communist guerrilla forces became a serious threat in the eyes of Chiang Kai-shek. In his effort to curtail the growth of the CCP armed forces, Chiang stationed about 200,000 of his best troops to blockade the Communists. The most typical of the CCP-KMT conflicts was the New Fourth Army Incident in January 1941, in which the CCP army's 9,000 troops were attacked and destroyed by KMT forces in Anhui Province. In his interview with Chiang Kai-shek, the Soviet ambassador questioned Chiang's assertion that the New Fourth Army had attacked government forces, asking how such a small army could attack government troops ten times its size. In protest, Molotov and Mikoyan cancelled a dinner arranged by the Chinese ambassador.[117]

The long-anticipated Soviet-Japanese Pact of Neutrality was signed on April 13, 1941. Among other things, the two countries recognized each other's puppet regimes, Manzhouguo and Outer Mongolia. The pact confirmed Chiang's view that the strategic value of the Soviet Union was dwindling. However, the American commitment to China by April 1941 had cushioned any shock the neutrality pact might have had on the Chinese. As Chiang put it, "The neutrality pact has no impact on us whatsoever and it would have had harmful effects had it been concluded one or two years ago."[118] By now, China depended almost totally on Washington rather than Moscow. With Japan's threat temporarily removed and the German threat rising on the horizon, the Soviets found little reason to pour resources into China, and its aid slackened and then came to a complete halt when Germany attacked Russia in June 1941.

Mutual suspicions, absence of a firm commitment from either side, and the increasing tensions in Europe had doomed the relationship from the very beginning to a quasi-alliance of an expedient nature. Yet, the Soviet military assistance proved to be a crucial factor in sustaining China's illusions and its will to fight. From 1937 to 1941, the Soviets sent altogether 904 planes and many other needed arms and munitions to China. At the height of Soviet involvement in China, there were 3,665 Soviet military personnel participating in the Chinese resistance war.[119] Without such a quasi-alliance and without Chinese illusions about Soviet intervention, it would perhaps have been unlikely for the Chinese resistance to last for as long as it did.

7

The United States:
The Last Best Hope, 1938–1941

The Chinese prewar perceptions of the United States as an arch foe of Japan were put to a test when the war came. The American policy failed to measure up to Chinese expectations in the first year of the war and thus, to the Chinese, America was a country of paradoxes and contradictions. It was a champion of the Nine Power Treaty and the Open Door, and yet it had refused to take any action to confront the Japanese aggression, embracing isolationism. However, Japan's expansion in China was expected to trigger an eventual conflict with the United States, and Chinese diplomatic efforts were directed toward hastening such a conflict. Sino-American relations became extremely crucial to China's survival after the Nazi-Soviet pact of 1939, and the Kuomintang government believed that the future of China was hinged on the support of the United States.

HOPES FOR AMERICA

When the Sino-Japanese War broke out, China appealed to the American government as well as to Britain and France to mediate the conflict in August 1937. Chiang hoped for close Anglo-American joint action to prevent the conflict from deteriorating into a war not of his own choosing. The Roosevelt administration did not see fit to play an active role in either mediating the conflict or protesting jointly with the British to Japan for violating the Nine Power Treaty. Nor did Chiang's repeated appeals to the United States to defend her own interests in the Far East receive much attention.[1] The Chinese public voiced resentment at the failure of the United States to openly champion China's cause.

The evacuation of the American embassy on board U.S. warships, for example, was regarded as a "betrayal, . . . and [an indication] that the United States was no longer the international friend of China."[2]

Expectations for a strong American show of support were perhaps part of the reason why in mid-August Chiang initiated hostilities in Shanghai, where foreign interests were concentrated. Yet no strong American policy was forthcoming. On September 14, after Japan blockaded its coastal lines, President Roosevelt, under pressures from domestic peace groups, announced that government-owned ships would not transport arms to China or Japan, and that private ships would do so at their own risk. With the Japanese domination of the sea, such a policy was obviously to the detriment of China. Ambassador Wang Zheng-ting protested to Secretary of State Hull. Because of this measure, 19 planes purchased by the Chinese government that were being transported on the USS *Wichita* had been removed from the ship, and the ambassador also mentioned that Du Pont had refused to sell TNT to China as a result.[3] Public opinion in China was outraged. *Dagongbao,* which had been generally friendly to the democratic powers, editorialized on September 28 that China could not forgive such a policy when China's survival was at stake. It also ridiculed "the Chinese who had indulged in pro-American dreams," to which the refusal to transport China's 19 planes was a reply. To the American government, it protested, "You enjoy your prosperity in the safe house; and we defend our rivers and mountains, and fight our war. Let us go our separate ways."[4] Such bitter disappointment was widespread.[5]

The Chinese attitude did not change until October 5, when Roosevelt compared Japan's action in China to an international disease of lawlessness that should be quarantined. What Roosevelt had in mind was a possible naval blockade of Japan to strangle the Japanese economy and thus force Japan to quit.[6] The Quarantine Speech "wholly and rapidly dispelled" Chinese disappointment, and Chiang Kai-shek himself was "moved by the speech." Chinese editorials were "uniformly enthusiastic and appreciative and frankly hopeful that isolationism has been abandoned."[7] The president's speech even made Fu Si-nian, a well-known intellectual and now a member of the National Defense Council, a believer in American idealism. He wrote Hu Shi, who was being sent to the United States to win support, that contrary to the cunning and opportunistic Britain, the United States had a real touch of idealism once mobilized.[8] From this point onward, the Chinese made a distinction between Roosevelt and the isolationist Congress and waited for the American idealism to materialize.[9]

IMPACT OF CHINESE RESISTANCE

Chiang's decision to fight raised China's strategic importance in terms of preventing Japan's hegemony in this part of the world and, in part, caused the United States to change its policy from acquiescing to Japan's expansionism to checking it by way of supporting China. Unable to act and yet unwilling to accept Japanese hegemony in the Far East, the United States had to find an alternative to counter Japan. Supporting China became an increasingly attractive option in 1938.

Was China able to resist the mighty Japanese war machine? At the beginning of the conflict, American military observers had serious doubts. Colonel Joseph Stilwell, the military attaché, and H. E. Overesch, the naval attaché, all maintained that Chiang Kai-shek would not fight Japan and would "eventually grant the Japanese demands." In Washington circles, Chinese defeats were also taken for granted.[10]

China's stubborn resistance in September and October came as a surprise to all and changed this traditionally negative attitude, forcing a reevaluation of China's military capability and strategic importance in the Far East. Captain Evans Carlson, an intelligence officer of the U.S. Marine Corps who was collecting intelligence for President Roosevelt, wrote favorable reports of the Chinese army.[11] Admiral Harry Yarnell, the commander in chief of the Asiatic Fleet, now expressed to Admiral Leahy his belief that the Chinese army will fight "for a long time" and "if properly led, her private soldiers are as good as any in the world." To safeguard U.S. commercial interests in the Far East, Yarnell recommended a plan for a naval-economic war to strangle Japan, an idea very similar to Roosevelt's naval blockade. In such a war, he suggested, "let China supply the manpower with American officers and equipment." Admiral Leahy, who passed Yarnell's reports to Roosevelt, shared his Open Door mentality and sense of inevitable conflict with Japan.[12] In spite of repeated defeats after the fall of Nanking, Americans in China maintained their confidence. Colonel Stilwell also reversed his earlier opinion and even predicted, before the Battle of Xuzhou began in late March, that "it is possible for China to win."[13]

The Chinese victory at Taierzhuang, a town about 30 kilometers northeast of Xuzhou, confirmed such confidence. Here on April 6, over half of the Japanese 5th and 10th Divisions was destroyed and the rest escaped north. It was the first Chinese victory since the war started and as Stilwell's office reported it, it smashed "the legend of the invincibility of the Japanese troops." Its impact on both Chinese morale and American confidence in China was tremendous. It firmly established the belief that, if sufficiently supplied, the

Chinese forces could indeed conduct a successful resistance. Major Barrett, assistant military attaché, gave the following conclusion to his superiors in Washington: "It appears as if the Japanese fly has at last got himself well entangled in the Chinese flypaper," and "the score in the present conflict is somewhat in favor of the Chinese."[14] Captain Carlson, who was in the midst of fighting at Taierzhuang, Admiral Yarnell, and Captain James McHugh, assistant naval attaché, all came to the same conclusion.[15]

The military reports of March and April did reach the highest American officials in Washington, who were no less partial and sympathetic than these military intelligence officers. The president and his cabinet were aware that "the Chinese continue to put up very stiff resistance." After the April victory, according to Harold Ickes, at a cabinet meeting, even the conservative State Department for the first time indicated that it was "not sure that Japan will win this war." As noted by Jonathan Utley, this realization sank "into the minds of the American foreign policy managers" at this time.[16]

Given these estimates about China's determination and ability to fight a long, drawn-out war, it was perhaps no coincidence that important American policymakers began to seriously explore avenues to aid China and to include China in their strategic conception of balance of power in the Far East. The $25 million aid granted in November 1938 was a good example.

Serious efforts between the Chinese and the U.S. governments regarding loans did not begin until mid-July when Chen Guang-pu, a Chinese banker, was invited by Henry Morgenthau to Washington to negotiate a loan with the U.S. government.[17] Morgenthau was the most enthusiastic supporter of China. In March and April, he had already bought 50 million ounces of Chinese silver and allowed China to use the proceeds to purchase military supplies. To make more money available to China, Morgenthau and Henry Wallace, secretary of agriculture, agreed in June to make a loan to China to buy flour and cotton gray goods. Most interesting was the argument used when presenting their case to Cordell Hull. Wallace contended that "China was going to win the war; in the future they would feel kindly disposed toward us on account of this loan."[18] After Hull refused to cooperate for fear of offending Japan, Morgenthau immediately bought another 50 million ounces of silver to boost China's resistance.[19] Morgenthau's rationale for aiding China could also be seen from a memo sent by his aide, Harry White. White justified the proposed loan internationally on two grounds. The first was the familiar sound of the Open Door: "It would assure the United States for many years to come a favored market among the 400 million people in China." Second, from a strategic standpoint, "anything we can do to help China in its resistance to Japan weakens Japan and thereby strengthens our defenses against possible enemies."[20] Morgenthau followed White's suggestions and persisted in his efforts to make the proposed loan.

There was some indication that Morgenthau was influenced by the Chinese. J. Lossing Buck, a Treasury agent in China, relayed the argument of General Li Zong-ren, the commander at the Xuzhou front who was responsible for the Taierzhuang victory, that "America's defense would be much easier and cheaper if she should use a small amount of the funds now going into battleships to finance China."[21] When Morgenthau asked President Roosevelt for a loan to China, he used Li's argument almost verbatim (see Morgenthau's October 17 letter to Roosevelt below). American military observers in China also accepted General Li Zong-ren's argument. Stilwell, after visiting the Chinese commander, argued that to supply "financial loans and military equipment is a much better defense for us than only the building of our own defense equipment." To strengthen Chinese will, Stilwell, Carlson, and McHugh called for a "more positive" American policy. J. Lossing Buck passed Stilwell and Carlson's opinions immediately to Morgenthau on September 6, adding his plea for a cash loan that China needed badly to purchase munitions and to maintain currency.[22]

Morgenthau's support was also linked to his concerns about worldwide aggressions and his belief that the United States was the only country to stop Japan. Europe was already controlled by the Nazis, Morgenthau told the president in late September. But Morgenthau was not willing to concede the Far East to Japan, and he emphasized many times to Roosevelt and others that aiding China was "our last opportunity," "the only chance" to contain aggression.[23] In early October, the fall of Wuhan and Canton was almost certain and would inflict a heavy blow to the Chinese. Troubled by the news of Munich and worried about a possible collapse of resistance, Morgenthau pressed Roosevelt once again for action. "By risking little more than the cost of one battleship," Morgenthau wrote Roosevelt on October 17, "we can give renewed vitality and effectiveness to the Chinese." The choice of the words *vitality* and *effectiveness* is very significant in that it clearly revealed the influence of the field military observers. More important to Morgenthau, a strong China became essential to national security so that the American president did not have to "fly to Tokyo and in a humble manner plead with the Kikado that he be content with half of the Philippines rather than wage war for the whole."[24]

Besides Morgenthau, others like William Bullitt, ambassador to France and a close friend of Roosevelt, and Hornbeck in the State Department were impressed by China's will to fight. Hornbeck was motivated by a deep fear of Japan controlling China and excluding the United States altogether from the Far East. He had received numerous reports about Japan's intention to abolish the Open Door. The State Department protested Japan's violation of the Open Door in early October, but met the latter's rebuff.[25] Supporting Chinese resistance became, to Hornbeck and many others, "the most practical course for us to follow." Hornbeck's philosophy was: "Better to have Chinese soldiers continue to fight Japan and to take now the small risk of an attack by the Japanese upon ourselves, than to take the risk of a stronger Japan."[26]

In mid-October, Chen's negotiations with Morgenthau ended in an agreement for a credit loan against delivery of Chinese tung oil for $20 million. By the time the agreement was presented to Roosevelt on October 24, Hankou and Canton had fallen several days earlier. The fall of these cities not only closed off 75 percent of supplies to China, but more important, they were terrible blows to Chinese morale, and there was a resurgence of talks about peace in Chongqing, China's wartime capital. China's will (not ability) to continue the resistance became more critical, and Roosevelt asked Chiang Kai-shek to give him assurances on this point. When Chiang Kai-shek replied on November 9 in the positive, Roosevelt gave the go-ahead signal, in spite of objections from his own government.[27] What is interesting to note here is that both President Roosevelt and American military observers in China regarded China as an instrument to safeguard American interests and based their aid on China's will and ability to resist Japan.

The timing for making the loan public on December 15, several days after Wang Ching-wei defected to champion peace, did have some positive impact on Chinese morale and attitudes toward the United States. To the Chinese, the significance of the loan lay in the fact that for the first time, America had started its assertive involvement in the Far East.[28] The Chinese praised these gestures of active policy. One called it "a prelude to active assistance to China." The widely read *Eastern Miscellany* called these actions "changes of Anglo-American attitudes toward Japan" and attributed this new favorable international situation in part to China's firm resistance. The Chinese political reading of the loan was expressed as "Money small, meaning big."[29]

TO CHANGE AMERICAN ATTITUDES

The Chinese government also aimed at winning the support of the American public, whose significant role in American politics was well understood by those Chinese who directed China's propaganda. At the beginning of the war, the Chinese government created the International Propaganda Bureau under the KMT Ministry of Information. Many Americans served in this office. For example, Dr. Frank Price, dean of the Theological Seminary at Nanking University, was in charge of publishing the *China Information Bulletin* in New York and later headed the Chengdu Editing Committee for propaganda materials.[30] The United States was the most important place for this bureau, whose activities included collaborating with pro-Chinese groups to impose embargoes on Japanese goods, disseminating information, and making contacts with high-level officials. For this reason, many people were sent to the United States to plead China's case. For example, Zhang Peng-chun, a university professor, and Hu Shi were dispatched to the United States in early 1938 and spoke to officials like Morgenthau and organizations such as the Foreign Affairs Association.[31] Nobody symbolized China's propaganda efforts more than Hu Shi, a student of John Dewey and probably the most prominent Chinese philosopher. Hu was appointed ambassador to Washington in August 1938. His appointment was obviously designed to make use of his reputation and connections in the United States.

The major aims of China's policy on the United States were spelled out in the Foreign Ministry's instructions to Hu. First, in case of a European war, China should reach an understanding with the United States to prevent British appeasement of Japan and to adopt a distant blockade of Japan in line with the Quarantine Speech. The second major aim was to urge the United States to revise neutrality laws so as to apply an arms embargo to Japan once Japan cut off China's lines of communication with the outside world. The third aim was to ask the American government to persuade industries not to sell gasoline and iron to Japan.[32]

The success of China's policy depended on its ability to change the isolationist sentiment in the United States. Wang Shi-jie, minister of information in charge of Chiang's foreign policy staff, considered the repeal of the neutrality laws the yardstick for America's active role in world affairs and "the target of China's diplomatic and propaganda activities."[33] Chiang Kai-shek especially asked Hu Shi to work on the isolationists because the Chinese regarded them as barriers to American support of China. The ambassador considered key political leaders most crucial in shaping public opinion and thought that China's diplomacy, in his words, should "shoot the horse and capture the king."[34] Chiang Kai-shek's foreign policy advisers recommended a similar approach, listing political parties, wealthy individuals, and business and labor leaders as objects of propaganda. Approaching American senators was specifically emphasized.[35]

Senator Key Pittman of Nevada, chairman of the Senate Foreign Relations Committee, was an ideal target of Chinese lobbying efforts. He had been openly sympathetic to China and had been a staunch opponent of Japanese aggression, advocating strong action to counter it.[36] Among other things, Pittman was a leading advocate of revising the Neutrality Act of 1937 and had cooperated closely with Roosevelt in his efforts. Pittman's bill was one of a dozen amendments introduced to amend the Neutrality Act. Yet it was designed primarily to help the British by abolishing the prohibition of arms and by putting all foreign purchases on the basis of "cash and carry." Moreover, it would give the president more discretionary power in determining the application of the new laws under consideration.

The Chinese were not entirely satisfied with the proposed Pittman bill. Since the sea lanes were completely dominated by the Japanese navy, "cash and carry" would hurt China, which lacked both cash and means to carry. What China wanted was not merely a revision of the neutrality laws but also an expansion of the list of prohibited war materials to include the gasoline and iron that Japan needed.[37] Chiang and the Foreign Ministry instructed Hu that Pittman's bill contained no distinction between the aggressor and its victim and asked him to talk with influential people to effect changes, Senator Pittman being the key figure.[38] Ambassador Hu not only wrote to Pittman but also prepared a formal memorandum to the State Department outlining the above Chinese concerns and emphasizing that China would be "the sole object and victim" of the proposed Pittman resolution.[39] In the meantime, China also noted its concern through diplomatic channels that under the new bill, the president would be obliged to proclaim a state of conflict between China and Japan and that, as a consequence, the cash-and-carry provisions would benefit Japan, a naval power.[40]

After hearing the Chinese concerns, Senator Pittman assured Hu that he would make changes so that the new laws would not be applied to the Sino-Japanese War.[41] In April, he introduced a resolution in the Senate authorizing the president to embargo specific war materials to a country violating the Nine Power Treaty. This was clearly a move against Japan. The Pittman bill had kindled excitement in China, though efforts at revising the neutrality laws stood little chance of success at this time.[42]

China's propaganda and lobbying efforts were supported by and coordinated with the American Committee for Non-participation in Japanese Aggression. The committee was set up in 1938 by people with close ties to China, and its honorary president was none other than the author of the Stimson Doctrine and one of the vice chairmen, Admiral Yarnell. Its executive director, Harry Price, a former professor at Yenching University and the brother of Frank Price who was also born in China, launched a public campaign for China's cause. The Chinese contributed financially to the committee's work. In addition, Zhang Peng-yuan,

Qian Duan-sheng, and Yu Jun-jie served as special agents coordinating activities with the committee.[43]

Though the efforts to reform the Neutrality Act produced little immediate result, the Chinese did find comfort in the termination of the U.S.-Japan commercial treaty of 1911. As Ambassador Hu reported to Chiang, the overwhelming majority of Americans sympathized with China, and terminating the commercial treaty represented a deterioration of U.S.-Japanese relations. The ambassador predicted that a complete breakup would come in the near future.[44] The Chinese at home hailed the American action as "the biggest blow to Japan so far," because 70 percent of its exports had gone to the Western hemisphere, and hoped that this would herald further American embargoes. In addition, the American action was thought to forestall a new tide of Anglo-French appeasement in the Far East.[45]

Japan's occupation of the Hainan Islands on February 10 prompted China to ask for active involvement of the Anglo-American powers. Chiang thought that this was Japan's most serious threat to the Anglo-American powers since the outbreak of the war and that it would cause a revival of the Nine Power Treaty. Consequently, Chiang publicly warned the British of Japan's strike at the Hainan Islands and its consequences to British lines of communication between Singapore and Hong Kong, terming it "the Manchurian Incident in the Pacific."[46] Most Chinese regarded Japan's occupation of the Hainan Islands with "a minimum of concern if not with a certain amount of complacency."[47] It was generally thought that it was British and American interests in the South Pacific rather those of China that were directly threatened. Consequently, it was the powers that ought to take drastic measures to counter Japan's invasion.[48]

Apparently Chiang Kai-shek considered it opportune to push for a strong British policy and proposed in March and early April a comprehensive plan of military and economic cooperation among Britain, France, and China in the Far East in case a European war broke out. Chiang's move was in part due to his fear of a Far Eastern Munich: he knew fully well the threat posed by the Rome-Berlin alliance to Britain and France and their inclination to appease Japan.[49] The British rejected Chiang's proposal.

To make such cooperation happen, China approached the United States for endorsement and support. Chiang's plan for military cooperation was presented to the American government on April 14.[50] Chiang Kai-shek was encouraged by the transfer of the American fleet from the Atlantic to the Pacific and considered it an indication of Roosevelt's determination to fight Japan. In late April the Foreign Ministry requested that the United States "at least confidentially show Britain, France, and the Soviet Union, at this particular juncture, its support for the plan of four-power cooperation, so that it could be successful." Three weeks later, the scheme met with the State Department's rejection.[51] Even after the American rejection, the Chinese Foreign Ministry still thought that the United States was merely waiting for an opportune moment to be more active.[52]

RELIANCE ON AMERICA

For the Chinese, the world in the fall of 1939 was a place of uncertainty. The Nazi-Soviet nonaggression pact of August 22 took the Chinese by surprise. The pact and the subsequent war in Europe created fears about a possible realignment of world powers and about British or Soviet appeasement of Japan at China's expense. The Chinese government was particularly frightened by a possible revival of the Anglo-Japanese alliance. It was troubled by the fact that the Shanghai customs (under British control) accepted the currency of the Japanese puppet regime.[53] As Chiang Kai-shek saw the consequences on August 29, "If the Anglo-Japanese alliance is revived, Russia will first compromise with Japan, and this will result in establishing a bloc of Germany, Italy, Russia, and Japan."[54] Chiang obviously feared that an Anglo-Japanese alliance would cause a domino effect of appeasement, especially in the Soviet Union.

Under these circumstances, the United States became the key to preclude such a devastating scenario. Unless the United States took measures to prevent a possible Anglo-Japanese alliance, Chiang's hopes for Japanese cooperation among China, Britain, France, and the Soviet Union would completely evaporate. Chiang instructed Ambassador Hu to warn Washington and personally told Ambassador Johnson that he had "completely reliable information that the British and Japanese governments were negotiating" to revive the alliance. He urged the United States to take the initiative toward the Soviet Union and to prevent British appeasement. Chiang's anxiety was serious and real. As Johnson reported, Chiang "spoke with an almost passionate vehemence" and with "more than his usual gravity."[55]

Ambassador Hu and Chen Guang-pu did not share Chiang's fears. Hu argued that although the Soviets did not want to fight Japan, the latter's military was suspicious of the former and compromises were not likely.[56] Hu and Chen advised Chiang that "a revival of the Anglo-Japanese alliance was absolutely impossible." Given Britain's dependence on the United States, the former dared not adopt a pro-Japanese policy or conclude the alleged alliance.[57] Chiang sent a most urgent telegram the next day. "This is not my own assumption, but a fact. If the United States does not give a warning now, Britain will instigate Japan to attack Russia, and this will probably lead to a pact of mutual assistance."[58]

The prospect of either Soviet or British appeasement of Japan was the most serious threat to China and was responsible for a major shift in the diplomatic center of gravity from Russia to America. An alignment of Russia, Germany, Italy, and Japan would have virtually sealed China's fate. Chiang made it very clear that he had decided to throw China's lot with America. He told Johnson that China depended on the United States and wanted to "associate China's future course" with her although he was very disappointed by the American indifference to his forecast of the British appeasement.[59] After the outbreak of the war in Europe, Chiang showed an inclination to identify with the democracies in general. On September 1, Chiang ordered Ambassador Koo to actively probe Ambassador Bullitt's idea of a United States-Britain-France-China alignment.[60] The next day he wrote in his diary: "Our country's only principle toward to the European war is to join the democratic bloc. Thus, in the eventual peace conference, the Sino-Japanese War could be solved together with the European war."[61] To forestall any British-French appeasement in the Far East, Chiang even wanted to declare war on Germany (see Chapter Six). Though such a drastic measure was dropped because of most high officials' fear that Russia might cut off aid, Chiang nonetheless made an offer of the support of Chinese manpower to Britain and France in mid-September.[62]

An easier way to get the United States actively involved in the Far East in this period of uncertainty was to ask for mediation. As early as May, Chiang Kai-shek believed that Japan would withdraw her troops from China if China stopped fighting. He asked Ambassador Johnson about a possible U.S. mediation and even invited him to be a mediator in the silver contro-versy in the Tientsin British concession, where the Japanese tried to gain control of Chinese silver deposits. Premier Kung also considered the Amer-ican role to be crucial in the silver crisis and ordered Chen Guang-pu to approach the U.S. government.[63] On September 27 the Chinese foreign minister, Wang Chong-hui, openly and unexpectedly stated that the United States was "in a favorable position to bring the Sino-Japanese hostilities to an early close."[64] The desire for American mediation seemed to be wide-spread. Even Sun Ke joined Ambassadors Wellington Koo and Guo Tai-qi in asking Chiang Kai-shek to place diplomatic emphasis on the United States, the only country "that can pressure Japan."[65]

In September Chiang Kai-shek sent four telegrams to Ambassador Hu in Washington urging President Roosevelt to mediate the Sino-Japanese War.

Though Hu and Chen Guang-pu were in favor of peace, Hu Shi considered the moment inopportune for such a move. Because they were asking for a loan of $75 million from Morgenthau and to talk peace at this time would jeopardize the American aid, they did not pursue any mediation of the Sino-Japanese War.[66]

The uncertainties of the fall of 1939 were also responsible for a renewed Chinese desire for a peaceful settlement in case the powers decided to appease Japan. The possibility of Soviet and/or Anglo-French appeasement of Japan would certainly leave China alone facing Japan while the United States was not fully committed to any international involvement. The Nazi-Soviet pact also resulted in British and French pressures on China to reach some sort of settlement with Japan.[67] Chiang approached the Germans for mediation at this time. When those efforts failed, Chiang engaged in clandestine contacts with the Japanese in Hong Kong that lasted for almost a year, until October 1940. China made many concessions, the most important of which included acquiescence to the loss of Manchuria and cooperation against the Soviet Union.[68] While these secret talks were designed to delay the establishment of Wang Ching-wei's puppet regime in occupied China or to bluff the Soviet Union and the United States, the fact that they originated in the wake of the Nazi-Soviet pact suggested an element of fear when a global appeasement of Japan loomed large.

In the wake of the Nazi-Soviet pact and the war in Europe, China had to rely on the United States and asked for more assistance in order to offset fears for the unknown future. Chiang outlined to Ambassador Koo in Paris Chinese plans for more loans. First, Chiang wanted the United States to continue purchasing silver and, second, he wished to borrow $50 million against tin delivery in the next five years and another $50 million for currency stabilization.[69] Hu Shi was also instructed to approach President Roosevelt directly. The American government continued to attach increasing strategic importance to the Chinese resistance and to view it as America's first line of defense against Japan, though priority was given to Europe. Therefore when Ambassador Hu asked for "another life-saving injection in the form of a loan" on September 8, President Roosevelt's reply was to do "everything for him that we can get away with." Morgenthau once again took the lead in proposing a loan to China.[70]

Negotiations between Chen Guang-pu and the administration for another loan began in late September 1939, when the old neutrality law still remained in effect. They were kept secret for fear that isolationists might find ammunition to attack Roosevelt's China policy. In December, during these negotiations, Chiang appealed directly to Roosevelt for immediate financial assistance to support the Chinese currency.[71] Because of America's preoccupation with the European war, a loan of $20 million against tin delivery was not concluded until March 1940, and the amount fell far short of Premier Kung's target of $75 million with Yunnan tin as security. Moreover, in late March, Kung was disappointed in his demand for a loan with no security, based on the fact that the United States did not ask for security in its loan to Finland. He argued that both were political loans and that there were domestic pressures on the Chinese government to obtain similar terms. After Chen and Hu vigorously objected to this last minute change on the grounds that China's credibility would be damaged, Kung dropped his demand.[72]

Such a meager loan was, as Chen Guang-pu put it, "a puzzle to our leaders at home."[73] The political atmosphere in Chongqing was full of anxiety over American assistance and of disappointment, even among the returned students from America, the most pro-American elements in China. Two thousand people expressed the hope that if the United States could not aid China now, at least it would not help Japan. Sun Ke compared America's $45 million loan so far to Russia's $250 million and warned that if America failed to act, China would be compelled to throw her lot with Russia completely. There was also a resurgent pro-German pressure on the Chinese government. The pro-German Chinese, led by Zhu Jia-hua, head of the Organization Department of the KMT, argued that the democracies were finished and that China should turn to Germany, which was likely to become a dominating world power and which would check Japan's ambitions in China through mediation. There was even public talk of peace with Japan. To the Chinese public, America was sympathetic in attitude but apathetic in action. One article called U.S. policy "gentleman's diplomacy" that only talked.[74]

CHINA AND THE FORMATION OF THE AXIS

The Anglo-French defeats in the summer of 1940 increased the possibility of the powers' appeasement of Japan. Submitting to Japanese pressure, Britain considered closing the Burma Road, China's only supply line to the sea, for three months. To prevent a British sellout of China, Chiang Kai-shek had to once again rely on the United States and pressed for U.S. naval cooperation with the British and the Soviets in the Far East. He refused to believe Ambassador Hu's opinion that the British decision was a temporary stalling tactic to gain time. Instead, he warned that unless the United States took immediate action, the consequences of Japan's advances in the South Pacific would jeopardize American security. More important, for the first time, Chiang formally proposed a grand coalition of China, Britain, the Soviet Union, and the United States under American leadership. Chiang emphasized to Ambassador Hu that "when the enemy sees close cooperation, especially between the Soviet Union and America, it will not dare make wanton moves."[75]

Though it did not meet Chiang's demands, the Roosevelt administration did move gradually to support both Britain (in the destroyer and naval base deal) and China. Another loan of $50 million against Chinese delivery of wolfram was concluded as a response to Japan's decision to move into French Indochina. The Chinese thought the sum was too small, and Chiang asked Soong, who was sent to Washington in June, to get as much propaganda value out of it as possible.[76]

The conclusion of the Tripartite Alliance on September 27 among Germany, Italy, and Japan further crystallized the world alignments of powers. The Chinese were insulted by Germany's recognition of Japan's new order in East Asia. The CCP and leftist opposition to the lingering ties with Germany became stronger. Even KMT officials around Chiang Kai-shek, such as Zhu Jia-hua, who had played an important role in establishing a close German-Chinese relationship, now urged Chiang Kai-shek to sever diplomatic relations with Germany and Italy and show complete solidarity with the democracies.[77]

Identifying with the Anglo-American democracies was in fact the policy Chiang had intended since the Nazi-Soviet pact. Now that the British appeasement of Japan appeared less likely and because the Soviet position was ambiguous, Chiang intended to better his bargaining position by adopting a wait-and-see attitude toward Germany, the Soviet Union, and the Anglo-American powers. Openly siding with the Anglo-Americans was desirable but dangerous in that such a move might alienate the Soviet Union and thus promote a Soviet-Japanese rapprochement. Such a policy, Chiang thought, could be adopted only when China's southwest, Singapore, and Malaya could hold out against Japanese attacks and China could link with Britain and the United States.[78] In other words, open and complete solidarity with the democracies depended on a firm American commitment and sufficient material support, a fair price the Anglo-American powers should pay.

As he was maximizing his diplomatic advantage, Chiang was actually happy to see Japan joining Germany and Italy. In his view, the Axis pact definitely reduced Japan's flexibility and made a Japanese-American conflict almost inevitable. He saw Japan's advance into Vietnam on September 22 as an indication of such a conflict. Chiang recorded in his diary that such a situation was just what he had hoped for for a long time. Chiang asserted that the victory over Japan was already a foregone conclusion. This new confidence was in part responsible for his terminating secret contacts with Japan from this point on.[79]

Chiang's desire to wait and see also revealed his awareness of the increasing strategic importance of China in the global conflict. Which side China would take was a vital concern to Anglo-American interests in the Far East. Therefore, Chiang constantly and consciously used his leverage to obtain aid. In an interview with the American ambassador, Chiang told Johnson that national morale was at a low point. To face up to both domestic and foreign enemies, Chiang asked for economic aid and military assistance in the form of airplanes, 500 of which should be delivered from the U.S. air force within the next three months. Ambassador Johnson endorsed Chiang's request and urged the American government to give it "the most serious consideration" as it came from "the head of a government that has nowhere to look now for help except to us."[80]

Ambassador Hu's analysis of the American policy immediately before the presidential election reinforced Chiang's confidence in American entry into the war and in his policy to wait until it happened. Hu informed Chiang on October 24 that "according to an insider's view, American entry into the war was only a matter of time. It is unavoidable. . . . In view of the present international situation, the United States will most likely get involved in war in the Pacific."[81] Consequently, Chiang's confidence in American aid and involvement remained unshaken even after the State Department replied to his request for alliance in the negative.

Such confidence gave rise to Chiang's comprehensive plan for an alliance among China, Britain, and the United States in late October. It called for a basic Anglo-Chinese alliance with American endorsement and, preferably, participation. It specified military cooperation between Chinese land forces and Anglo-American naval and air forces. In addition, Chiang proposed a joint Anglo-American economic commission to work in China and asked for a $200 to 300 million loan and for a lease of 500 to 1,000 airplanes annually with 200 to 300 delivered by the end of the year. Chiang intended to present his plan to the American ambassador after the American presidential election.[82]

The reelection of Roosevelt aroused much joy and excitement in China. For Chiang Kai-shek and other government leaders, Roosevelt's reelection seemed to have assured them of continued and increasing American support for years to come, since Roosevelt could be relatively free of domestic political pressures. They oriented China's foreign policy completely to the American orbit. Premier Kung told Ambassador Hu that the "time has come for our diplomatic maneuvers. . . . Whether in diplomacy, economy, or in obtaining military supplies, we shall *focus everything on Washington.*"[83] The public was equally elated. In a letter to the newly reelected American president, the National Association of Gentry wrote: "We wish that you might have visited any one of hundreds of Chinese cities on the evening of Election Day to witness the universal spontaneous outburst of deep feeling."[84]

T. V. Soong found Chiang's optimism and comprehensive plan of alliance impractical. He pointed out that it was almost impossible for the United States to participate in military cooperation, and he was doubtful that even the British would be willing to conclude an alliance with China. As for the $200 to 300 million loan, Soong thought it was unwise to push for such a huge sum in a rash manner. However, Chiang ignored Soong's opinion and presented his "Sino-Anglo-American Plan of Cooperation" to Johnson on November 9, several days after Roosevelt won his election.[85]

In an apparent attempt to woo Americans to accept his proposal, Chiang suggested orally in the same interview that upon recovery of Chinese ports from Japan, he would make an arrangement for the Anglo-American navies to use these ports for 10 to 20 years. This was the first time Chiang had made such an offer, and it was a politically risky proposition considering the anti-imperialist resentment of the Chinese people in the past three decades. It showed how far Chiang would go to obtain American backing for consolidating his regime in the face of both Communist and Japanese threats.[86]

As Chiang was moving closer to the United States, he was narrowing his diplomatic options with regard to the Soviet Union and Germany. Now Chiang in fact staked his political future on the United States. This was one of the reasons for his anxious persistence for American support, "the only way to avoid compromising [with Japan] in the face of pro-German, Japanese peace, Communist groups."[87] Chiang's anxiety was so visible that Johnson considered his proposal "to be the appeal of a man who has lost confidence in his ability to contend any longer with a domestic situation which he feels he cannot control."[88] It was out of the question, given the grave European situation and the American policy not to precipitate a conflict with Japan in late 1940, that Chiang's scheme could possibly be entertained. Naturally, the American government rejected Chiang's proposal for an alliance and a joint declaration of principles and was willing only to discuss "various features" of his plan.[89]

At this moment, diplomatic leverage was placed in Chiang's hands. German foreign minister Ribbentrop notified Chinese ambassador Chen Jie that Germany's domination of Europe had been secured and that the Tripartite powers would soon defeat the democracies. Though desirous of friendly relations with China, Germany was obligated by treaty to follow Japan in recognizing Wang Ching-wei's regime in Nanking. Ribbentrop then offered to mediate between China and Japan and also expressed the hope that China would join the Tripartite Alliance.[90]

Chiang Kai-shek played this German card and Japan's impending recognition of Wang's puppet regime by notifying the American ambassador and thus indicating that there was an alternative open to him.[91] This move was designed to accelerate American aid, since neither Japanese nor Chinese politics would permit a peace settlement acceptable to both. Despite the slow pace of American aid, Chiang still remained very hopeful and never gave up his insistence upon an American endorsement of the Anglo-Chinese alliance.[92]

The German diplomatic maneuvers and the Japanese recognition of Wang's regime did worry Roosevelt. Although he had given priority to the survival of Britain and intended to maintain peace in the Pacific, Roosevelt could not afford a Chinese collapse and Japanese domination in the Far East. Suspecting that something was going on between Chiang and Wang's regime, Roosevelt quickly ordered his subordinates on November 29 to grant China a $100 million loan within 24 hours, half of which was to support the Chinese currency; the other half was to be a loan with tin and wolfram as security. The loan was made public the next day when Japan formally recognized Wang's regime. Chiang appeared relatively satisfied for now with the arrangement, though his targets were not reached. The United States was, in Chiang's words, "a friend in need, a friend indeed."[93]

The American commitment to China had a ripple effect upon China's international position. Ten days after the American loan, the British announced a loan of 10 million pounds to China. In addition, the Soviets expressed to Chiang their willingness to resume the slackened aid programs. Chiang attributed all these changes to the American action.[94]

In any event, the American loan signalled further American commitment to China and gave rise to "a wave of unprecedented optimism" in Chongqing. The Chinese convinced themselves that China had come to be inseparably linked with the democratic powers and would receive increasingly effective support. On New Year's Day, 1941, the foreign minister proclaimed:

> China and the United States are in complete accord with regard to the stand they have taken in the Far East. . . . China looks to America as one of her true friends in this hour of distress. Whether you want it or not, the role of leadership is being forced upon the United States.[95]

CHINA, CURRIE, AND LEND-LEASE

To commit the United States to underwriting China's economic system and the entire war, T. V. Soong managed to persuade Lauchlin Currie, economic adviser to Roosevelt, to undertake a trip to China in January 1941. The Chinese saw in Currie's trip an opportunity to influence Roosevelt. Soong stated its significance to Chiang: "First, . . . [Currie] will help you to determine policy. Second, once he returns to his post, he will be around the president every day. Probably, this will strengthen American economic and financial assistance to us. Moreover, he can be a private channel between you and the president."[96] Roosevelt approved of Currie's trip, knowing well that "their purpose is to enlist your aid more than anything else," but considering it worthwhile.[97]

Though Currie's mission was to gather facts about the Chinese economy and make recommendations, the explosive CCP-KMT relationship and the possibility of a civil war caused concern among U.S. government officials. The CCP-KMT United Front since 1939 existed only in name. As the war with Japan reached a stalemate, Chiang began to pay more attention to his old enemy, and conflicts between the government and Communist forces escalated because of Chiang's fear of rapid Communist expansion. The Communist forces had grown tenfold by 1940 from 400,000 to 500,000 men, though most of them were behind Japanese lines. From July 1940 onward, Chiang began to alert Ambassador Johnson that the Communist threat to his government was a bigger danger than was Japan, and that if the American government did not support China with large amounts of aid, the Soviet Union might abandon its noninterference policy and support the Communists. Chiang never hid his intention to strike against the Communists.[98]

America's aid of November 1940 and growing commitment to China had the effect of strengthening Chiang's determination and power against the Communists. In January 1941 Chiang's forces trapped and destroyed the headquarters of the Communist New Fourth Army south of the Yangtze River and arrested its commander. Though the American government desired Chinese unity, neither its representatives in China nor officials in Washington, up to this point, did anything to prevent such large-scale fighting between the Kuomintang government and the CCP. Certain private Americans, such as the pro-Communist reporter Edgar Snow and Captain Evans Carlson, opposed Chiang's attacks, but key U.S. officials in China, especially Ambassador Johnson and Captain McHugh, were receptive to the KMT version of the story.[99]

Chiang's determination to crush the Communists revealed his belief that Japan was only one of the enemies and could be deterred and confronted by the United States, while no foreign power would eliminate the Communist threat for him. Chiang's keen sense of survival in the Chinese political arena, which few foreigners understood, induced him to give priority to postwar considerations at a much earlier stage. Yet the irreconcilable nature of the CCP-KMT conflict was not understood by Currie, who expressed opposition to the disruption of Chinese unity. In his first meeting with Chiang, Currie considered the Chinese Communists no different from American socialists and praised their policies toward peasants, women, and Japan, making it clear that Roosevelt urged common unity. Chiang could not accept the American thesis on Chinese communism. He contended that the CCP was a puppet of the Comintern and that the CCP opposed China's cooperation with Britain and the United States. Chiang strongly implied that the American view was a result of Communist propaganda.[100]

The American visitor's view on the CCP-KMT relationship remained essentially unchanged. In his report to Roosevelt, Currie attributed the New Fourth Army incident and the CCP-KMT conflict in general to the central government's alarm over Communist expansion. He considered the situation serious and thought that pressures from the United States and Britain as well as the importance of aid from Russia would dissuade Chiang from precipitating actual conflict. As a means to contain the CCP-KMT conflict and to institute political and economic reforms, Currie suggested that a liberal American adviser be sent to Chiang, backed by his government and able to deliver or withhold dollars. Currie's views were fully shared by Roosevelt, who repeatedly pressured Chiang to accept the CCP, though Chiang steadily held his ground.[101]

Currie's trip was turned by the Chinese into a great occasion of canvassing for American assistance. In addition to his interviews with numerous government officials, Currie was surrounded by petitions, articles, memos, and all kinds of arguments during his one month visit. For example, members of the National Political Council presented him with a list of enormous problems China was facing and pleaded that China's survival depended on aid from America. The People's Foreign Relations Association reminded Currie that recent Japanese peace overtures to the United States were "sugar-coated words" to cover up their planned expansion into the South Pacific. It urged the United States to take immediate action by adopting a system of American-British-Chinese cooperation, increasing aid to China, and winning over the Soviet Union. Otherwise, "one day's permit for the enemy's free action becomes a root of trouble for several generations."[102]

Currie's trip was a success from the Chinese point of view. Chiang, who distrusted the State Department for its appeasement tendency toward Japan, now opened a direct channel to President Roosevelt. Chiang told T. V. Soong that Currie had been "very favorably impressed by conditions here, and when he returns to the United States he will surely prove to be of the greatest assistance to our cause."[103] After the trip, Currie became an ardent, if not "the greatest," supporter of China within Roosevelt's inner circles.[104] Chiang's relationship with him, as Owen Lattimore, the American political adviser to Chiang sent in June 1941, put it, was of "a frank and personal kind impossible in relations with an ambassador of even the most friendly and trusted nation."[105]

Shortly after Currie's return, the U.S. Congress passed the Lend-Lease Act and Currie was put in charge of channelling lend-lease materials to China. On China's side, T. V. Soong was designated as the official representative in charge of lend-lease materials through his newly set up agency, the China Defense Supplies. Before the passage of lend-lease, Soong had been engaged in the task of procuring American war materials since his arrival in June 1940. Chiang had been interested in getting modern airplanes to take control of Chinese skies from the Japanese. General Mao Bang-chu of the Chinese air force and Claire Chennault, a former U.S. air force colonel serving under Chiang Kai-shek, were also sent to assist Soong in obtaining airplanes and recruiting American pilots. The American and British governments agreed to transfer to China 100 P-40s assigned for Britain. And in April Roosevelt openly approved the recruitment of U.S. military personnel for service in China.[106] In the recruitment of American pilots and other matters of aid, Currie, along with many administration officials and with the approval of Roosevelt, assisted Chinese efforts all the way.

In Chinese eyes, their de facto alliance with the United States had been settled by the November 1940 loan and the passage of lend-lease. The American decision in early 1941 to fortify Guam and the Philippines together with the similar British action at Singapore greatly encouraged Chiang Kai-shek. He regarded a Japanese conflict with the Anglo-American powers as unavoidable and attributed, quite perceptively, the Anglo-American determination to China's four-year resistance.[107]

THE DREAM OF ALLIANCE COME TRUE

With the perceived strategic importance of China's resistance, the Chinese government considered it opportune to raise its international prestige and status by abolishing the unequal treaty system, which had been the fundamental cause of conflict between revolutionary China and the imperialist powers a decade ago. The agitation to abolish unequal treaties had remained relatively dormant throughout the 1930s although there had been brief moments of talk about the problem.[108] This renewed interest in utilizing the goodwill of Britain and the United States had been inspired partly by the Japanese action. In recognizing the puppet regime of Wang Ching-wei, Japan announced its intention to relinquish extraterritorial rights in China. Window dressing notwithstanding, Japan's move could have had a great deal of propaganda impact on the Chinese, who had always regarded the unequal treaty system as a national humiliation. If Wang's regime in Nanking succeeded first in abolishing these treaties, it would further its claim as the legitimate government of China and could undermine Chinese resistance. How could Chiang justify his alliance with the Anglo-American powers, which still enjoyed imperialist privileges and were unsympathetic to China's struggle for equality among nations?

Zhang Zhong-fu proposed that China ought to take advantage of the present opportunity to demand two things. First, China and the Anglo-American nations should reach an agreement in principle to abolish all unequal treaties after the Sino-Japanese War. Second, Britain and the United States should also issue a statement pledging assistance for China's economic construction during and after the war.[109] The Chinese government adopted such a policy but decided to approach the matter very cautiously. Foreign Minister Wang Chong-hui spoke in public on December 16, 1940, about China's hope to abolish the unequal treaties and to put an end to China's semicolonial status by legal means.[110]

In April 1941 the KMT Central Standing Committee passed a resolution instructing the newly appointed foreign minster, Guo Tai-qi, who had been ambassador to Britain, to raise the question of abrogation of unequal treaties officially with the American government on his way home.[111] In their meetings with Secretary of State Hull, Guo and Ambassador Hu were given favorable responses. Hornbeck was disposed to granting China's request as "moral encouragement."[112] In the final exchange of letters between the foreign minister and the secretary of state, Hull stated that the United States would be willing to negotiate a relinquishment of extraterritoriality by lawful and orderly processes after the war.[113] Thus, the United States had agreed in principle to relinquish its privileges under the old treaties and to restore diplomatic relations completely on equal footing. Britain soon followed suit. There were opinions, pro and con, in the United States about the abrogation of privileges, and the final completion of the process was not announced until 16 months after China and the Anglo-American powers had become formal allies.

The German attack on the Soviet Union in June crystallized the European war into two opposing blocs. In the Pacific, Japan moved into southern Indochina, and the United States responded by freezing Japanese assets on July 25, which amounted to a full economic embargo. The Chinese government looked upon the new international development as a good opportunity to revive its push for a bona fide military alliance of China, the Soviet Union, Britain, and possibly the United States in the Pacific.

China was concerned that the Soviet Union might cease to be a deterrent to Japan as a result of the German-Soviet war. Chiang Kai-shek, therefore, urged the United States to send aid to the Soviet Union so as to strengthen its Far Eastern position and prevent Japan from any possible southward move against Kunming, capital of Yunnan Province. Keeping Japan occupied in the north or preferably in confrontation with the Soviet Union was what most Chinese wanted.[114] Chiang Kai-shek informed Roosevelt through Currie that the Soviets had repeatedly expressed their desire to conclude a definite military arrangement with China against Japan. He suggested that the situation was "ripening for a military pact among China, Russia and Great Britain with the friendly support of the United States." In his reply, Roosevelt was careful not to be drawn into a commitment and told Chiang that his attitude toward either a bilateral or trilateral alliance was favorable, but he could not accept any responsibility.[115]

Now that the Chinese had come to regard China as an important strategic factor needed by the powers, they expected to be treated as an equal. Consequently they deeply resented the fact that for four years, China had not won a single ally and had been isolated while other countries had formed alliances. This resentment and the demand for equal treatment of China surfaced in July and August 1941. Chiang insisted that the United States invite China to participate in the military talks on joint defense among the Americans, the British, and the Dutch to "show that they gave us equal treatment."[116] Zhang Qun, governor of Sichuan Province, stated that in order to raise Chinese morale, the powers would have to "bring China into the international councils *now*."[117] As Owen Lattimore reported, the Chinese felt that the democracies had regarded China as inferior and unworthy of being their ally. On August 2, under tremendous domestic pressure, Chiang Kai-shek presented Roosevelt with two choices: either the president should suggest to Britain and Russia that they propose an alliance with China; or America, Britain, and Holland should invite China to participate in their already existing Pacific defense conferences.[118] Currie, as usual, was very sympathetic to Chiang's demand. He proposed to Roosevelt that he go to Moscow via Chongqing and thus create an impression of "representing

China," because he was widely regarded by the Chinese as their man. In so doing, Chiang's "internal critics who are charging that the Western powers are only using China for their own ends" would be silenced.[119]

The Chinese thought that Japan was a common threat to all concerned Pacific powers and that China had done more than its share of fighting single-handedly for four years. It was time others did their fair share. This general feeling was shared within Chiang's government. Apparently its purpose in advocating a foreign alliance was to let others defeat Japan, and to conserve energy for postwar political control of China.[120]

The demand for an alliance and for equality came at a time when Japan was negotiating with the United States. China had been confident that the United States would confront Japan uncompromisingly and stand firm on the question of China in the negotiations. As the talks continued in September, anxiety about a possible Japan-U.S. modus vivendi began to emerge. Despite Secretary Hull's assurances that the United States would consult the Chinese government in any negotiations affecting China, suspicions remained. The early confidence gave way to the fear of a Far Eastern Munich.[121]

There seemed to be little question of Chiang's confidence in the United States, whose commitment to China grew stronger and stronger as the Far Eastern situation developed. Unlike others, Chiang did not believe it possible for the United States and Japan to compromise.[122] The American military mission to China in October, headed by General John Magruder, further strengthened Chiang's confidence. Military talks were held about the common defense of the South Pacific and Yunnan among Britain, the United States, and China.[123] As demanded by Chiang the previous November, an Anglo-American economic mission headed by Sir Otto Niemeyer, a director of the Bank of England, and H. Merle Cochrane of the U.S. Treasury also arrived in October.[124]

Chiang's confidence in the United States remained unshaken until late November, when he was suddenly alarmed by the American intention to reach an agreement with Japan. In November, Japan made a last ditch effort to solve the diplomatic impasse with the United States by sending a special envoy, Kurusu Saburo, to join Ambassador Nomura. The United States rejected Japan's proposal that Japan would withdraw from southern Indochina in exchange for American relaxation of economic pressures on Japan. In spite of this, Secretary Hull responded to Kurusu's suggestion for a temporary modus vivendi with a similar proposal. Hull explained his proposal in a meeting with the ambassadors from China, Britain, and Australia: the United States would ease economic embargoes in return for

Japan's withdrawal of troops from Vietnam, with only 2,000 to 3,000 remaining, and a pledge not to attack in other directions. Ambassador Hu was, in Hull's words, "disturbed as he always is when any question concerning China arises not entirely to his way of thinking," and objected that since these "other directions" included the southeast and the northeast but not the Chinese front, Japan would be encouraged to step up offensives against Chinese resistance.[125]

Chiang Kai-shek and Foreign Minister Guo strongly objected to any relaxation of economic pressures on Japan before it withdrew all troops from China, warning that otherwise Chinese resistance would collapse instantly. "I cannot believe," Chiang cabled Hu, "that the United States could even entertain such an idea." Two days later, Hull ignored the Chinese objection and told Hu that he was going to present Japan with a proposal that would allow 25,000 instead of 2,000 to 3,000 Japanese troops in Vietnam. The arrangement was supposed to last for three months.[126] Chiang Kai-shek's reaction was violent upon hearing the news on November 25. Lattimore reported that he "never saw him really agitated before." Chiang cabled to Currie his opposition to the proposed relaxation of the embargo and the freezing of Japanese assets and also instructed Soong to convey his concern to two other supporters of China, Navy Secretary Knox and War Secretary Stimson. "The morale of the entire people will collapse and . . . a most tragic epoch in the world will be opened," Chiang warned. Much to the annoyance of Secretary Hull, Chiang mobilized every possible connection in Washington to change the American position.[127]

For all intents and purposes, China had become totally dependent on the United States by the end of 1941. A slight sign of compromise by the American government would arouse uproar and fears in China. Therefore, Chiang's repeated warnings of collapse of resistance, albeit a smart negotiation tactic, did show genuine concern about resistance as well as about his power and prestige. The concern for Chinese resistance was perhaps part of the reason why the British also opposed a Japanese-American modus vivendi. Churchill voiced his concern to Roosevelt on November 25.[128] These last-minute efforts to prevent Japanese-American understanding played a role in forcing Washington to abandon the proposed plan. The next day, instead of the draft for a modus vivendi, Hull presented Japan with an ultimatum, including demands that the latter withdraw completely from China. Chiang felt greatly relieved.[129]

The American ultimatum to Japan prevented any compromise and resulted in the Japanese attack on Pearl Harbor on December 7, 1941. When the news arrived, Chongqing became a joyful and cheering city, after having lived with daily Japanese bombing for three years. In the streets, people were excited by the news; in government, officials congratulated one another; in the generalissimo's headquarters, Chiang Kai-shek "sang an old opera air, and played the Ave Maria all that day," perhaps for the first time since the war.[130] At last, the powers had gone to war with Japan! China's diplomatic efforts in the last ten years and sacrifices since 1937 had at last been redeemed and her hopes fulfilled by the formation of a grand alliance. China declared war on Japan and the other two Axis powers on December 9.

Epilogue

CHINA'S DIPLOMACY AND THE
ORIGINS OF THE PACIFIC WAR: A SPECULATION

In his recent book *The Origins of the Second World War in Asia and the Pacific,* Iriye suggests: "The tragic road to the war needs to be put in a global and comparative perspective" and asks: "What were the forces, inside each country and in the world at large, that made for so much violence, conflict, and war in the 1930s?"[1] The analysis in this book is an attempt to understand the Chinese part of that violent process leading to the war. In essence, the coming of the Pacific War for the Chinese was a self-fulfilling prophecy. Chiang Kai-shek and other Chinese had been predicting such a conflict ever since the Manchurian Incident. Based on their understanding of the nature of imperialism, they believed that the powers' economic interests were jeopardized by Japan's attempt to establish hegemony in East Asia and that an inevitable conflict would occur in the 1930s. Similarly, they also viewed Japan's threat to the Soviet Union as a catalyst for war. Albeit it also served as an excuse for Chiang Kai-shek's government to deal with its domestic rivals first, such a belief became the rationale for its foreign policy.

China's belief in an inevitable war between Japan and other powers was an illusion more than anything else, since the powers were neither ready nor willing to confront Japanese expansionism from 1931 to 1937. It was questionable whether they would have done so had there not been the unexpected Chinese resistance during the Sino-Japanese War after 1937. The assumption that their conflict of interests was irreconcilable was not based on solid ground. The same was true of the Chinese hopes for alliances with the Soviet Union, the United States, and Britain. If anything, these powers regarded Chinese hopes and maneuvers simply as the old Chinese tactics of playing barbarians against each other and had no intentions "of pulling chestnuts out of fire for China."[2]

When the powers failed to rescue China, the Chinese government sometimes adopted a flexible attitude—for example, the gradualist policy between 1934 and 1935—and also kept open the secret channels of communication with Japan after 1937. But it was subject to heavy public pressure that doomed any pursuit of such flexibility. Domestic politics and public opinion in China greatly limited diplomatic leverage and alternatives available to the government. Therefore, Chiang Kai-shek had to pursue more vigorously his beliefs about Japan's conflict with the powers.

The question of the validity of these Chinese beliefs aside, the consequences of such beliefs were most important. Diplomatically, they became the operating basis for fighting the war: counting on the assistance and eventual intervention by the powers. Without these beliefs in and hopes for an internationalization of the war, it would have been next to impossible for China's war efforts to last as long as they did. The timely material assistance rendered by the Soviet Union and later by the United States at various critical moments before Pearl Harbor had the effect, dialectically speaking, of strengthening and vindicating these beliefs and thus sustaining the war.

The effect of the resistance war on the powers was even more significant in that it affected the strategic planning of every one of them. For Japan, it was an unexpected disaster that drained valuable resources into a war it did not intend to fight and weakened its position vis-à-vis other powers; for the Soviet Union, on the other hand, the war was a godsend, an opportunity that it had tried but was unable to obtain for years and that reduced the threat from both east and west; similarly for the Anglo-American powers, it offered an opportunity to defend their interests by supporting China but without actual military involvement.

In a sense the war transformed the traditional relationship between China and the powers into one of mutual dependence. China became a strategic factor to be reckoned with and in fact came to be viewed by Anglo-Americans and the Soviets as the first line of defense for their security and interests in the Far East.[3] Therefore, supporting China became the most economical policy for defense and became the logic for both the Soviet Union and the Anglo-American powers; accommodation with Japan in this new situation became a less attractive alternative. Little wonder that both Stalin and Roosevelt wanted to keep China in war. The Soviets changed their policy of supporting China against Japan only after it concluded the Nazi-Soviet pact, securing a relatively safe west, and attempted to reach an understanding with Japan.

In the literature on the origins of the Pacific War the subject is treated, naturally enough, in a bilateral context of Japanese-American relations. *Pearl Harbor as History* (1973) stands out as a monumental reminder. Some scholars emphasize the European factor and the support America gave Britain by protecting its Far Eastern possessions. Therefore, Japan's southward move and membership in the Axis alliance were unacceptable to Washington and thus were insurmountable barriers to a peaceful settlement.[4] Others, while not denying the importance of the European factor, put strong emphasis on American policy to support China and regard the first loan in 1938 as a turning point.[5] The latter view raises the question of why there was a change of policy from tolerating Japan's aggression before 1937 to a policy of confronting it, a question that the European emphasis is not able to answer, since there was no serious need to protect the European colonies from Japan's threat in 1938.

Scholars agree that the actual American interests in China were very small and many in Washington believed that they were not worth fighting a war. Given this fact and concerns with Europe, it is even more puzzling that the United States did not adopt a policy of compromise. A possible reason might be that the Chinese resistance revived the concept of the Open Door as vital to American economy and society. Prior to 1937, American policymakers, following the spirit of the Lansing-Ishii agreement, were realistic enough to tolerate Japan's special position in the Far East. There was no forceful policy against the violation of the Open Door in Japan's conquest of Manchuria and after. For all intents and purposes, the Open Door was a dead letter. China's decision to fight and its ability to endure the war was something unprecedented and a new factor in the configurations of the power balance. In spite of military defeats, China's resistance enabled Americans to think that America's weakness and inability to keep alive the Open Door could now be compensated by supporting China. Apparently those behind the 1938 loan to China—Morgenthau, Hornbeck, and others— followed this line of reasoning. Even those who opposed the loan, for example, Cordell Hull, did not differ much in basic beliefs. Hull, like everyone else, reversed his initial doubts about China's ability to resist Japan and came to believe that Japan would be bogged down in China. His strategy as opposed to that of the activists was to wait for the destruction of Japan without involving the United States.[6] The belief that China could carry on resistance if well supplied led to the American policy of not compromising with Japan, since China's resistance would weaken Japan militarily and economically. Thus the chances for the United States to uphold the Open Door depended on supporting China. This kind of thinking preceded events in 1940. Once conceived, the American position was to remain fairly consistent.

In any event, without Chinese beliefs in the powers' inevitable conflict with Japan, there would hardly have been a sustained resistance; without such resistance, there would hardly have been the Soviet and American support for China, and the later uncompromising American policy toward Japan and the outbreak of the Pacific War. In the final analysis, the Chinese perceptions about inevitable conflicts between Japan and other powers were indeed important. Fact and fancy make history. The story of China's foreign relations in the 1930s is a good case in point.

NOTES

Notes to Introduction

1. For a partial list of the studies of the Far Eastern policies of the powers, see James Crowley, *Japan's Quest for Autonomy: National Security and Foreign Policy, 1930-1938* (Princeton: Princeton University Press, 1966); Michael Barnhart, *Japan Prepares for Total War* (Ithaca: Cornell University Press, 1989); Dorothy Borg, *The United States and the Far Eastern Crisis of 1933-1938: From the Manchurian Incident through the Initial Stage of the Undeclared War* (Cambridge: Harvard University Press, 1964); Michael Schaller, *The US Crusade in China, 1938-1945* (New York: Columbia University Press, 1979); Jonathan Utley, *Going to War with Japan* (Knoxville: University of Tennessee Press, 1985); Ann Trotter, *Britain and East Asia, 1933-1937* (Cambridge: Cambridge University Press, 1975); Wm. Roger Louis, *British Strategy in the Far East, 1919-1939* (Oxford: Clarendon Press, 1971); Bradford Lee, *Britain and the Sino-Japanese War, 1937-1939* (Stanford: Stanford University Press, 1973); Peter Lowe, *Great Britain and the Origins of the Pacific War: A Study of British Policy in East Asia 1937-1941* (Oxford: Clarendon Press, 1977); Aron Shai, *Origins of War in the East: Britain, China and Japan, 1937-1939* (London: Croom Helm, 1976); Stephen Endicott, *Diplomacy and Enterprise: British China Policy, 1933-37* (Vancouver: Manchester University Press and University of British Columbia Press, 1975); George P. Fox, *Germany and the Far Eastern Crisis, 1931-1938: A Study in Diplomacy and Ideology* (Oxford: Clarendon Press, 1982); and Christopher Thorn, *The Limits of Foreign Policy: The West, the League and the Far Eastern Crisis of 1931-1933*, 1st American ed. (New York: Putnam, 1973).
2. William C. Kirby, *Germany and Republican China* (Stanford: Stanford University Press, 1984); John Garver, *Chinese-Soviet Relations, the Diplomacy of Chinese Nationalism, 1937-1945* (New York: Oxford University Press, 1988); John Hunter Boyle, *China and Japan at War*, (Stanford: Stanford University Press, 1972); and Gerald Bunker, *The Peace Conspiracy* (Cambridge: Harvard University Press, 1972); Parks Coble, *Facing Japan: Chinese Politics and Japanese Imperialism, 1931-1937*, (Cambridge: Harvard East Asian Council, 1991).

Notes to Chapter 1

1. See Iriye's 1978 presidential address at SHAFR, "Culture and Power: International Relations as Intercultural Relations," *Diplomatic History,* 2 (Spring 1979): 115-128. For a most recent survey on political science literature on this subject, see Richard Little and Steve Smith, eds., *Belief Systems and International Relations* (Oxford: Basil Blackwell, 1990). See also Holsti's study of John Foster Dulles, "The Belief System and National Images: A Case Study," in James N. Rosenau, ed., *International Politics and Foreign Policy* (New York: Free Press, 1969): 543-550.

2. Yaacov Y. I. Vertzberger, *The World in Their Minds: Information Processing, Cognition, and Perception in Foreign Policy Decision-making* (Stanford: Stanford University Press, 1990), 260.

3. When analyzing public opinion in the United States, Ernest May defined the public as "comparatively well-to-do, well-educated, well-read, and politically active public." See *American Imperialism: A Speculative Essay* (New York: Atheneum, 1968), 24. This is especially true of the Chinese public opinion in the 1930s.

4. Tang Shou-chang, *Diguozhuyi Qinlue Zhongguo Tongshi* [A History of Imperialist Aggression in China] (Shanghai: Dadong Shuju, 1929); Huang Xiaoxian, *Diguozhuyi Qinlue Zhongguo Shi* [A History of Imperialist Aggression in China] (Shanghai: Commercial Press, 1928); and Chen Tong-he, *Diguozhuyi Qinlue Zhongguo Shi* [A History of Imperialist Aggression in China] (Shanghai: Shijie Shuju, 1927), 5-16.

5. Dai Ji-tao, *Daijitao Xiansheng Liangge Zhongyao De Jianghua* [Two Important Speeches by Mr. Dai Ji-tao] (n.p.: Huangpu Military Academy, 1927), 21-22.

6. John Gittings, *The World and China, 1922-1972* (New York: Harper and Row, 1974), 30.

7. See Michael Hunt, *The Making of a Special Relationship: The United States and China to 1914* (New York: Columbia University Press, 1983), 189, 203. Also see Marilyn Young, *Rhetoric of Empire* (Cambridge: Harvard University Press, 1968) for the Chinese role in the formation of the Open Door Policy.

8. See Liang Qi-chao, "On General Situation of National Competition" (1903), *Yinbingshi Heji* (Beijing: Zhonghua Shuju, 1989), 2: 10-35, and "General World Situation and China's Future" (1908), ibid., 3:307. Also another piece, "On the Development of Imperialism and the Future of the World in the 20th Century" in Liang's newspaper *Qingyibao* in *Xinhai Geming Qianshinian Jian Shilun Xuan Ji* [Selected Articles in the Ten Years Prior to the Republican Revolution], vol. 1 (Hong Kong: Sanlian Shudian, 1963), 53-58. Gidding's book was published in 1901 (New York, Macmillan) and Kazuomi's was translated into Chinese in 1895(?). For more information, also see Harold Shiffrin, *Sun Yat-sen and the Origins of the Chinese Revolution* (Berkeley: University of California Press, 1968), 283-286.

9. For Liang's views on trust, see "Big Trusts in the 20th Century," *Yinbingshi,* 2:33-61. Also see Martin Bernal, *Chinese Socialism to 1907* (Ithaca: Cornell University Press, 1976), 144-147. For Sun's earlier views, see Shi Zhen-ding,

Guofu De Waijiao Zhengce [The Founding Father's Diplomatic Policy] (Taibei: Youshi Shudian, 1965), 92 and Shiffrin, *Sun Yat-sen,* 332; A. James Gregor and Maria Hsia Chang, "Marxism, Sun Yat-sen, and the Concept of Imperialism," *Pacific Affairs* 55, no. 1 (Spring 1982): 71.

10. Chester C. Tan, *Chinese Political Thought in the Twentieth Century* (New York: Doubleday, 1971), 186. Tan mentions that Chu's concept formed a contrast with Lenin's theory of imperialism. This is certainly true as far as Chu continued to hold his old ideas. Lenin's book on imperialism was translated into Chinese in September 1919 and Chu died exactly one year later. It was not clear that in his last year of busy political and military life Chu had any time to read Lenin's thesis. The fact that Chu began to learn Russian in his later years may suggest a possibility that he might have been influenced by Lenin had he lived into the 1920s.

11. For example, Liu Wen-hai, *Jinshi Daguojiazhuyi* [Big Countryism in the Modern Age] (Shanghai: Commercial Press, 1925). He treated the subject as overdetermined by a cluster of factors, such as migration to the new world, commerce, naval problems, and the development of capitalism and Christianity. He argued that though imperialists all aimed at subjugation of other people and lands, there were basically two kinds of imperialists. The first kind were Social Darwinists who believed in the survival of the fittest. The second kind were racists who argued that imperialism was carrying on civilization and "bearing the white man's burden."

12. For Sun's views on imperialism see his lecture No. 4 on nationalism, Sun Yat-sen, *San Min Chu I* [The Three Principles of the People] (Calcutta: Chinese Ministry of Information, 1942), 57. Also see Kuang-sheng Liao, *Anti-foreignism and Modernization in China, 1860-1980* (Hong Kong: The Chinese University Press, 1984), 86-88 and Shu-Chin Tsui, "The Influence of the Canton-Moscow Entente upon Sun Yat-sen's Political Philosophy," *The Chinese Social Political Science Review* (Peking) 18, no. 1(1934): 96-145. Both Liao and Tsui argued that Sun was not influenced by Lenin's theory of imperialism. However, Sun's change of attitude toward foreign investments, for example, certainly indicated some Soviet influence.

13. Wang Ching-wei, *Guominhuiyi Guoji Wenti Caoan* [Draft Resolution of the National Congress] (n.p.: Guoji Wenti Yanjiu Hui, 1927), 6-7.

14. Liao Zhong-kai, *Liaozhongkai Ji* [Works of Liao Zhong-kai] (Peking: Zhonghua Shuju, 1983), 259.

15. See Tan, *Chinese Political Thought,* 196-198.

16. See Gittings, *The World and China,* 32.

17. Ma Zhe-min, *Guoji Diguozhuyi Shilun* [A History of International Imperialism] (Shanghai: Kunlun Shudian, 1929).

18. Yang You-jong, *Jinshi Guoji Wenti Yu Zhongguo* [Recent International Problems and China] (Shanghai: Taidong Tushuju, 1928), 2-3, 8-9. For others, see Gao Er-song, *Diguozhuyi Yu Zhongguo* [Imperialism and China] (Shanghai: Xinwenhua Shushe, 1924).

19. Dong Lin, *Diguozhuyi Yu Zhonghua Minzu* [Imperialism and the Chinese Nation] (Shanghai: Guangming Shuju, 1929), 166-167. All the four theories

Dong comments on in this book were Marxist including those of Lenin and Hilferding. Though he defines imperialism as expansionism and aggression, Dong considers the motive to be economic.

20. For example see Hu Sheng's *Imperialism and Chinese Politics* (Beijing: Foreign Languages Press, 1955) and his article, "Guanyu Jindai Zhongguo Yu Shijie De Jige Wenti [Several Problems about Modern China and the World]," *People's Daily* (overseas edition) (October 26, 1990), 2.

21. Li Yun-han, *Zhongguo Xiandai Shilun He Shiliao* [Articles and Materials on Modern Chinese History] (Taibei: Commercial Press, 1979), 537.

22. Chen Xing-tang, "Jiuyiba Qianhou De Fengjiangjun" [General Feng around the Time of the 9.18 Incident], *Lishi Dangan* [Historical Archives] 3(1982): 110-115.

23. For the tactics of anti-imperialism in the 1920s, see Xu Yi-jun, "On the Anti-imperialist Diplomatic Tactics of the National Government during the Period of Canton and Wuhan," *Jindaishi Yanjiu* [Studies on Modern History] 3(1982): 31-48.

24. Zhou Geng-sheng, *Zhanshi Waijiao Wenti* [Wartime Diplomatic Problems] (Chongqing: Political Dept. of National Military Affairs Commission, 1938), 53.

25. Zhang Zhong-dong, *Cong Zhuzhang Heping Dao Zhuzhang Kangzhan De Hushi* [Hu Shi: From Advocating Peace to Advocating War] (Taibei: Institute of American Culture, Academia Sinica, 1983), 98.

26. *Sue Pinglun* [The Soviet Russia Review] 1, no. 1 (October 1931): 1-10.

27. For example, see Han Qing, "The Second World War and Its Impact on Russia and China," ibid., 2-3, no. 2 (1932): 58.

28. Ye Yu, "An Observation of China's Diplomatic Way Out from the Perspective of World Realistic Situation," *Waijiao Yuekan* [Diplomatic Monthly] 3, no. 6 (December 1932): 188.

29. Editorial, "The Threat of A Japanese-Russian War," *Eastern Miscellany* 30, no. 23 (December 1933): 3.

30. For the discussion records, see *Diplomatic Monthly* 2, no. 2 (February 1933): 2-12, 17-20.

31. Letter from the Northeast People's Anti-Japanese Salvation Association to the Nanking government, October 11, 1931, see State Department decimal file, 711.93/261, National Archives, Washington, D.C.

32. See *Soviet Russia Review* 2, no. 1(1932): 145-146. For Feng's views, see his *Zhongguo Yu Erci Dazhan* [China and the Second (world) War] (Tientsin: Shishi Chubanshe, 1935), 214-219. The book was written with the assistance of many young left-minded scholars.

33. For Zhang Chong and Li Chang-qing's views, see *Shishi Yuekan* [Current Affairs Monthly] 8, no. 2 (1933), 77.

34. *Xian Zongtong Jianggong Sixiang Yanlun Zongji* [A Complete Collection of Former President Chiang's Thoughts and Speeches], 40 vols., ed. Qin Xiao-yi (Taibei: Party History Committee of the Kuomintang, 1984), 12: 102; also see Chen Li-fu, "Recollections about Participating in Preparations for the Resistance War," *Zhuanji Wenxue* [Biographical Literature] 31, no. 1 (July 1977): 45-51. Chiang's efforts to establish an alliance with the Soviet Union are dealt with in Chapter Four.

35. Wang Diao-pu, "The Basic Diplomatic Policy and Attitude That Should Be Adopted," *Diplomatic Monthly* 3, no. 4 (October 1933): 157-164.

36. Hu Huan-yong, "Studying China's Foreign Relations from a Geopolitical Perspective," *Waijiao Pinglun* [Diplomatic Review] 3, no. 7 (July 1934): 45-54.

37. Jiang Ting-fu, "On Foreign Aid," *Diplomatic Monthly* 1, no. 3 (September 1932): 13-17.

38. Peck to Secretary of State, January 9, 1933, *Foreign Relations of the United States,* 1933, 3: 39-40. Hereafter cited as *FRUS.*

39. Zhang Zhong-fu, "Sino-Soviet Restoration of Relations and the Future of China's Diplomacy," *Diplomatic Monthly* 2, no. 1 (January 1933).

40. Sun Lin-sheng, "The Relations among China, Japan, Russia and the United States," *Eastern Miscellany* 31, no. 3 (December 1934): 18. This was the most widely shared theme in periodicals and writings of the same kind are numerous, for an example, see Yao Ping, "Yuandong Lieqiang de Duili Yu Woguo Waijiao Fangzhen" [The Conflicts among the Powers in the Far East and Our Diplomatic Principle], *Guofang Luntan* [National Defense Forum] 3, no. 11 (April 1935).

41. Lin Bo-sheng, *Duiri de Liangtiao Luxian* [Two Lines Regarding Japan] (Shanghai: Zhonghua Ribao 1935), 17-18.

42. *Chinese Affairs* 5, no. 6 (August 1933): 78.

43. Feng Yu-xiang to Chiang Kai-shek, October 23 and December 11, 1935, *Jiang Feng Shujian* [Chiang Feng Correspondences] (Shanghai: Zhongguo Wenhua Xintuo Fuwushe, 1946), 1-3.

44. Hu Han-min, *Yuandong Wenti Yu Dayazhouzhuyi* [The Far Eastern Problem and the Pan Asianism] (Guangzhou: Zhongxing Xuehue, 1935), 54-55.

45. See Fu Qi-xue, *A Diplomatic History of China,* 388-389; *Riben Dalu Zhengce De Zhenmianmu* [The True Face of Japanese Continental Policy] (Shanghai: Shenghuo Shudian, 1938); Memo on the Tanaka Memorial prepared for Chinese delegation to the League of Nations, 1932, Wellington Koo Papers, Box 6, Columbia University. Some contemporary Chinese scholars on both sides of the Taiwan Straits still believed in its existence; see *Zhongguo Jindai Duiwai Guanxishi Ziliao Xuanji* [Selected Materials on Modern Foreign Relations of China] (Shanghai: Shanghai Rimin Chubanshe, 1977), 2:141 and Li Yun-han's chapter in Paul K. T. Shih, ed., *Nationalist China during the Sino-Japanese War, 1937-1945* (New York: Exposition Press, 1977). A scholarly study by John J. Stephan shows that the Tanaka Memorial is a fake; see "The Tanaka Memorial (1927): Authentic or Spurious?" *Modern Asian Studies* 7, no. 4 (1973): 733-745.

46. See *Zhonggguo Jindaishi Duiwai Guanxishi Ziliao Xuan Ji* [Selected Materials on Modern Foreign Relations of China], vol. 2, comp. by History Department, Fudan University (Shanghai: Rimin Chubanshe, 1977), 259.

47. Wilbur, "Military Separatism and Process of Reunification under National Regime, 1927-1937," in *Crisis in China,* ed. Ping-ti Ho and Tang Tsou (Chicago: University of Chicago Press, 1968), 203-276.

48. For a representative piece with this view, see Wu Qian-yao, "The Crisis of World War and Redivision of the World," *Shenbao Yuekan* [Shenbao Monthly]

3, no. 7 (July 1934): 15-18. Virtually all the articles written before 1937 had similar views.

49. See Jiang Gong-huai and Zhang Yue-hua, "An Analysis on the Pacific Situation," ibid., and also see Yuan Dao-feng's article on the possibility of World War II, *Eastern Miscellany* 33, no. 12 (June 1936): 145-150.

50. Ma Xing-ye, "The American Attitude during the Second World War," in Zhang Nai-qi, ed., *Dierci Shijie Dazhan Yu Zhongguo* [The Second World War and China] (Shanghai: Qingnian Xiehui Shuju, 1936), 77-78. For similar views, also see Wang Ji-yuan, "Contradictions among the Imperialists and China's Political Diplomacy," *Shenbao Monthly* 3, no. 7 (July 1934): 25-29 and Geng Dan-ru, "A Perspective on Anglo-American-Japanese Competition in the Pacific," *Shishi Monthly* 12, no. 6 (June 1935): 432-437.

51. Hu Shi-jie, "Japanese-German Alliance, Anti-Sovietism and the World War," *Soviet Russia Review* 10, no. 1 (1936): 5-7.

52. Fu Si-nian, "The Possibility of a Japanese-Soviet Conflict," *Duli Pinglun* [Independent Review], 116: 2-4.

53. Tang Yue-liang, "An Observation of the Far Eastern International Reality," *Qinghua Zhoukan* [Qinghua Weekly] 38, no. 5 (October 1932): 47; Bei Chen, "We Need a Second World War," ibid., 37, no. 1 (February 1932): 24.

54. See editor's summary of the forum, *Shenbao Monthly* 1, no. 2 (August 1932): 4.

55. There were six articles in this forum on the Pacific situation, *Eastern Miscellany* 30, no. 6 (March 1933): 5-43.

56. In addition to books on a future war by Zhang Nai-qi and Feng Yu-xiang mentioned earlier, there were at least 20 books of such a kind in circulation by 1935, some of which were translations from American or Japanese works. For a list of these books, see Ping Xin, comp., *Quanguo Zongshumu* [National Bibliography of Books] (Shanghai: Shenghuo Shudian, 1935), 174-176 and also see Zhang Nai-wen, *1936* (Shanghai: Yuehua Tushushe, 1935). Alerting and urging preparations for world war was a very popular theme in the periodical literature. For example, see Jiang Jian-ren (political director of the Air Force), "Weilai Zhanzheng Yu Zhongguo Qiantu" [The Coming War and China's Future], *Kongjun* [Air Force] 141 (August 1935). Japanese writings on Japanese-American war are described in John Stephan, *Hawaii under the Rising Sun* (Honolulu: University of Hawaii Press, 1984), 55-68.

57. Wang Xing-hun, "My Observations of the Second World War," *Independent Review,* 187 (1936): 7-14.

58. See Keiji Furuya, *Jiangzongtong Milu* [The Secret Records of President Chiang] 15 vols. (Taibei: Zhongyang Ribao, 1977), 8: 45.

59. Chiang's speech to military officers, 1931, see Qin Xiao-yi, ed., *Zongtong Jianggong Dashi Changbian Chugao* [Major Events in the Life of Former President Chiang], 8 vols. (Taibei: n.p., 1978), 2: 192. Hereafter cited as *DSCB*.

60. Chiang Kai-shek, *Kangzhan Bisheng Shijiang* [Ten Speeches on the Certainty of Victory in the Resistance War] (Canton: Xinzhongguo Chubanshe, 1938), 1-2. This speech was first made in 1934 and reprinted in 1938.

61. For Chiang's diary, see Qin Xiao-yi, ed., *DSCB,* 3:218.

62. Ole R. Holsti, "Cognitive Dynamics and Images of the Enemy," in John C. Farrell and Asa P. Smith, eds., *Image and Reality in World Politics* (New York: Columbia University Press, 1967), 16.

Notes to Chapter 2

1. The following works contain descriptions about Chinese reactions to the Manchurian Incident: Pao-chin Chu, *V. K. Wellington Koo* (Hong Kong: Chinese University Press, 1981); Christopher Thorne, *Limits of Foreign Policy: the West, the League and the Far Eastern Crisis of 1931-1933* (New York: Putnam, 1973); Westel Willoughby, *The Sino-Japanese Controversy and the League of Nations* (Baltimore: Johns Hopkins University Press, 1935); Liang Jing-dun's *Jiuyiba Shishu* [A History of the Manchurian Affair] (Taibei: Shijie Shuju, 1968); Xian Yi-shi et al., *Jiuyiba Shibian Shi* [A History of the Manchurian Incident] (Shenyang: Liaoning Renmin Chubanshe, 1981); Donald Jordan, *Chinese Boycotts versus Japanese Bombs* (Ann Arbor: University of Michigan Press, 1991); Parks Coble, *Facing Japan: Chinese Politics and Japanese Imperialism, 1931-1937* (Cambridge: Harvard East Asian Council, 1991).

2. Record of meeting no. 106 of the KMT Central Executive Committee, September 19, 1931, *Zhonghua Minguo Zhongyao Shiliao Chubian: Duiri Kangzhan Shiqi* [Important Historical Documents on the Republic of China during the Anti-Japanese War], edited by Party History Committee of the Kuomintang Central Committee (Taibei: Party History Committee, 1981), supplement, 1: 277-278. Hereafter cited as *SLCB*. Chiang Kai-shek's diary entry, September 20, ibid., 275, 281.

3. Liang Jing-dun, *A History of the Manchurian Affair,* 109; another telegram of "nonresistance" is mentioned in Hong Fang, "Zhang Xue-liang at the time of September 18 Incident," *Wenshi Ziliao Xuanji* 6: 24. It was dated August 16, 1931, and it advised Zhang to avoid armed conflicts with Japan and not to resist even if the Japanese army tried to make trouble in the northeast. Chiang told him not to put his temporary anger above the interest of the nation.

4. Pao-chin Chu, *V. K. Wellington Koo,* 122.

5. Chiang to Liu Zhen-nian, divisional commander at Yantai, Shandong Province, September 21 and Chiang's speech at a KMT Party rally, September 22, *SLCB,* supplement, 1: 282-283.

6. For Chiang's speech on November 28, see *Jiang Zongtong Ji* [Works of President Chiang], vol. 1, comp. by Guofang Yanjiuyuan (Taibei: Lianhe Chuban Zhongxin, 1968), 577.

7. This news conference was held by students from Peking, and they were influenced to some extent by the underground Communists. For a personal recollection, see Liu Jing, "Recall the student patriotic movements around 'the September 18,' " *Zhongguo Xiandaishi* [Modern Chinese History], comp. by People's University, vol. 6 (1982): 79-85.

8. *"9.18"—"1.28"* Shanghai Junmin Kangri Yundong Shiliao [Materials on the Resistance Movements by Shanghai Army and People during the Period from September 18 (1931) to January 28 (1932)], compiled by History Institute of Shanghai Academy of Social Sciences (Shanghai: Academy of Social Sciences Press, 1986), 111-149. Hereafter cited as *SHSL*. For student anti-Japanese activities and the CC Clique involvement, see Jordan, *Chinese Boycotts,* Chapter Six.

9. William L. Tung, *Revolutionary China: A Personal Account, 1926-1949* (New York: St. Martin's Press, 1973), 116.

10. For Soong-Shigemitsu talks, see *Documents on British Foreign Policy,* 2nd series, 8: no. 534 and also, Sara R. Smith, *The Manchurian Crisis, 1931-1932: A Tragedy in International Relations* (New York: Columbia University Press, 1948), 37-38. Here Soong himself and China's communication to the League of Nations asserted that Shigemitsu contacted Soong first and proposed the joint commission. Wu Xiang-xiang suggests that Soong proposed the idea first in his *Dierci Zhongri Zhanzheng* [The Second Sino-Japanese War] (Taibei: Zonghe Yuekanshe, 1973), 85.

11. Keiji, *The Secret Records* 8: 32, 43.

12. Wellington Koo, *Guweijin Huiyilu* [Memoirs of Wellington Koo] (Peking: Zhonghua Shuju, 1985), 1: 417; Chiang to Zhang, October 6, 1931, *SLCB,* supplement, 1: 291.

13. Smith, *The Manchurian Crisis,* 38.

14. Koo to Zhang Xue-liang, October 14, 15, and 16, 1931, *Minguo Danan* [Republican Archives], vol. 1 (1985): 11-13.

15. Shen Yun-long, *Huang Ying-bai,* 1: 458.

16. *SLCB,* 6, part 1: 263.

17. Ibid., 264; For these discussions, see Willoughby, *The Sino-Japanese Controversy,* 52-72.

18. Koo to Zhang, October 16, 1931, *Republican Archives,* vol. 1 (1985): 14, 15.

19. Johnson to Secretary of State, October 17, 1931, 1931, *FRUS,* 1931, 3: 219.

20. Koo to Zhang, October 22 and October 23, 1931, *Republican Archives,* vol. 1 (1985): 17-18; also see *SLCB,* 6, part 1: 266.

21. Yung Kwai to Secretary of State, September 21, 1931, *FRUS,* 1931, 3: 24.

22. Koo's conversation with U.S. consul in Tianjin, October 10, 1931, ibid., 151; Soong's conversation with U.S. consul in Nanking, October 12, 1931, ibid., 170; *SLCB,* supplement, 1: 296.

23. See Xian Yi-shi, et al., *Jiuyiba Shibian Shi,* 174.

24. Keiji, *The Secret Records,* 8: 45.

25. For the report, see Wellington Koo Papers, Columbia University, Box 6, F.26; also see Chen Tian-xi, ed., *Daijitao Ji* [Works of Mr. Dai Ji-tao] (Taibei: Central Committee of the Kuomintang, 1959), 1: 373-374.

26. Record of the preliminary session, October 26, 1931, *Lishi Dangan* [Historical Archives], vol. 2 (1982): 72.

27. Koo to Zhang, November 26, 1931, *Republican Archives,* vol. 2 (1985): 5; Chiang to Zhang, December 8 and 9, 1931, *SLCB,* supplement, 1: 312-313; National Government to Zhang Xue-liang, December 25 and 30, ibid., 313.

28. Chen Hong-min, "Chronological History of Hu Han-min," *Republican Archives,* vol. 1 (1986): 120, 121.

29. "Mr. Eugene Chen's account of the history of his relations with the Japanese during the last half of 1931," British Foreign Office, *Documents on British Foreign Policy,* 2nd series (London: Her Majesty's Stationary Office, 1965), 9: 148-149. For factional struggles after the Manchurian Incident, see Donald A. Jordan, "Place of Chinese Disunity in Japanese Army Strategy during 1931," *China Quarterly,* vol. 109 (March 1987): 42-63.

30. Peck to Secretary of State, January 8, 1932, *FRUS,* 1932, 3: 15; *Zhonghua Minguoshi Jiyao* [Chronological Events of the Republic of China], January-June 1932 (Taibei: Zhonghua Minguo Shiliao Yanjiu Zhongxin, 1980), 100. Hereafter cited as *MGJY.*

31. Chiang Kai-shek, "The Northeast Problem and the Policy toward Japan," January 11, 1932, *SLCB,* supplement, 1: 317-319.

32. Li Yun-han, *Zhongguo Xiandai Shilun He Shiliao* [Articles and Materials on Modern Chinese History] (Taibei: Commercial Press, 1979), 300; "On Severing of Diplomatic Relations," *Dagongbao,* January 17, 1932.

33. See State Department central files, China: Internal Affairs, 1930-39, microfilm reel no. 4 (Frederick, Md.: University Publication of America, 1983).

34. Guo Da-Jun, "The Changes of Policy of the KMT government from 9.18 to 8.13," *Zhongguo Xiandaishi* [Modern Chinese History], comp. People's University, 1, no. 6 (1985): 119; He to Wu, January 31, 1932, *SHSL,* 271; Luo Wen-gan, He Ying-qin, and Chen Ming-shu to Cai Ting-kai, February 13, 1932, ibid., 278.

35. Peck to Secretary of State, January 27 and 29, 1932, *FRUS,* 1932, 3: 78-79, 92; Luo Wen-gan's note to Johnson, February 3, 1932, ibid., 193.

36. Sun and Chen's statement was published by Guo Min News Agency; see Cunningham and Peck to Secretary of State, February 27 and April 4, respectively, ibid., 454-455, 663.

37. Guo Tai-qi to Luo Wen-gan, February 14, 1932, *Geming Wenxian* [Revolutionary Documents], ed. Party History Commission of the Kuomintang (Taibei: Zhongyang Wenwu Gongyingshe, 1965), 36: 1535, 1567-1568. Hereafter cited as *GMWX.*

38. Luo Wen-gan to Wellington Koo, February 14, 1932, ibid., 1539.

39. See *MGJY,* 713-714, 722-723, 728-729.

40. Luo Wen-gan to Wellington Koo, July 23, 1932, Koo Papers, Box 23, F15.

41. He Jun, "Lun Yijiuerjiu-Yijiusanjiu Nian de Zhongsu Guanxi" [On Sino-Soviet Relations, 1929-1939], master's thesis, Nanking University, 1986, 30.

42. Draft proposal on restoration of Sino-Soviet relations in CPC, May 1932, Koo Papers, Box 23, F15.

43. Yan to Foreign Ministry, March 18, 1932; two of Koo's telegrams to Wang, Chiang, Luo and Soong, undated (approximately late March or early April), ibid., Box 23, F15; for opinions of the miliary staff, see He Jun, "On Sino-Soviet Relations," 31-32.

44. Draft proposal on restoration of Sino-Soviet relations in CPC, May 1932, and Koo's Special Instructions to Hussey for the four principles on the Manchurian

solution, Koo Papers, Box 23, F15. Also see "Jiejue Dongan Banfa Dagang Caoan" [the proposed draft solution of the Manchurian problem], which Wang sent to Koo on June 28, ibid., Box 6, F26.

45. Wang's conversation with Lytton, June 20, 1932, ibid., Box 4.

46. See He Jun, "On Sino-Soviet Relations," 31-32.

47. See Wellington Koo's "General Instructions" to Hussey, Koo Papers, Box 23, F15 and Qin Xiao-yi, ed., *DSCB,* 2: 212, 222.

48. Luo Wen-gan to Wellington Koo, July 23, 1932, and Wang's telegram to Foreign Ministry, June 20, see Koo Papers, Box 23, F15. Also see Aitchen K. Wu, *China and the Soviet Union* (New York: John Day Company, 1950), 214.

49. See Koo's "Some points orally explained to Mr. Hussey," and also Koo to Luo, July 1, 1932, Koo Papers, Box 23, F15. For Hussey's background and his close relations with Koo, see Harry Hussey, *My Pleasures and Palaces: An Informal Memoir of Forty Years in Modern China* (Garden City, NY: Doubleday, 1968).

50. Luo to Koo, June 29, July 1, 3, 20, 23 and 26, Koo Papers, Box 23, F15. Hussey, *My Pleasures,* 309-313.

51. See He Jun, "On Sino-Soviet Relations," 33-34.

52. For Chiang's diary, see Qin Xiao-yi, ed., *DSCB,* 2: 245.

53. For a complete list of invitees to the conference, see *MGJY,* 137-138.

54. See Shen Yun-long, "Recalling the National Conference on Crisis," *Zhuanji Wenxue* [Biographical Literature] 30, no. 6 (June 1967): 102, 103.

55. See *Independent Review* 45 (April 5, 1932), and for his position on China's modernization, see Charles R. Lilley, "Tsiang T'ing-fu: Between Two Worlds, 1895-1935," Ph.D. dissertation, University of Maryland, 1979, 410, 416.

56. Jiang Ting-fu, "A Recollection of Participating in the National Conference on Crisis," *Jiangtingfu Xuanji* [Selected Works of Jiang Ting-fu] (Taibei: Qingwen Chubanshe, 1968), 1: 10.

57. See the second part of Shen's article in *Biographical Literature* 31, no. 1 (July 1977): 107; also see Proposal no. 36, National Conference on Crisis Documents, Box 2.2.798, Second Historical Archives, Nanking, China.

58. Proposal no. 64, and Gong's proposal no. 36, section 6. Practically every proposal mentioned the United States as the most important ally in fighting Japan, e.g., see Proposal no. 59; for opinions on Germany, see the summary letter by the secretariat of the conference, ibid.

59. Ibid., Proposal no. 63.2261

60. *SLCB,* 6, part 1: 649-650.

61. Ibid. 647-648; also see *Diplomatic Monthly* 1, no. 4 (October 15, 1932).

62. For a collection of a wide range of Chinese newspapers' reactons, see *Public Opinion toward the Report of the League Enquiry Commission on Sino-Japanese Dispute,* ed. Kan-li Kiang (Nanking: International Relations Committee, 1932); also see *SLCB,* 6, part 1: 717; See Tientsin *Yishibao*'s editorial on October 4, 1932; Gong Ci-jun's article on the report in *Diplomatic Monthly* 1, no. 4; Shanghai *Shenbao* and *Shishi Xinbao* editorials of the same period; *Eastern Miscellany* 28, no. 23 (December 10, 1931): 288; "Nature of the League of Nations," ibid., 29, no. 3; *Qinghua Zhoukan* [Qinghua Weekly] 38,

no. 5 (October 21, 1932): 5; Also see *Diplomatic Monthly* 1, no. 4; "On the Draft Report of the League of Nations," editorial, February 1933, see Zeng Xu-bai, *Tawanbao Pinglun Ji* [Comments of *Dawanbao*] (July 1933), 220.

63. Zhang Zhong-dong, "*Cong Zhuzhang Heping Dao Zhuzhang Kanzhan De Hushi*" [Hu Shi: From Advocating Peace to Advocating War] (Taibei: Institute of American Culture, 1983), 98; For Ting's article, see *Diplomatic Monthly* 1, no. 4; Wang Zuo-yan's article in ibid.; Lilley, "Tsiang Ting-fu," 411.

64. The *Independent Review* group urged resistance this time. See volume 13 of the magazine, which published many articles along the these lines.

65. For orders to enforce North China fighting, see *SLCB*, supplement, 1: 563, 597; for Chiang's request that Zhang go to the front, see ibid., 607. Several of Chiang's telegrams to He Ying-qin, Huang Shao-hong, Yang Jie, etc., showed his intention to hold onto the Peking-Tientsin area at almost any cost, see ibid., 642-643. Also see Huang Shao-hong, "Changcheng Kangzhan Gaishu" [A Brief Description of the Great Wall Resistance], in *Wenshi Ziliao Xuanji* [Selected Historical Materials], ed. Wenshi Ziliao Yanjiu Weiyuanhui, 14: 11. Hereafter cited as *WSZL*. Huang was minister of internal affairs and chief of staff of Chinese forces in North China. The estimate of casualties, 20,000 to 30,000, is derived from two sources. First Wang Ching-wei wrote Wellington Koo on May 16 mentioning casualties "more than 20,000"; see Koo Papers, Box 24, F20. Second, the government casualty figure was 18,335. But this is the only available figure from 5 of the 9 armies (30 divisions, both central and regional) and those from the other 4 armies, which suffered heavy casualties, were unaccounted for. Therefore, 20,000 to 30,000 is a reasonable estimate. See Liu Feng-han, *Kangri Zhanshi Lunji* [Analyses of the War of Resistance] (Taibei: Datong Tushu Youxian Gongsi, 1987), 66-72.

66. For Chiang's letter, see Shen Yun-long, *Huang Yingbai Xiansheng Nianpu* [A Chronological History of Mr. Huang Ying-bai] (Taibei: Lianjing Chuban Shiye Gongsi, 1976), 2: 497, and also Wu Xiang-xiang, 112.

67. Johnson to Secretary of State, March 19 and April 1, 1933, *FRUS*, 1933, 3: 242, 266.

68. Koo, *Memoirs,* 2: 178, 183, 189, 191-192; Peck to Johnson, April 1, 1933, State Department decimal file, 793.941/6260.

69. See Willoughby, appendix no. 4, 724.

70. Peking to Johnson, April 3, 1933, State Department decimal file, 793.94/6259.

71. See Shimada Toshihiko, "Designs on North China, 1933-1937," in *China Quagmire,* ed. James W. Morley, (New York: Columbia University Press, 1983), 36-37; Wu Xiang-siang, *Second Sino-Japanese War,* 126-128 and *FRUS,* 1933, 3: 278-288; Keiji, *The Secret Records,* 9: 91.

72. Hornbeck's memo of May 16, 1933, *FRUS,* 1933, 3: 325-326. For another memo of May 9, 1933, see *Franklin D. Roosevelt and Foreign Affairs,* ed. Edgar B. Nixon, vol. 1 (Cambridge: Belknap Press, 1969), 103-107; see Dorothy Borg, *The United States and the Far Eastern Crisis of 1933-1938* (Cambridge: Harvard University Press, 1964), 34-35.

73. Wang to Huang and He, May 18, 1933, Huang Fu Papers, Columbia University, Box 19, no. 124.

74. For Karakhan's letter to Konstantin Iuren'ev, May 17, 1933, see George Alexander Lensen, *The Damned Inheritance: The Soviet Union and the Manchurian Crises, 1924-1935* (Tallahassee: Diplomatic Press, 1974), 223-224.

75. Ju Zheng's speech at government weekly memorial, May 15, 1933, *SLCB,* supplement, 2: 264-265; for government reactions and protests to the Soviet Union, see ibid., 266-271; for public opinion, see Zuo Zhou, "Negotiations about the Sale of the CER," *Eastern Miscellany* 30, no. 15 (August 1933): 1.

76. Huang to Chiang, May 23, 1933, Wang to Huang, Wang to He, May 25, 1933, and Wang's telegram to He, telling him the decisions of the National Defense Council, May 23, 1933, *SLCB,* supplement, 1: 645-648.

77. Koo, *Memoirs,* 2: 225-226; Luo Wen-gan to Koo, June 5, 1933, Koo Papers, Box 24, F20.

Notes to Chapter 3

1. For studies of the British appeasement, see William R. Rock, *British Appeasement in the 1930s* (New York: W. W. Norton, 1977), Chapter Four.

2. For the most recent descriptions on the policy of appeasement, see Coble, *Facing Japan,* chapters 5-7; for Nanking's diplomatic efforts and Feng Yu-xiang's opinion, see next chapter.

3. For descriptions of political factionalism, see Tien Hung-mao, *The Government and Politics in Koumintang China, 1927-1937* (Stanford: Stanford University Press, 1972), 67-71. According to the author, many provincial governors belonged to this loosely connected group, for example, Chen Yi of Fujian, Huang Shao-hong of Zhejiang, and Xiong Shi-hui of Jiangxi. Also included here were Wu Ding-chang, minister of industry, Zhang Jia-ao, minister of railway, Wong Wen-hao and Jiang Ting-fu, both high officials in the Executive Yuan.

4. See Jiang Ting-fu (Tsiang Ting-fu), "Reminiscence," Chinese Oral History, Columbia University, 153-154, and also see *Selected Works of Jiang Ting-fu,* 3: 61; also see Li Yun-han, "Kangzhan Qian Zhongguo Zhishifenzi De Jiuguo Yundong" [Chinese Intellectuals' Salvation Movement before the Resistance War], in *Zhongguo Jindai Xiandai Shilunji* [Articles on Modern Chinese History], ed. Committee for Chinese Cultural Revival Movement, 26 (Taibei: Taiwan Commercial Press, n.d.), 1: 384.

5. Zhang Zhong-fu, *Zhongguo Guoji Guanxi* [China's International Relations] (Shanghai: Shijie Shuju, 1933), 183-184.

6. Hu to Wang, December 20, 1933, ibid., 226-227; also see Hu's "The Chinese Diplomatic Policy in New World Situation," *Independent Review* 78 (Nov. 26, 1933).

7. Wang to Hu Shi, April 23, November 22, and December 25, *Hushi Laiwang Shuxin Xuan* [Selected letters of Hu Shi], ed. Institute of Modern History, Chinese Academy of Social Sciences, vol.2 (Peking: Zhonghua Shuju, 1979), 210-211, 220-221, 228-229; Wang also showed his convictions about

the effect of a future war on China on many other occasions; see "Wang Ching-wei's opinion regarding the rumor about Soviet-American restoration of diplomatic relations and that Russia and Japan would go to war," (This telegraph was written in late 1933), Yiban Ziliao Bufen, 1924-1936 (general materials part), vol. 3, *Diaocha Ziliao Mulu* [Contents of Investigation Materials], 136, Yangmingshan KMT Party History Commission, Taibei. Wang published many of his gradualist views in articles and books; for example, *China's Problems and Their Solution* (Shanghai: China United Press, 1934), 116-123.

8. Keiji, *The Secret Records*, 9: 90, 115; also see Chiang's telegram to Chen Ji-tang, May 20, 1933, *DSCB*, 2: 312.

9. Zhang Qun to Huang Fu, June 13, 1933, Papers of Huang Fu, microfilm reel 12, Box 20, Columbia University.

10. For Wang's telegram, see Foreign Ministry to Soong, Koo, and Guo Tai-qi, June 29, 1933, Koo Papers, Box 23, F1 and also see Koo, *Memoirs*, 2: 243-244.

11. Chiang's phrase in Chinese reads: Yi Heri Yanhu Waijiao. See Chiang's diary, July 14, 1933, *DSCB*, 2: 2337.

12. Koo, *Memoirs*, 2: 243-244. Koo's *Memoirs* contained many conversations in which he tried to promote American-Soviet cooperation, e.g., 98-99; also see memo by Secretary of State, *FRUS*, 1933, 3: 495. China's ambassador to the Soviet Union, Yan Hui-qing, relayed China's official position to the American Secretary of State while they met in London in July 1933.

13. For descriptions of this faction, see Lin Han-sheng, "A New Look at Chinese Nationalist 'Appeasers,' " in Alvin D. Coox and Hilary Conroy, eds., *China and Japan: Search for Balance since World War I* (Santa Barbara: ABC-CLIO, 1978), 214.

14. "Summary of a discussion relative to the formulation of a foreign policy for the immediate future," Koo Papers, Box 23, F1, Columbia University, 3. This was the consensus view of Soong's meeting with ambassadors Koo, Guo, and Yan.

15. Ibid., 4-7.

16. Soong's conversation with Hornbeck, August 8, 1933, State Department decimal file, 711.93/302; also see Borg, *The United States and the Far Eastern Crisis*, 63-65, 70-71; Trotter, *Britain and East Asia*, 65.

17. Huang to Zhang Qun, September 6, 1933, Huang Papers, microfilm reel 12, Box 20.

18. Yang Yong-tai to Huang Fu, September 6, 1933, ibid.

19. Records of September 6 Conference, microfilm reel 10, Box 20, ibid.

20. Memo by counselor of U.S. legation in China, October 3, 1933, *FRUS*, 1933, 3: 419-420; also see Howard L. Boorman, ed., *Biographical Dictionary of Republican China* (New York: Columbia University Press, 1970), 3: 151.

21. See Koo, *Memoirs*, 2: 274.

22. Tang You-ren to Huang Fu, November 3 and 4, 1933, Huang Papers, Box 20; memo by Johnson, November 9, 1933, see *FRUS*, 1933, 3: 450-451.

23. See James Sheridan, *Chinese Warlord, the Career of Feng Yu-hsiang* (Stanford: Stanford University Press, 1966), 270-271.

24. See Guo Xu-yin, "Reevaluating Feng Yu-xiang's Relations with the CCP," *Zhongguo Xiandaishi* [Modern Chinese History], compiled by People's University, 3 (1990), 207-208. Top leaders who were CCP members include Zhang Mu-tao, Wu Hua-zi, Ji Hong-chang, Xuan Xia-fu and others.

25. Feng, *China and the Second World War,* 112-113, 210-220.

26. Feng left his troops to his generals in August 1933 and retired to Mount Tai. His generals continued to fight on until they were defeated in late 1933. For the coordinated attacks on Feng's forces, see *Zhongguo Xiandaishi Dashiji* [A Chronology of Major Events in Modern Chinese History] (Harbin: Heilongjiang Sheng Chubanshe, 1984), 128-129.

27. Li Ji-shen, one of the leaders of the rebellion, sent his brother to persuade Hu Han-min to join the new government but was reprimanded. Hu and the Southwest faction did not support the movement. See Chen Hong-min, "The Chronological Records of Hu Han-min," in *Republican Archives* 1 (1986), 132. For the positions of other Southwest generals, see Ballantine's dispatch to Secretary of State, *FRUS, 1933,* 3: 473 and also see Tong Te-kong and Li Tsung-jen (Li Zong-ren), *Memoirs of Li Tsung-ren* (Boulder, Colo.: Westview Press, 1979), 300-301.

28. For an analysis of the foreign policy orientation of the Fujian government, see Eastman, *The Abortive Revolution,* 108-109. For its declaration of People's Rights, see *Guowen Zhoubao* [National News Weekly] 10 (Nov. 27, 1933), 47; it disavowed the validity of the unequal treaties and pledged to realize complete tariff autonomy.

29. See Johnson to Secretary of State, November 28, 1933, *FRUS, 1933,* 3: 473.

30. For Huang's telegram to Chiang Kai-shek, November 21, and Huang to Chiang and Wang, December 31, 1933, see Shen Yun-long, *Huang Ying-bai,* 663, 675.

31. Yang Yong-tai to Huang Fu, September 1934, Huang Papers, Box 20.

32. See Trotter, *Britain and East Asia,* 80.

33. Vice Minister Xu Muo informed Johnson of the position of the Chinese government, Johnson to Secretary of State, May 5, 1934, *FRUS, 1934,* 3: 164 see also, Trotter, *Britain and East Asia,* 85.

34. Borg, *The United States and the Far Eastern Crisis,* 79-80, 87.

35. Peck to Secretary of State, April 26, 1934, *FRUS, 1934,* 3: 139; Ballantine to Secretary of State, April 29, 1934, ibid., 147.

36. Do Niu, "The Changes of the American Far Eastern Policy and Our Diplomacy to the United States,' *Waijiao Pinglun* [Diplomatic Review] 3, no. 6 (May 1934): 26-28.

37. See *Zhongguo Jindai Duiwai Guanxishi Ziliao Xuanji* [Selected Materials on China's Modern Foreign Relations], comp. by History Department, Fudan University, 2, no. 1 (Shanghai: Shanghai Rimin Chubanshe, 1977), 264-265.

38. Qin Xiao-yi, ed., *DSCB,* 3: 31.

39. Fu Qi-xue, *A Diplomatic History of China,* 460-461; also see Li Zhen-hua, comp., *Jindai Zhongguo Guoneiwai Dashiji* [Chronological Events inside and outside Modern China], Jindai Zhongguo Shiliao Series, ed. Shen Yun-long, 67 (Taibei: Wenai Chubanshe, 1979), 5657; *Shenbao Monthly* 3, no. 5 (May 1934): 8; Fan Zhong-yun, "The International Situation and China after the Japanese Declaration on China," ibid., 15-18.

40. Tang's conversation with Johnson, March 19, 1934, State Department decimal file, 793.94/6593, National Archives, Washington, D.C.
41. Huang to Wang, November 21, 1933, Huang Fu Papers, Box 3, Hoover Institution, Stanford, California.
42. Huang to Wang, April 19, 1934, see Shen Yun-long, *Huang Ying-bai*, 728.
43. Johnson to Secretary of State, April 18, and Wang Ching-wei's conversation with Johnson, May 10, 1934, *FRUS, 1934*, 3: 113-114, 173-174.
44. See Shen Yun-long, *Huang Ying-bai*, 723.
45. See Morley, *China Quagmire*, 70-71. For the assasination attempt, see Qin Xiao-yi, *Dashin Changbian*, 3: 51.
46. *SLCB,* supplement, 3: 615-616.
47. *SLCB,* supplement, 3: 620, 635.
48. For Chiang's talk with the Investigating and Planning Committee on March 7, see Qin Xiao-yi, ed., *DSCB*, 3: 19 and for his speech on March 18, see ibid., 3: 25.; for Chiang's speech to army officers, see Qin Xiao-yi, ed., *Xianzongtong Jianggong Sixiang Yanlun Zongji* [Complete Collection of Thoughts and Speeches of Former President Chiang] (Taibei: Party History Commission, 1984), 12: 303-304.
49. For Wang's speech on January 23, see Huang Papers, Box 20.
50. For Chiang's interview with a Japanese reporter, February 24, 1935, see *SLCB,* supplementary, 1: 639; also see Wu Xiang-xiang, *The Second Sino-Japanese War,* 182.
51. Keiji, *Secret Records,* 10: 29.
52. It is interesting to note that exactly at this time, Chiang began his overtures to the Soviet Union. For more information, see Chapter Four.
53. Chiang's telegram to Wang Ching-wei, February 11, 1935, Shen Yun-long, *Huang Ying-bai,* 846.
54. See Crowley, *Japan's Quest,* 211, and Wu, *The Second Sino-Japanese War,* 204; for Wang's report to Chiang, see Chiang's diary entry, May 24, 1935, Qin Xiao-yi, ed., *DSCB*, 3: 190.
55. For the dubious attitude of the Japanese military toward Chiang's appeasement policy and their determination to promote an autonomous North China and to support other anti-Chiang regional groups as decided in December 1934 by foreign ministry and military services, see Morley, *The China Quagmire,* 78, 97-98.
56. Chiang to Wang, June 9, 1935, *SLCB,* supplement, 1: 679-680.
57. Wang to Chiang, June 8, 1935, ibid., 1: 678.
58. He sent two urgent telegrams to Chiang, and to Chiang and Wang, June, 9, 1935, ibid., 680-681.
59. Wang to H. H. Kung, June 10, 1935, *Republican Archives* 2 (1989): 27.
60. Chiang to He, June 13, *SLCB,* supplement, 1: 684.
61. See Wu, *The Second Sino-Japanese War,* 180; Chiang to He, June 17 and June 21, 1935, *SLCB,* supplement, 1: 686-687.
62. Hoare to Lindsay, June 14 and Clive to Hoare, June 15, 1935, *Documents on British Foreign Policy,* 1919-1939, second series, 20: 532-534. Hereafter cited as *DBFP.*

63. Paul Haggie, *Britannia at Bay: the Defence of the British Empire against Japan, 1931-1941* (Oxford: Clarendon Press, 1981), 84.

64. Johnson to Secretary of State, June 17, 1935, *FRUS*, 1935, 3: 257.

65. Lindsay to Hoare, June 17, 1935, *DBFP*, 2nd series, 20: 535-536.

66. See Borg, *The United States and the Far Eastern Crisis*, 149-150.

67. See Wang Yi, "German Attitude to Mediating Sino-Japanese Relations in 1935," *Jindaishi Yanjiu* [Studies on Modern History] 5 (1984), 181-182. For detailed descriptions of Sino-German relations in the 1930s, see Kirby, *Germany and Republican China* and Fox, *Germany and the Far Eastern Crisis of 1933-1938*.

68. Chiang to He, June 21, 1935, *SLCB*, supplement, 1: 688.

69. For this plan, see Second Historical Archives, 787.1633, Nanking, China.

70. Chiang to Lin Wei and Zhu Pei-de, March 1, 1933, Chiang to Chen Yi, June 7, 1933, and Chiang to Liu Shi, February 12, 1935, *SLCB*, supplement, 3: 295-300; Chiang to He, June 26; Chiang to Liu Shi, June 27, 1935, ibid., supplement, 1: 690-691.

71. Chiang's Speech, "Sichuan should be the base for national revival," March 4, 1935; Chiang to Kung, May 28; Chiang's diaries, May 2 and 31, *SLCB*, supplement, 3: 329-335. Also see Ishijima Noliyuki's paper presented at a conference on Republican archives and Republican history in Nanking, 1987, Min Guo Dang An Yu Min Guo Shi Xue Shu Tao Lun Lun Wen Ji [Papers on Republican Archives and History] (Peking: Archive Press, 1988), 288-297.

72. De Wang, "My Evil Colluding Activities with the Japanese before the Resistance War," *WSZL* 63 (1979), 25. De Wang was the head of the Mongolian independence movement supported by the Japanese in late 1935 and onward.

73. For details of these negotiations, see Zhang Qun to Huang Fu, [August] 28, 1935, Huang Papers, microfilm reel 10, Box 20. Also in Huang's papers was an undated document, "Zhechong Shixiang [Negotiations Items]" which included 1) China would exchange information on the Chinese Communist Party and the Comintern; 2) both countries abolish hostile activities against each other; and 3) economic cooperation. This document may indicate a plan worked out by Huang Shao-hong and Chiang Kai-shek in the summer of 1935. Chen Gong-bo's memoir, *Ku Xiao Lu*, mentions that Wang Ching-wei gave his approval of a plan to deal with Japan at this time while he was recuperating in Qingdao; see page 333.

74. For Jiang Zuo-bin's report to foreign ministry, September 8, 1935, see Wu, *The Second Sino-Japanese War*, 209; according to Konoe, the military matters referred to the conclusion of a military agreement; see *Selected Materials on Modern Foreign Relations of China*, 279.

75. Chiang to Song, *SLCB*, supplement, 1: 713.

76. Chiang to Song, November 20, ibid., 714-715.

77. Chiang to Shang Zhen; Cheng Xi-keng to Foreign Ministry, November 20, ibid., 715, 718.

78. Ibid., 717.

79. Qin Xiao-yi, ed., *DSCB*, 3: 229.

80. For his report see, *SLCB,* supplement, 3: 659.
81. Wang to Chen Bi-jun, July 13, 1936, *Jindaishi Ziliao* [Materials on Modern China] 60 (1986), 119-120.
82. Diary entry, December 31, *SLCB,* supplement, 1: 742.
83. For details of the origin of Hebei-Charhar Political Council, see Chiang's report to the Central Political Council, December 12, 1935, ibid., 739-740; for critical analysis, see Chang Kai and Cai De-jin, "On Hebei-Chahar Political Council," *Studies on Modern History* 4 (1985), 140-161; Li Yun-han, *Kangzhan Qian Huabei Zhengzhi Jushi Shiliao* [Materials Regarding North China Political Situation before Resistance War] (Taibei: Zhengzhong Shuju, 1982), 197-202. Li's article is apologetic of Chiang's appeasement policy.
84. For details of students' opposition to the autonomous movement and the December 9 demonstrations, see John Israel, *Student Nationalism in China, 1927-1937,* 111-128.
85. January 15, 1936, *SLCB,* supplement vol. 1, 747.
86. *Guowen Weekly* 47, December 2, 1935.
87. *Shenbao Monthly* 4, no. 12 (December 15, 1935).
88. *Dazhong Shenghuo* [Mass Life] 1 (December 21, 1935): 6.

Notes to Chapter 4

1. For more information on salvation groups, see Zhou Tian-du, ed., *Jiuguohui* [Salvation Associations] (Peking: Academy of Social Sciences, 1981). This collection of declarations, articles, telegrams, and documents on the salvation movement is a useful sourcebook. Also see Chiang Kai-shek, *Soviet Russia in China: A Summing-up at Seventy* (New York: Farrar, Straus, and Cudahy, 1957), 67.
2. Zhou, *Salvation Associations,* 73.
3. Margo S. Gewurtz, *Between America and Russia: Chinese Student Radicalism and the Travel Books of Tsou Tao-fen, 1933-1937* (Toronto: University of Toronto-York University Joint Center on Modern East Asia, 1975), 10, 29.
4. See Zhou, *Salvation Associations,* 52-53; Mu Xin, *Zou Tao-fen* (Hong Kong: Sanlian Shudian, 1959), 154.
5. For a brief biography of Du, see Yu Yi-fu and Guan Meng-jue, "A Short Biography of Du Chong-yuan," *Sian Shibian Ziliao* [Materials on the Sian Incident], comp. by Institute of Modern History (Peking: Chinese Academy of Social Sciences, 1981), 247-259; also see Hu Yu-shi, "Wei Quan Min Kang Zhan Ben Zou Hu Hao," [Working Tirelessly for National Resistance], *WSZL* 106 (1986): 11-12.
6. Guo Xu-yin and Sheng Mu-zhen, "A Review of the Political Positions of the National Salvation Association," *Contemporary Chinese History,* comp. by People's University, vol. 7 (1985): 87; Sha Qian-li, "Recalling the Case of the Seven Gentlemen of the Salvation Association," *WSZL* 89 (1983): 2-3. Zou

Tao-fen was not yet a Communist as late as 1938. Zhou En-lai greeted Zou in Wuhan as a friend and said: "The Salvation Association's stand on resisting Japan is the same as ours and I respect the courage of the Seven Gentlemen." See Jin Chong-ji, ed., *Zhou Enlai Zhuan* [A Biography of Zhou En-lai] (Peking: Remin Chubanshe and (CCP) Central Committee Document Press, 1989), 413.

7. Zhou, *Salvation Associations,* 98-99; also see Hu, "Working tirelessly," 18. The Salvationists in general had a strong inclination toward the Soviet Union and a much less favorable attitude toward the capitalist powers. See for example, Zhang Nai-qi's article in Zhang Nai-qi, et al., *Zhongri Wenti Jianghua* [Speeches Regarding the Sino-Japanese Problem] (Shanghai: n.p., September 1935), 9.

8. See Sha Qian-li, *Recalling the Salvation Association* (Peking: Wenshi Ziliao Chubanshe, 1983), 2-3; Sun Xiao-cun, "Huiyi Feng Yuxiang Jiangjun Dui Jiuguohui De Zhichi" [Recalling General Feng Yu-xiang's Support for the Salvation Association] *WSZL* 89 (1983): 47-50.

9. Guo and Sheng, "A Review of the Political Positions," 90.

10. Sha, *Recalling,* 18.

11. Mu Xin, *Zou Tao-fen* (Hong Kong: Sanlian Shudian, 1959), 178; for Pan's influence, see Hu Yu-shi's article.

12. See Zhou, *Salvation Associations,* 87-88.

13. Lo Yun-shu and Wang Jin-xia, "Shilun Zhongguo Gongchandang Yu Liangguang Shibian" [On The Chinese Communist Party and the Two Guang Revolt], *Guangxi Shehui Kexue* [Guangxi Social Sciences] 4 (1988): 194-217; also see, Yang Kui-song, "The Formation," 87, in the same source.

14. Zhang Nai-qi, "Our Lessons from the Southwest Incident," in Zhou, *Salvation Associations,* 138. At the same time, the salvation leaders also rejected the view that the Southwest leaders were old-style warlords.

15. Wilson to Secretary of State, June 12, 1936, *FRUS,* 1936, 4: 204.

16. Howe to Eden, June 23, 1936, *Documents on British Foreign Policy,* 2nd series, 20: 885-886. Also see Chen Ming-zhong, "Shilun Yijiusanwu, Yijiusanliu Nian Zhongri Huitan" [On Sino-Japanese Negotiations in 1935 and 1936], *Republican Archives* 2 (1989): 115.

17. Chiang's Speech at Second Plenary Session of the Fifth Congress, July 15, 1936, *SLCB,* supplement, 3: 666.

18. Zhou, *Salvation Associations,* 122-123.

19. Mu Xin, 160-163. This proposed political council never materialized before the war.

20. Shen Yun-long, *Events and Personages in Modern History,* 372.

21. Peking Cultural Circles to National Government, November 24, and Li to Nanking leaders, November 25, 1936, see Zhou, *Salvation Associations,* 209-210; Feng to Chiang, November 26, 1936; Chiang to Feng, the date should be somewhere in the neighborhood of December 2 or 3, 1936, see *Republican Archives* 2 (1985): 27-28; Zhang Xue-liang's speech before a Sian mass meeting, December 17, 1936, see *Sian Shibian Ziliao Xuanji* [Selected Documents on the Sian Incident], comp. by History Department, Northwestern University, et al. N.p., 1979, 123-124.

22. Accounts of the worldwide united front policy of the Comintern are many. But for a description of CCP and its relations to the Comintern's policy, see Shum Kui-kwong, *The Chinese Communist Road to Power: the Anti-Japanese United Front, 1935-1945* (New York: Oxford University Press, 1988); Lyman Van Slyke, *Enemy and Friend: The United Front in Chinese Communist History* (Stanford: Stanford University Press, 1967); Gregor Benton, "The Second Wang Ming Line," *China Quarterly* 61 (March 1975): 61-94; The best article summing up the late Chinese literature on the United Front in China is John Garver, "The Origins of the Second United Front: The Comintern and the Chinese Communist Party," ibid. 113 (March 1988): 29-59. Newly opened materials on the Chinese Communist party have been researched by Chinese scholars and the results are a series of books and articles on this subject which have made previous studies obsolete, e.g., see Xiang Qing, *Gongchanguoji Yu Zhongguo Geming Guanxishi Lunwenji* [Papers on the Relations between the Comintern and the Chinese Revolution], and *Gongchanguoji He Zhongguo Geming Guanxi Shigao* [A History of Relations between the Comintern and the Chinese Revolution] (Peking: Peking University Press, 1988); an opposite view to Xiang's is advanced by Li Yi-bin, "Guanyu Bijiang Kangri Fangzhen Xingcheng Wenti" [On the Formation of the Principle of Forcing Chiang to Resist Japan] *Lishi Yanjiu* [Study on History] 4 (1989): 212-232.

23. See Xiang Qing, *Papers,* 184-185; Garver, "The Origins," 31-35. For this document, see *Selected Materials on Contemporary Chinese History,* 330-331.

24. There are conflicting views on the Comintern instructions brought to the CCP by Lin Yu-ying (Zhang Hao). Garver supplements Benton and argues that Lin transmitted a policy of "unite with Chiang to resist Japan." But the records at CCP Politburo meetings at Wayaobao in December 1935 show that Lin still insisted on "resist Japan and attack Chiang." The time gap between Lin's departure from Moscow over land to Wayaobao through enemy-controlled territories may explain the policy difference later between Wang Ming's gestures to Chiang and Lin's position. See Li Yi-bin, "Forcing Chiang to resist Japan," 214-215; Braun, 52-53, 157, 168; Garver, 35-37.

Mao had been a pragmatist deriving his theories and strategies from reality in China rather than following orders from Moscow. As early as 1928, Mao attributed his success in establishing the first Communist base in the Jinggang Mountains to the fact that "the prolonged splits and wars within the White regime provide a condition for the emergence and persistence of one or more small Red areas under the leadership of the Communist party." See Mao Ze-dong, "Why is it that Red political power can exist in China?" *Selected Works of Mao Ze-dong,* vol. 1 (Peking: Foreign Languages Press, 1967), 65.

25. Mao Ze-dong, "On tactics against Japanese imperialism," in *Selected Works,* 156-159; For this Wayaobao Conference, see Yang's article cited above and see also Slyke, 58-59 and Braun, 153-157.

26. Luo Rui-qing, Lu Zheng-cao, and Wang Bingnan, *Zhou En-lai and the Xi'an Incident: An Eyewitness Account* (Peking: Foreign Languages Press, 1983), 27-35.

27. Xiang Qing, *Papers,* 190-191; Garver, "The Origins," 41-42.

28. The CCP Party Center's "Instructions about the Two Guang Military Move to Resist Japan" to Peng De-huai, et al., June 20, 1936, *Dierci Guogong Hezuo De Xingcheng* [The Formation of the Second CCP-KMT Cooperation] (Peking: CCP Party History Materials Press, 1989), 104-105. Liu Zhong-rong, Li Zong-ren's representative reached Wayaobao in the winter of 1935. During the revolt, Li Zong-ren's representative, Qian Shu-kang, reached CCP's headquarters and carried Mao's letter back to Guangxi. See Zhang Tong-xin, *Wang Jiang Hezuo Shiqi De Guomin Zhengfu* [The Nationalist Government during the Period of Wang-Chiang Cooperation] (Harbin: Heilongjiang Renmin Chubanshe, 1988), 418, and also Lo and Wang, "The Two Guang Revolt," 201, 203-205.

29. For a good description of the CCP Politburo discussions on the change of policy in August and September, see Li, "Forcing Chiang to resist Japan," 218-231; also see Garver, "The Origins," 37-43.

30. Edgar Snow, *Red Star Over China* (New York: Grove Press, 1968), 87-89.

31. Bullitt to Secretary of State, January 8, 1935, *FRUS, 1935*, 3: 7. The Soviet Union noticed Nanking's fear of Japan as the most important barrier in Sino-Soviet relations. For example, Litvinov expressed such an opinion to Ambassador Bullitt on March 14, 1934. See Orville H. Bullitt, ed., *For the President, Personal and Secret: Correspondence between Franklin D. Roosevelt and William C. Bullitt* (Boston: Houghton Mifflin Co., 1972), 78. For Chiang's concern about the CCP's Red Army, see ibid., 100.

32. Foreign Ministry to Huang Fu, March 9, 1934, Huang Fu Papers, Box 20.

33. See Jiang Ting-fu, *Jiang Ting-fu Huiyilu* [Memoirs of Jiang Ting-fu], 152-155; also see He Jun, "On Sino-Soviet Relations," 57-58.

34. Bullitt to Secretary of State, May 14, 1935, *FRUS, 1935*, 3: 166.

35. For border incidents, see Hata Ikuhiko, "The Japanese-Soviet Confrontation, 1935-1939," in James W. Morley, ed., *Deterrent Diplomacy: Japan, Germany and the USSR, 1935-1940* (New York: Columbia University Press, 1976), 133.

36. He Jun, "On Sino-Soviet Relations," 75-76.

37. Charles R. Kitts, "An Inside View of the Kuomintang: Chen Li-fu, 1926-1949," Ph.D. dissertation, Johns Hopkins University, 1978, 63-64.

38. As Chiang later recorded in his diary, December 1, 1937, "the original purpose of alliance with Russia was to threaten the Japanese." See Qin Xiao-yi, ed., *DSCB*, 4: 147.

39. Bogomolov to Foreign Ministry, December 19, 1935, Komissiia po izdaniiu diplomaticheskinkh dokumentov, *Dokumenty Vneshnei Politiki SSSR* [Documents on Soviet Foreign Policy, 1936-38] (Moscow: Political Literature Publishing House, 1973), 18: 599. Hereafter cited as *DSFP*.

40. Ibid., 599-600.

41. Foreign Ministry to Bogomolov, December 28, 1935, ibid., 602.

42. Bogomolov to Foreign Ministry, January 22, 1936, *DSFP*, 19: 35-38.

43. Cheng Tian-fang, *A History of Sino-Russian Relations* (Washington D.C.: Public Affairs Press, 1957), 190; Chen Li-fu, "Recollections about Preparations for Resistance War," *Biographical Literature* 31, no. 1 (July 1, 1977): 48; See Garver, "The Origins," 45.

44. Foreign Ministry to Bogomolov, December 28, 1935, *DSFP,* 18: 601-602.

45. *DSFP,* 19: 35-38.

46. See Chiang Kai-shek, *Soviet Russia in China,* 69; also He Jun, "On Sino-Soviet Relations," 85; Bogomolov was some sort of persona non grata in Nanking because he made extensive contacts with Chiang's opponents, such as Feng Yu-xiang, Sun Ke, and many others. He alleged that Chiang had agreed to the Soviet-Outer Mongolian treaty. Chiang lost his temper when he heard this. See Jiang Ting-fu's notes about his conversation with Litvinov, "Records of Ambassador Jiang Ting-fu's talks with the Soviet foreign ministry officials," *Republican Archives* 4 (1989): 23. For Chiang's comments on the Soviet-Outer Mongolia agreement, see his diary entry, April 1, 1936, Qin Xiao-yi, ed., *DSCB,* 3: 285-286.

47. Weng Wen-hao, "Recollections of Visits to Britain, Germany, and the Soviet Union in 1937," *WSZL* 1 (1960): 63.

48. Jiang Ting-fu, *Memoirs,* 191-193.

49. For Koo's conversation with Litvinov, see Koo to Foreign Ministry, October 10, 1936, Koo Papers, Box 24, F17; also see David Dallin, *Soviet Russia and the Far East* (New Haven: Yale University Press, 1942), 67.

50. *DSFP,* 19 (November 7, 1936): 542-548.

51. Ambassador Jiang after arriving in Moscow in mid-November tried to discuss the possibility of a military pact. But the Soviets ducked the issue and throughout December no progress was made. See Records of Jiang Ting-fu's conversations with Litvinov, November 19; with Stomaniakov, December 3 and 9, 1936; with Bogomolov, February 16, 1937, *Republican Archives* 4 (1989): 21-29. Also see He Jun, "On Sino-Soviet Relations," 89-90.

52. For Chiang's thoughts on a possible German-Soviet or Japanese-Soviet war, see his diary entry, March 14, 1936, Qin Xiao-yi, *DSCB,* 3: 281.

53. Deng Wen-yi, *Congjun Baoguo Ji* [Joining the Army and Requiting the Nation] (Taibei: Zhengzhong Shuju, 1979), 71.

54. The intermediary was Chen Xiao-qin. See his "Some Recollections of KMT-CCP Negotiations before the Sian Incident," in Museum of Chinese Revolutionary History, *Dangshi Yanjiu Ziliao* [Study Materials for Party History], vol. 3 (Chongqing: Sichuan Renmin Chubanshe, 1982): 567-571; the best article on initial contacts between the KMT and the CCP is Yang Kui-song's "Guanyu Yijiusanliu Nian Guogong Liangdang Mimi Jiechu Jingguo De Jige Wenti" [Several Problems Concerning KMT and CCP Secret Contacts], *Studies on Modern History* 1 (1990): 245-265.

55. Jin Chong-ji, *Zhou Enlai Zhuan* [A Biography of Zhou En-lai] (Peking: Rimin Chubanshe, 1989), 315-316.

56. Yang, "Several problems," 264-265. For Zhou's letter, see Chen Li-fu's article, 46-47. Chen's chronology was wrong. Zhou's letter could not have been written in September 1935.

57. He Li, "Kangzhan Qijian de Guogong Guanxi" [The KMT-CCP Relations during the Resistance War], *Studies on Modern History* 2 (1983): 29; for preliminary issues in negotiations in October, see *SLCB* 5, no. 1: 63-64.

58. Zhang Qun's diplomatic report to the Second Plenary Session of the Fifth Congress of KMT, July 10, 1936, see *SLCB,* supplement 3: 664-665.
59. Feng's diary, September 8, see Zhang Tong-xin, *Jiang Wang Hezuo De Guomin Zhengfu* [The National Government under Chiang-Wang Cooperation] (Harbin: Heilongjiang Rimin Chubanshe, 1988), 422.
60. *FRUS,* 1936, 3: 323, 357.
61. Records of Zhang-Kawagoe negotiations, October 19 and 21 and November 10, *Republican Archives* 2 (1988): 27-30, 32; For Chiang's idea on regaining sovereignty in North China as a price for anticommunist cooperation, see Qin Xiao-yi, ed., *DSCB,* 3: 351; For Zhang Qun's recollections, see Zhang Qun, *Wo Yu Riben Qishi Nian* [Japan and I in the Past Seventy Years] (Taibei: Institute of Sino-Japanese Relations, 1980), 61-76.
62. Record of negotiations, September 15, *Republican Archives,* 26.
63. See Zhang, *Japan and I,* 63.
64. See Zhang Qun's diplomatic report to the Third Plenary Session of the Fifth KMT Congress, *SLCB,* supplement, 3: 691-692; Records of negotiations, September 15, *Republican Archives,* 27.
65. Chiang's conversation with Kawagoe, October 8, *SLCB,* supplement, 3: 675.
66. Chiang to He, September 18, 1936, *SLCB,* supplement, 3: 673-675; Chiang to He, September 24, Qin Xiao-yi, *DSCB,* 3: 331-332.
67. See Zhang, *Japan and I,* 67.
68. Koo, et al., to Foreign Ministry, September 26, 1936, *Lugouqiao Shibian Qianhou De Zhongri Guanxi* [Sino-Japanese Relations around the Marco Polo Bridge Incident], ed. Institute of Diplomatic Studies, Vol. 4, Diplomatic Materials Series (Taibei: n.p., 1966), 59. Hereafter cited as *LGQ*. Also see Koo to Zhang, November 26, Koo Papers, Box 23, "China's International Relations;" *FRUS,* 1936, 3: 326-327, 393.
69. For the professors' statement, see *LGQ,* 129-131.
70. *FRUS,* 1936, 3: 345.
71. Chiang to Yan, October 21, *SLCB,* supplement, 3: 677-678.
72. See Johnson's telegram to Secretary of State, December 14, 1936, *FRUS,* 1936, 3: 422; Zhou Kai-qing, *Sianjieduan Zhi Zhongri Wenti* [The Present Sino-Japanese Problem] (Nanking: Zhongxin Pinglun She, 1936), preface.
73. For scholarly accounts of the Sian Incident, see Tien-wei Wu, *Sian Incident: A Pivotal Point in Modern Chinese History* (Ann Arbor: University of Michigan Press, 1976); Li Yun-han, *Xian Shibian Shimo* [A Study of the Sian Incident] (Taibei: Jindai Zhongguo Chubanshe, 1982); Susan Fu Tsu, Ph.D. dissertation, "A Study of Chang Hsueh-liang's Role in Modern Chinese History," 1980; Mi Zhan-chen, *The Life of General Yang Hu-cheng* (Hong Kong: Joint Publishing Co., 1981). The best account of the Sian Incident from the PRC is perhaps *Xian Shibian Jianshi* [A Concise History of the Sian Incident] published in 1986 by Wenshi Press which contains valuable and authoritative primary sources and objective analyses. Zhang Xue-liang made a confession in 1968 acknowledging that he was tricked by the Communists. But given the fact that he was under house arrest, it is hard to accept this as

truth. See Zhang Xue-liang, "Penitent Confession on the Xi'an Incident," *Chinese Studies in History* 22 (Spring 1989): 64-76.

74. See Tien-wei Wu, *The Sian Incident,* 5, 22 and also see Ying De-tien, *Zhang Xueliang Yu Sian Shibian* [Zhang Xue-liang and the Sian Incident] (Hong Kong: n.p., 1981), 20. Ying was one of the closest assistants of Zhang Xue-liang.

75. Shen Bo-chun, *Xian Shibian Jishi* [Records of the Sian Incident] (Hong Kong: n.p., 1980), 18. Shen was a participant in the Sian Incident.

76. Ying, *Zhang Xue-liang,* 51. Negotiations took place in early March 1936. Also see, Qian Zhi-guang, "Around Lochuan Negotiations," in *Zhonggong Dangshi Ziliao* [Materials on History of the CCP], comp. CCP committee on historical materials] 10 (1984): 122-138. Qian was a participant on the CCP side.

77. Jin Chong-ji, *A Biography of Zhou En-lai,* 308-310; Ying, *Zhang Xue-liang,* 57; Li, "Forcing Chiang to resist Japan," 218-219. Zhou En-lai admitted Zhang's influence in an interview with Zhang's brother, Zhang Xue-ming, in 1961.

78. Shen Bo-chun, "The Process of Winning Zhang Xue-liang to Join the Resistance," in *Sian Shibian Qinliji* [Witnesses to the Sian Incident], ed. Wu Fu-zhang (Peking: Zhongguo Wenshi Chubanshe, 1986), 56-57.

79. See *The Formation of the Second CCP-KMT Cooperation,* 445 and also Jiao Ji-hua, "Zhang Xue-liang's Secret Talks with the Soviet Ambassador," *Witness to the Sian Incident,* 9-10. The author was an officer in General Staff of the Military Commission in charge of Soviet intelligence. He was the go-between who arranged the meeting for Zhang.

80. Wu Tien-wei, *The Sian Incident,* 58; Ying, *Zhang Xue-liang,* 82-83.

81. Zhang to Chiang, September 23, 1936, *SLCB* 5, no. 1: 147.

82. See *Sian Shibian Ziliao Xuanji* [Selected Materials on the Sian Incident], comp. by History Dept., Northwestern University, et al., n.p., n.d., 108.

83. H. H. Kung, "Recalling the Sian Incident," *Biographical Literature* 10, no. 3 (March 1967): 83.

84. Jiang Ting-fu, *Memoirs,* 198-199.

85. See Kitts, "Ch'en Li-fu."

86. Ambassador Jiang to Foreign Ministry, December 14, 15, 17, see Kung's recollection in *Biographical Literature* 10, no. 3: 84.

87. The Red Army generals' telegram to KMT government, December 15, *Sian Shibian Ziliao Xuanbian* [Selected Materials on the Sian Incident], edited by Second Historical Archives, Yunnan Archives, and Shaanxi Archives, (Peking: Dangan Chubanshe, 1986), 43-44; Ding Yong-nian, "About Our Party's Policy of Peaceful Solution to the Sian Incident," *Dangshi Yanjiu Ziliao,* vol. 11, 1982. The author illustrates with documentation that the CCP arrived at an independent decision for a peaceful solution. He points out that the so-called Moscow Telegram on December 13 Chang Kuo-tao's *The Rise of the Chinese Communist Party, 1928-1938,* vol. 2 was in fact news from TASS. The Comintern did send instructions to the CCP on December 16, and yet, due to equipment failure, the CCP could not decipher the cable. By the time the Comintern's instructions were finally received on December 20, the CCP had

already reached a decision for peaceful solution of the Sian Incident. See *Zhou Enlai Nianpu* [A Chronological History of Zhou En-lai], ed. Wenxian Jianjiushi of the Central Committee of the CCP (Beijing: Renmin Chubanshe and Zhongyang Wenxian Chubanshe, 1989), 335; Jin Chong-ji, *A Biography of Zhou En-lai,* 325-330; and *A Concise History,* 78-80.

88. For a survey of public reactions, see Wu Tien-wei, *The Sian Incident,* 120-124; for Salvationists' attitude, see Sha, *Recalling,* 49.

89. Feng to Zhang, December 13, 1936, see *Selected Materials on the Sian Incident,* 149.

90. Feng's diary entry, December 25, 1936, see *Republican Archives* 4 (1986): 37.

91. *FRUS,* 1938, 3: 174.

92. Chiang to Gu Zhu-tong, February 16, 1937, ibid., 264.

93. Chen Bu-lei to Chiang, May 8, 1937, and Zhang Chong's talks with Zhou En-lai and Mao Ze-dong, ibid., 266-268; also see Jin Chong-ji, *A Biography of Zhou En-lai,* 360-365.

94. Wang Chong-hui's report, July 8, 1937, *SLCB,* 3: 325-326; for information on the loan proposal, see Zhou You-cun, *Zhong-Su Guanxi Neimu* [The Inner History of Sino-Soviet Relations] (Hong Kong: Shidai Chubanshe, 1950), 55.

95. Jiang to H. H. Kung, July 15, 1937, *Republican Archives* 4 (1991): 6.

96. Bogomolov to Foreign Ministry, May 7, 1937, *DSFP,* 20: 232-233.

97. Johnson to Secretary of State, March 9, 1937, State Department decimal file, National Archives, 711.93/350.

98. See Zhang Qun's talk with a member of the Japanese economic delegation, March 17, 1937, *LGQ,* 117.

Notes to Chapter 5

1. See Crowley, *Quest for Autonomy,* 330-331.

2. Chiang to Xu Yong-chang, etc., July 8 and July 9, and to Song Zhe-yuan, July 9, *SLCB,* 2, part 2: 32, 35-37. For Chiang's remarks on the He-Umetsu Agreement, see Tao Xi-sheng, *Chaoliu Yu Diandi* [Currents and Drops] (Taibei: Zhuangji Wenxue Chubanshe, 1964), 148. For Chiang's thoughts on the escalation of war, see his diary entry, July 12, 1937, Qin Xiao-yi, ed., *DSCB,* 4, part 1: 75.

3. For Song's peace efforts, see Yang Xuan-cheng to He Ying-qin, July 22, *GMWX,* 106: 164-165; Chiang sent numerous telegrams to Song since the conflict, for a most representative one, see Chiang to Song, July 13, *SLCB,* 2, part 2: 43.

4. Records of Meetings of the High Military Staff (hereafter MHMS), July 12, 1937. These were a series of meetings held at the residence of He Ying-qin, the minister of war. Practically all high military and civilian leaders except Chiang and Wang Ching-wei attended the meetings. Their records are published in *Republican Archives* 2 and 3, 1987. These records supplemented

documents on the Chinese responses to the Marco Polo Bridge Incident and they reveal the Chinese strategic decisions for the 19 days following the Incident, July 14, 1937.

5. Bogomolov to Foreign Ministry, July 13, 1937, *DSFP,* 1937, 20: 375-376.

6. Wang Chong-hui to Chiang, July 11 and 12, 1937, *LGQ,* 210, 214. On July 12, Japanese embassy officials called on Wang Chong-hui to express their concern over the troop movements. Wang again proposed that both China and Japan stop their troop movements, but the Japanese side did not agree to the withdrawal of troops or the halting of troop movements. See Wang's conversations with the councillor, Hidaka, and military attachés of the Japanese Embassy, July 12, 1937, ibid., 222-225.

7. British Embassy to the Department of State, July 13, 1937, *FRUS,* 1937, 3: 158; State Department to the British Embassy, July 13, ibid., 159-160.

8. Borg, *The United States and the Far Eastern Crisis,* 292-293.

9. Qin Xiao-yi, ed., *Xianzongtong Jianggong,* 14: 584.

10. Keiji, *Secret Records,* 11: 22-23.

11. Johnson to Secretary of State, July 25, 1937, *FRUS,* 1937, 3: 257-258.

12. *Shenbao,* weekly supplement, vol. 2, No 31.

13. Keiji, *Secret Records,* 9: 90.

14. "National Defense War Plan A, 1937," *Republican Archives,* 1987, 4: 40-44. As a contrast to War Plan A, Plan B envisioned an offensive gesture for the Chinese army, see ibid., 1988, 1: 34-36.

15. See Diary entry, July 31, 1937, *Hu Shi De Riji* [Diary of Hu Shi], vol. 2 (Peking: Chonghua Shuju, 1985).

16. Chiang's speech, August 18, 1937, *SLCB,* 2, part 1: 45.

17. Wang Shi-jie, *Wang Shijie Riji* [Diary of Wang Shi-jie], ed. Modern History Institute, Academica Sinica (Taibei: Modern History Institute, 1990), 1: 97.

18. For an account of the military campaigns at Shanghai and Nanking, see Hsi-sheng Ch'i, *Nationalist China at War: Military Defeats and Political Collapse, 1937-1945* (Ann Arbor: University of Michigan Press, 1982), 141-145 and also Frank Dorn, *The Sino-Japanese War, 1937-1941: From Marco Polo Bridge to Pearl Harbor* (New York: Macmillan, 1974), 74; Chiang to Zhang Zhi-zhong, August 16, *SLCB,* 2, part 2: 170; Order No. 4, Chinese High Command, August 20, see *Republican Archives* 1 (1987): 30.

19. Dorn, *The Sino-Japanese War,* 74; Order no. 4, Chinese High Command, August 20, see *Republican Archives* 1 (1987): 30.

20. Eastman, *Abortive Revolution,* 235.

21. See *Memoirs of Li Zong-ren,* 329. Li's foreign policy adviser, Gan Jie-hou, explained right after the Shanghai campaign that the defense of the city was motivated by international reasons; see Gan Jie-hou, *Kangzhan Zhong Junshi Waijiao De Zhuanbian* [Changes in Military and Diplomatic Affairs during the Resistance War] (Shanghai: Qianjinshe, January 1938), 31-32. Wang Ching-wei in 1940 even attributed China's foreign policy during this period to Chiang Kai-shek's determination "to fight to make an impression on the world" (Zhan Gei Guoji Kan) and confidence that the Soviet Union would join the war in

three months and the powers would stop the Sino-Japanese conflict; see Hu Lan-cheng, *Zhan Nan He Yi Buyi* [To Fight Is Difficult and So Is to Reach Peace] (Shanghai: Zhonghua Ribao, 1940), Wang's introduction.

22. Borg, *The United States and the Far Eastern Crisis,* 304, 306.

23. Chiang to Li Zong-ren, et al., December 6, 1937, *SLCB,* 2, part 2: 219.

24. Chiang's diary entry, December 13, 1937, Qin Xiao-yi, ed., *DSCB,* vol. 4, part 1: 150.

25. Kung to Nanking government, August 16, 1937, *LGQ,* 345.

26. Resolutions of the National Defense Council, no. 3, August 26, 1937, ibid., 348.

27. Wellington Koo engaged in numerous diplomatic maneuvers at the beginning of the League Council session. However, while the British representative Anthony Eden and the French Delbos were privately sympathetic to China, they were by no means ready to assume any responsibility to punish Japan. See Koo, *Memoirs,* 2: 474-484.

28. Chinese delegate to Foreign Ministry, September 18, 1937, *LGQ,* 349.

29. Koo, *Memoirs,* 2: 493.

30. Ibid., 495.

31. Bradford A. Lee, *Britain and the Sino-Japanese War,* 53.

32. For the League resolutions, see *LGQ,* 359.

33. Chen Bu-lei to Vice Foreign Minister Xu Mo, October 6, 1937, ibid., 367-369.

34. Foreign Ministry to Chinese Embassy at Paris, October 24, 1937, ibid., 403.

35. Nicholas R. Clifford, *Retreat from China: British Policy in the Far East, 1937-1941* (Seattle: University of Washington Press, 1967), 39; Borg, *The United States and the Far Eastern Crisis,* 406.

36. See *Zhongguo Waijiaoshi Ziliao Xuanji* [Selected Materials of Chinese Diplomatic History], comp. by Diplomatic College, Peking, 3: 133-134; Dorn, *Sino-Japanese War,* 76-78.

37. Foreign Ministry to Chinese Embassy in Brussels, November 13, 1937, *LGQ,* 407; Koo, *Memoirs,* 652; see Kung's two telegrams to Koo on November 15, and another two on November 19 and 20, Koo Papers, Box 26, F40.

38. Shi Guo-gang, "After the Brussels Conference," *Eastern Miscellany* 34, no. 20 (November 1937): 2-3.

39. See Chiang's diary entry, November 24, 1937, Qin Xiao-yi, ed., *DSCB,* vol. 4, part 1: 146.

40. For detailed description of close German-Chinese relations, see William Kirby, *Germany and Republican China,* Chapter Seven.

41. Gan, *Changes in Military and Diplomatic Affairs,* 38-39.

42. Zhou En-lai, et al., *Kangzhan Zhong De Xin Xingshi Yu Xin Zhengce* [New situation and new strategy in the Resist-Japan War] (Hankow: n.p., 1938), 117.

43. Fox, *Germany,* 238, 265. On November 5, Trautmann transmitted the Japanese terms: 1) an autonomous Inner Mongolia; 2) a demilitarized zone in North China to be administered by officials appointed by Nanking friendly to Japan; 3) cessation of anti-Japanese policies; 4) common struggle against communism; 5) reduction of customs duties; and 6) respect of rights of foreigners.

44. Fox, *Germany*, 271-272.

45. Wang Ching-wei, "Take an Example," in *Heping Fangong Jianguo Wenxian* [Documents on Peace, Anti-Communism and Reconstruction of the Nation] 1 (Nanking: Propaganda Dept., 1941), 6-7. This article was published by Wang, who had defected from Chongqing in March 1939. It is an account of the 54th meeting of the National Defense Council and its credibility was proved by the fact that Wang was accused of leaking top government secrets by Wu Zhi-hui, a top KMT official, in his *Dui Wang Ching-wei Ju Yigeli De Jinyijie* [An Explanation to Wang Ching-wei's "Take an Example"] (Guilin: Zhanwang Shudian, January 1939). For Chiang's diary entry, see Keiji, *Secret Records,* 11: 98.

46. See Fox, *Germany,* 272; Wang, "Take an Example," 7. Also see Chen Bu-lei, *Huiyilu* [Memoirs] (Shanghai: Ershi Shiji Chubanshe, 1949), 97.

47. Stalin and Voroshilov to Chiang Kai-shek, December 5 [?], and Chiang to Stalin, December 6, 1937, *SLCB*, 3, part 2: 339-340.

48. Johnson to Secretary of State, December 3, 1937, *FRUS*, 1937, 3: 750-751. Kung also asked Wellington Koo's opinion on the powers' reaction to the German mediation; see Kung to Koo, December 2 and 3, and Koo's reply to Kung, December 4, 1937, Koo Papers, Box 26, F40. Koo opposed relying on the Germans alone and still advocated mediation by the United States if possible and a joint mediation by Germany and the powers if there were no choice.

49. The new terms included: abandonment of pro-Communist, anti-Japanese, and anti-Manzhouguo activities and cooperation with Manzhouguo in anti-communism; setting up demilitarized zones and special regimes in these zones; economic cooperation among Japan, Manzhouguo and China; and China's necessary reparations to Japan. See Fox, *Germany, 277.*

50. See Qin Xiao-yi, ed., *DSCB*, vol. 4, part 1: 154, 156.

51. Foreign Ministry to Chinese ambassador to the Soviet Union, Jiang Ting-fu, December 28, 1937, *LGQ*, 497.

52. Johnson to Secretary of State, December 28 and December 31, 1937, *FRUS,* 1937, 842, 847. Roosevelt later denied that he used the term "lenient."

53. Foreign Ministry to Chinese Embassy in Tokyo, January 2, 1938, *LGQ*, 498.

54. Ibid., 499-502.

55. Lin Han-sheng, "Wang Ching-wei and the Japanese Peace Efforts," Ph.D. dissertation, University of Pennsylvania, 1967, 217. For a good account of these peace advocates, see John Hunter Boyle, *China and Japan at War, 1937-1945: Politics of Collaboration* (Stanford: Stanford University Press, 1972), 167-172.

56. Lin Han-sheng, 219; For behind-the-scene peace activities, a valuable Chinese source is Cai De-jin, ed., *Zhou Fuo-hai Riji* [Diary of Zhou Fuo-hai] (Peking: Academy of Social Sciences Press, 1986); for plans to reopen diplomatic channels in three months and continuous activities, see diary entries, August 16 and 31, page 19 and 24. Also see *Selected Letters of Hu Shi,* 363-364.

57. Twenty-seventh meeting of the *MHMS,* August 6, 1937, in *Republican Archives* 3 (1987): 13; Gan, *Changes in Military and Diplomatic Affairs,* 23. For the popularity of the idea of protracted war, see Jin Pu-sen, "On KMT's

Military Strategy in the Resistance War," in *Minguo Dangan Yu Minguoshi Xueshu Taolunhui Lunwen Ji* [Conference Papers on Republican Archives and Republican History], ed. Zhang Xian-wen, Chen Xing-tang, and Zheng Hui-xin (Peking: Dangan Chubanshe, 1988), 374-386.

58. Diary entry, October 6, *Diary of Zhou Fuo-hai*, 43.

59. Sun Ye-fang, *Quanmin Kangzhan De Lilun Jichu* [Theoretical Foundation for National Resistance] (Shanghai: n.p., November 12, 1937): 11-12; Zhou En-lai, et al., *New Situation*, 111-112, 117; Zhang Tie-sheng, "The three pillars in the peace camp and our resistance war," *Kangzhan Sanrikan* [Resistance Tri-daily] 52 (March 9, 1938): 6-7.

60. Tao Xi-sheng, "The sabotaged collective security," *Public Opinion,* December 22, 1937, in his *Ouzhou Junshi Yu Taipingyang Wenti* [The European Equilibrium and the Pacific Problems] (Wuhan: Yiwen Yanjiuhui, June 1938), 6-7.

61. Tao Xi-sheng, "The change and nonchange in the international situation," January 5, 1938, see ibid., 10-11. For similar opinions, see, for example, a pamphlet published by Zhou Fuo-hai and Tao Xi-sheng's Arts and Literature Institute, Zhang Yi-ding, *Woguo Guoji Guanxi Yu Kangzhan Qiantu* [Our Foreign Relations and the Future of the Resistance War] (Wuhan: Yiwen Yanjiuhui, June 1938), 43-44.

62. "Comments on Current Events," February 21-March 24, 1938, *U.S. Military Intelligence Reports,* microfilm reel no. 2.

63. For Feng's attitude toward the Soviet Union during the war, see Guo Xu-yin and Pan Ji-Xian, "Feng Yu-xiang Carried out the Spirit of Sun Yat-sen's Three Policies during the Resistance War," in Zhang Xian-wen, et al., eds., *Conference Papers,* 764-776.

64. Wang's speech, "Three Points We Should Pay Attention to during the Resistance War," January 23, 1938. See *Ruhe Jiuwang Tucun* [How to Achieve Salvation and Survival] (Hong Kong: Nanhua Ribao, April 1938), 113; Tao, "Another illusion," in *European Equilibrium,* 12.

65. Tao, *Currents and Drops,* 159.

66. Tao, "The formation of a new international balance," January 15, 1938, *European Equilibrium,* 15-16.

67. Zhang Zhong-shi, "The positive change in the British and American Far Eastern policy."*Kangzhan Sanrikan* 31 (December 26, 1937): 6-8; Jin Zhong-hua, "We should not be pessimistic about the international situations," ibid., 37 (January 16, 1938): 3; Hu Qiu-yuan, "On the eve of international storm," in *Sujian Yu Chengtan* [Punish Treason and Corruption] (Hankou: Shidai Ribao, 1938), 4-6.

68. See Tao, "The formation of a new international balance," 16. Partially due to the war atmosphere, peace advocates generally could not openly argue their views. For Zhou's views, see diary entries, October 1 and 11, 1937, *Diary of Zhou Fuo-hai,* 41, 46.

69. See Chiang's diary entries, January 3, 12, 28, 1938, Qin Xiao-yi, ed., *DSCB,* vol. 4, part 1: 161, 163, 173.

70. Chiang's speech to army officers, January 11, 1938, *SLCB*, 2, part 1: 66.

71. Tao Xi-sheng to Hu, December 31, 1938, *Selected Letters of Hu Shi,* 397. This letter was written when Tao defected with Wang and was intended to justify his desertion and his peace policy.

72. For detailed descriptions of Gao's meetings with Japanese counterparts, see Gerald Bunker, *The Peace Conspiracy: Wang Ching-wei and the China War, 1937-1945* (Cambridge: Harvard University Press, 1972), 76-77.

73. Boyle, *China and Japan at War,* 179.

74. Gong De-bo, *Wang Zhaoming Toudi Panguo Mishi* [The Secret History of Wang Zhao-ming's Surrender to the Enemy and Betrayal of the Nation] (Taibei: n.p., 1963), 53.

75. For Wang's refusal to lead the peace movement in early 1938, see Tao Xi-sheng, *Currents and Drops,* 166; for the Italian ambassador's effort to persuade Wang to force Chiang out of power and to visit Japan secretly to enter China into the anticommunist pact, see Cai De-jin, "Wang Ching-wei Jituan Panguo Toudi de Qianqian Houhou" [The story of the Wang Ching-wei clique's betrayal of the nation and surrender to the enemy], *Studies on Modern History* 2 (1983): 189-190.

76. For details see Boyle, *China and Japan at War,* 156.

77. Boyle, *China and Japan at War,* 184-187; Also see Jin Xiong-bai, *Wang Zhengquan De Kaichang Yu Shouchang* [The Beginning and the End of the Wang Regime], vol. 5 (Hong Kong: Chunqiu Zazhishe, 1964): 8-9. Bunker, *The Peace Conspiracy,* 86.

78. The letter carrier for Kung, Jia Cun-de, wrote a recollection "Sketches of H. H. Kung's colluding activities with Japanese bandits" in *WSZL* 29 (1962): 67-78. He not only carried telegrams and letters for Kung but also participated in some of the talks. According to him, he continued to negotiate with Japan as Kung's representative through 1940.

79. Shi Le-qu, "A surrender plot of Chiang during the resistance war," *WSZL* 1 (1960): 65-67. Shi was an official of the Central Bank sent to Hong Kong. He was ordered to take care of the documents for the negotiations. Not only did he read these documents but also enjoyed a close relationship with Xiao, who confided in him. Xiao asserts that it was he who insisted on adding the return of Manchuria and Inner Mongolia to China as a condition. He argued that anticommunism was the most important concern of Japan and that since China had conceded this point, Japan should not mind restoring China's sovereignty in these two areas. Chiang reluctantly agreed to add this condition to the list, but told Xiao to be flexible. Another person, Yan Bao-hang, also heard Xiao talking about these negotiations and Chiang's leaving Manchuria and Inner Mongolia out of the discussions; see ibid., 86.

80. Chiang's orders, September 28 and October 14, *SLCB,* 2, part 1: 121-122. The name of the negotiator is not mentioned. But judging from the time of negotiations, August-October 1938, perhaps Xiao was the only high-level official carrying on the work. According to Shi's recollection, Xiao was given direct telephone access to Chiang, a privilege few people had; Chiang to Kung, October 18, ibid., 123-124.

81. Johnson to Secretary of State, July 27, 1938, *FRUS,* 1938, 3: 238-239; Chiang to Roosevelt, ibid., 312-313; Chen Bu-lei to Hu, October 15, Book 146, 65,

Morganthau Diary, Franklin D. Roosevelt Library, Hyde Park, New York. Professor Wu Xiang-xiang also mentions that using the Anglo-American powers to solve the Sino-Japanese problem was one of Chiang's basic diplomatic policies at this time; see Wu, *The Second Sino-Japanese War*, 1: 461.

82. Diary entries, July 26 and October 15, *Diary of Zhou Fuo-hai*, 129, 170.

83. Zhang Zhong-fu to Hu Shi, August 24, 1938, *Selected Letters of Hu Shi*, 377; *FRUS*, 1938, 3: 320.

84. Shou Kang, ed., *Wang Ching-wei Chezhi Jingguo* [The Process of Wang Ching-wei Being Fired] (s.l.: n.p., 1939), 1.

85. For a good study of this institution and its functions, see Lawrence Nae-lih Shyu, "The People's Political Council and China's Wartime Problems, 1937-1945," Ph.D. dissertation, Columbia University, 1972; also see, Shen Yun-long, "The Origin and Achievements of the People's Political Council," in his *Events and Personages*, 369-385.

86. Madame Sun, et al. to Lin Sen, Chiang, and Sun Ke, October 27, 1938, in Nicholson's report to Morganthau, *Morganthau Papers*, Book 148, 44.

87. For the Communist motion, see *Guomin Canzhenghui Wenxian Huibian* [Records of People's Political Council] (Chongqing: Chongqing Chubanshe, 1985), 1: 331-332.

88. Ibid., 334-336.

89. *Kangzhan Zhong De Zhongguo Zhengzhi* [The Chinese Politics during the Resistance War] (Yanan: Shishi Wenti Yanjiuhui, 1940), 173.

90. Tao to Hu Shi, December 31, 1938, *Selected Letters of Hu Shi*, 397.

91. Feng Yu-xiang, *Feng Yu-xiang Huiyilu* [Memoirs of Feng Yu-xiang] (Hong Kong: Wenhua Chubanshe, 1949), 83, 84-87; as he had done before, Feng wrote a memo for Chiang after their talk recording his opinion. This can be found in *Jiang Feng Shujian* [Correspondence between Chiang and Feng] (Shanghai: Zhongguo Wenhua Xintuo Fuwushe, 1946), 79-78.

92. For a detailed description of the negotiations between Wang's people and the Japanese before his defection and for Wang's collaboration with Japan since 1939, see Boyle's book; also Bunker's *The Peace Conspiracy* and Jin's book.

93. Hu's conversation with Hornbeck, State Department decimal file, 893.51/6908.

94. Chiang's diary entry, November 11, 1938, Qin Xiao-yi, ed., *DSCB*, vol. 4, part 1: 226.

95. Sun Ke to Yang Jie, Chinese ambassador to the Soviet Union, January 27, 1939, *Republican Archives* 1 (1985): 51.

Notes to Chapter 6

1. Sun Ke, *Zhong Su Guanxi* [Sino-Soviet Relations] (Shanghai: Zhonghua Shuju, 1946), 16.

2. John Garver, "Chiang Kai-shek's Quest for Soviet Entry into the Sino-Japanese War," *Political Science Quarterly* 102, no. 2 (Summer 1987): 302.

3. Jiang to Foreign Ministry, July 15, 1937, *LGQ,* 484-485; also see Jiang to Wang Chong-hui (foreign minister), July 16 and Jiang to H. H. Kung, July 15, *Republican Archives* 4 (1991): 5-7.

4. Bogomolov to Foreign Ministry, July 19, 1937, *DSFP,* 1937, 20: 393-94.

5. Ibid., 394. According to one Chinese report, Kliment Voroshilov, Soviet defense commissar, told General Yang that Bogomolov had made four errors of judgment about China's situation, and one of them was that Chiang Kai-shek did not have the determination to resist. See Yang's report to Chiang, November 12, 1937, *SLCB,* 3, part 2: 337.

6. Bogomolov to Foreign Ministry, July 23, 1937, *DSFP,* 400-401.

7. Bogomolov to Foreign Ministry, July 26, 1937, ibid., 405.

8. Chiang's conversation with the French ambassador, July 27, 1937, *LGQ,* 486.

9. Litvinov to Bogomolov, July 31, 1937, *DSFP,* 430.

10. See Garver, "Quest for Soviet Entry," 302.

11. Bogomolov to Foreign Ministry, August 18, 1937, *DSFP,* 463.

12. Hu Yu-zhi, "Retrospect and Prospect of Sino-Soviet Nonaggression Pact," *Eastern Miscellany* 34, no. 16-17 (September 1, 1937): 15-16; also see *Zhongguo Kangzhan Yu Sulian* [Chinese Resistance and the Soviet Union], Zhong Su Wenhua Zazhishe [Sino-Soviet Magazine] series, ed. Wei Ling, vol. 1 (Wuhan: Dazhong Chubanshe, 1938), 47-48.

13. Record of the first meeting, September 9, 1937, *Republican Archives* 3 (1987): 32; third meeting, September 14, ibid., 37.

14. Wilson to the Secretary of State, October 16, 1937, *FRUS,* 1937, 3: 616.

15. See Wang Ching-wei's introduction in Hu, *To Fight Is Difficult and So Is to Make Peace.*

16. Foreign Ministry to Chinese embassy in Moscow, September 22, 1937, *LGQ,* 488.

17. Jiang Ting-fu's conversation with the American charge d'affaires in the Soviet Union, December 21, 1937, *FRUS,* 1937, 3: 827. Bogomolov was reportedly executed after returning to the Soviet Union for encouraging Chinese hope of Soviet intervention. Although Bogomolov might have been a convenient scapegoat for the Soviet refusal to intervene militarily, he did seem to have some idea about limited military involvement. He presented a plan of direct military aid to China by utilizing Outer Mongolia, and his plan was supported by the Soviet military leaders in the Far East. See Davis to the Secretary of State, November 23, 1937, *FRUS,* 1937, 3: 712.

18. He Yao-zu to Chiang, September 7, 1937, *SLCB,* 3, part 2: 329-330.

19. *History of Soviet Foreign Policy, 1917-1945,* comp. by A. Beryozkin, et al. (Moscow: Progress Publishers, 1969), 336; Koo, *Memoirs,* 2: 476, 492.

20. Yang and Zhang to Chiang, November 1, 1937, *SLCB,* 3, part 2: 334.

21. For trade figures, see Harriet L. Moore, *Soviet Far Eastern Policy, 1931-1945* (Princeton: Princeton University Press, 1945), 115.

22. Yang and Zhang to Chiang, November 12, 1937, *SLCB,* 3, part 2: 335-336.

23. Zhang Chong to Chiang, November 18, 1937, ibid., 338.

24. Stalin to Chiang, December (1-5?), 1937, ibid., 339.

25. Yang to Chiang, December 21, 1937, *Republican Archives* 1 (1985): 45; also see Yang to Chiang, January 5, 1938, *SLCB,* 3, part 2: 474.

26. Aron Shai, *Origins of War in the East: Britain, China and Japan, 1937-1939* (London: Croom Helm, 1976), 115, 120.

27. Conversation between Litvinov and Jiang Ting-fu, December 21, 1937, *DSFP,* 20: 679.

28. Jiang Ting-fu, *Memoirs,* 201. Also see, Henderson to Secretary of State, December 21, 1937, *FRUS,* 1937, 3: 827-828.

29. Shen Zhi-yuan, *Zhong Su Huzhu Lun* [The Theory of Sino-Soviet Cooperation] (Shanghai: Shanghai Zazhi Gongsi, April 1938), 22-28, 38-39.

30. Gan Jie-hou, *Sue Weishenmo Haiwei Canzhan* [Why Hasn't Soviet Russia Joined the War Yet?] (Shanghai: Qianjinshe, July 1938), 4-5, 8-18.

31. Stalin and Voroshilov to Chiang, December, *SLCB,* 399-340; diary entry, December 16, James McHugh Papers, Box 11, F-12, Cornell University.

32. Fu Si-nian to Hu Shi, October 11, *Selected Letters of Hu Shi,* 2: 365; Koo, *Memoirs,* 3: 36-37. Sun attacked those anti-Soviet elements in late July 1937, see *GMWX,* 106: 285.

33. Henderson to Secretary of State, February 5, 1938, *FRUS,* 1938, 3: 70.

34. Koo, *Memoirs,* 3: 38.

35. Stomoniyakov's talk with Sun, January, 21, 1938, *DSFP,* 21: 43-44.

36. Sun to Chiang, February 7, 1938, *SLCB,* 3, part 2: 407.

37. Henderson to Secretary of State, February 5, 1938, *FRUS,* 1938, 3: 70.

38. Sun's report, *SLCB,* 407.

39. Conversation between Litvinov and Sun, February 9, 1938, *DSFP,* 21: 68-69.

40. Wilson to Secretary of State, April 5, 1938, *FRUS,* 1938, 3: 136.

41. See Garver, "Quest for Soviet Entry," 311.

42. Conversation between Sun and Stomonyalov, May 19, 1938, *DSFP,* 21: 279.

43. Chiang to Stalin, May 5, and Stalin and Voroshilov to Chiang, May 10, 1938, *Republican Archives* 1 (1985): 46-47.

44. Aitchen K. Wu, *China and the Soviet Union: A Study of Sino-Soviet Relations* (New York: John Day Company, 1950), 268.

45. Bullitt to Secretary of State, July 1, 1938, *FRUS,* 1938, 3: 210; Koo, *Memoirs,* 136-137.

46. Conversation between Lugants Orelski and Chiang, June 14, 1938, *DSFP,* 21: 334.

47. Japanese estimates: Soviets 1,200 killed and 4,300 wounded; Japanese 526 killed and 913 wounded. Soviet estimates: Soviets 236 killed, 611 wounded; Japanese 600 killed, and 2,500 wounded. See Alvin D. Coox, *The Anatomy of a Small War: The Soviet-Japanese Struggle for Changkufeng/Khasan, 1938* (London: Greenwood Press, 1977), 285.

48. See *Diary of Zhou Fuo-hai,* 138.

49. Jiang Ting-fu, *Memoirs,* 211-212; Comments on Current Events, August 17, microfilm reel no. 3, *U.S. Military Intelligence Reports: China, 1911-1941* (Frederick, Md: University Publications of America, 1983); *Shenbao,* July 24, *Xingbao,* August 6 in Wang Zhong-shu, ed., *Zhanggufeng Shijian Niaokan* [A

Bird's-eye View of Zhanggufeng Incident] (Changsha: Shangwu Yinshuguan, July 1938), 164-189.

50. Chiang to Yang, July 27, 1938, *SLCB,* 3, part 2: 342; Qin Ziao-yi, ed., *DSCB,* 4, part 1: 238.
51. Kung to Koo, August 2, 1938, Koo Papers, Box 26, no. 47.
52. Kung's conversation with Ganin, July 30, 1938, *DSFP,* 21: 410-411.
53. Kung to Koo, August 2, 3, and 4, 1938, Koo Papers, Box 26, no. 47.
54. Chiang to Koo, August 6, 1938, ibid.
55. Koo, *Memoirs,* 3: 170.
56. Sun to Chiang, August 7, *SLCB,* 3, part 2: 408; for Litvinov's remarks, see Koo's *Memoirs,* 3: 100-101.
57. Sun to Chiang, *SLCB,* 3, part 2: 408.
58. Litvinov to Lugants Orelski, August 21, 1938, *DSFP,* 21: 442; Koo, *Memoirs,* 3: 171.
59. J. Lossing Buck's interview with Chen Guang-pu, August 15 and September 2, *Morganthau Diary,* Book 138, Franklin D. Roosevelt Library, Hyde Park, New York.
60. Qin Xiao-yi, ed., *DSCB,* 4, part 1: 241.
61. Chiang to Yang, October 1, 1938, *SLCB,* 3, part 2: 343.
62. Yun Gong, "On the Soviet Foreign Policy from the Perspective of Chinese Resistance War," *Eastern Miscellany* 35, no. 20 (October 16, 1938): 18.
63. Litvinov to Lugants Orelski, October 9, 1938, *DSFP,* 21: 570.
64. Yang to Chiang, October 16, *Republican Archives* 1 (1985): 49; Lugants Orelski to Foreign Ministry, October 27, 1938, *DSFP,* 21: 608-609.
65. Sun to Yang, January 27, 1939, *Republican Archives* 1 (1985): 51.
66. Yang to Chiang, February 23, ibid., 31: also see Clifford, *Retreat from China,* 133.
67. Foreign Ministry to Hu, April 10, *Hu Shi Ren Zhumei Dashi Qijian Wanglai Diangao* [Telegraphic Correspondences of Hu Shu during His Ambassadorship to the United States] (hereafter cited as *HSDG*), in Zhonghua Minguoshi Ziliao Conggao [Historical Materials on Republican China Series], comp. Institute of Modern History, Chinese Academy of Social Sciences (Peking: Zhonghua Shuju, 1978), 15; Koo, *Memoirs,* 3:413-414.
68. Foreign Ministry to Koo, March 24, Koo Papers, Box 37; Halifax to Clark Kerr, April 13, *DBFP,* 3rd Series, 9: 5-7.
69. Chiang to Sun, April, 1939, *SLCB,* 3, part 2: 409; Chiang to Sun, April 25, ibid., 410.
70. Chiang to Sun, May 7, ibid., 411.
71. Sun to Chiang, May 14 and Sun to Kung, May 15, ibid., 513-514. For Stalin's remarks, see Aitchen Wu, *China and the Soviet Union,* 269.
72. Sun to Chiang, May 14, *SLCB,* 3, part 2: 513-514.
73. See Chiang's diary entries, June 3, 17, August 4, Qin Xiao-yi, ed., *DSCB,* 4, part 1: 366, 371, 393; Zhang Chong-fu, "The Two Most Important International Questions at Present" and Liu Guang-yan, "Six International Issues at Present," *Waijiao Yanjiu* [Diplomatic Studies] 1, no. 3-4 (July 1939): 1. Liu considered the Soviets more active in seeking agreement than the British. Liu's view was

more representative of general Chinese public opinion on the ongoing Soviet-British negotiations in Moscow.

74. Chiang to Stalin and Voroshilov, August 3, *SLCB,* 3, part 2: 426.

75. Chiang to Sun, August 17, ibid., 426-427.

76. Sun to Chiang, August, ibid., 427.

77. Zhou Zi-ya, "Du Fr Husnxi Yu Shijie Dazhan" [Soviet-German Relations and World War], *Diplomatic Studies* 5, no. 1 (September 1939): 38.

78. Guo Chang-lu, "Causes and Repercussions of the Soviet-Germany Pact," ibid., 43.

79. Chiang Kai-shek, *Soviet Russia in China* (New York: Noonday Press, 1968), 91; *Su De Zhanzheng Hou De Zhongguo Gongchandang* [The Chinese Communist Party after the German-Soviet War], ed. Research Institute of Current Affairs [Shishi Wenti Yanjiushe] (n.p.: August, 1941), 3-5.

80. Chiang's diary entry, August 23, Qin Xiao-yi, ed., *DSCB,* 4, part 1: 396.

81. Chiang to Guo, August 29, *SLCB* 3, part 2: 105.

82. See John Garver, *Chinese-Soviet Relations, 1937-1945: Diplomacy of Chinese Nationalism* (New York: Oxford University Press, 1988), 92-93.

83. Diary entry, September 2, Qin Xiao-yi, ed., *DSCB,* 4, part 1: 406.

84. Diary entries, September 2, 4, 5, 8, *Diary of Wang Shi-jie,* 2: 143-147. The decision to recall the ambassador seemed to be circumvented by Kung, Wang, and others who let the order die. See the above diary.

85. See Qin Xiao-yi, ed., *DSCB,* 4, part 1: 410-411.

86. Shao Yu-lin, "The Japanese New Diplomatic Moves after the Soviet-German Pact," *Diplomatic Studies* 5, no. 1 (September 1939): 20. This notion seemed to be entertained by many people; for example, see Xie Yi-cheng, "The Soviet-German Joining of Hands and the Far Eastern Diplomacy," ibid., 15.

87. For descriptions of the Nomonhan fighting, see Alvin D. Coox, *Nomonhan: Japan against Russia, 1939* (Stanford: Stanford University Press, 1985) and also see Hosoya Chihiro, "The Japanese-Soviet Confrontation, 1935-1939," in James W. Morley, ed., *Deterrent Diplomacy: Japan, Germany and the USSR, 1935-1941* (New York: Columbia University Press, 1983), 129-178.

88. Sun to Chiang, September 13, *SLCB,* 3, part 2: 430.

89. Sun to Chiang, September 17, *SLCB,* 3, part 2: 431-432.

90. Sun to Foreign Ministry, September 16, 1939, Koo Papers, Box 37.

91. Sun to Chiang, September 18, *SLCB,* 3, 2: 432-433.

92. Foreign Ministry to Hu Shi, September 5, *HSDG,* 23; diary entry, September 7, *Diary of Wang Shi-jie,* 2: 146; Foreign Ministry to Koo, September 6, 1939, Koo Papers, Box 37.

93. Chiang to Hu, September 18, 1939, *SLCB,* 3, part 1: 89; Yang to Chiang, September 2, ibid., 3, part 2: 345-346; Zhang to Chiang, September 5, ibid., 346.

94. Yang to Chiang, September 23, ibid., 348-349.

95. Conversation with Jiang Ting-fu, September 20, McHugh Papers, Box 3, F-1.

96. Diary entry, November 1, Qin Xiao-yi, ed., *DSCB,* 4, part 1: 435.

97. Chiang's conversation with Paniushkin, November 8, *SLCB,* 3, part 2: 351-354.

98. Weng to Hu, November 11, *Selected Letters of Hu Shi,* 439.

99. Wang to Hu, November 7, *HSDG,* 26.

100. Chiang to He, January 31, 1940, *SLCB,* 3, part 2: 521; He Ying-qin's report to Chiang Kai-shek, March, 28, 1941, ibid., 531.

101. Dai to Chen Bu-lei, December 6, *Dai Jitao Ji* [Works of Mr. Dai Ji-tao], ed. Chen Tian-xi (Taibei: Central Committee of the KMT, 1959), 1: 377.

102. Wang Shi-jie's diary entries, December 6, 7, 9, *Diary of Wang Shi-jie,* 2: 193-196.

103. Yang to Chiang, January 9, 1940, *SLCB,* 3, part 2: 362-363.

104. He to Chiang, January 10 and 12, ibid., 363-365.

105. He to Chiang, January 13 and 19, ibid., 366-367.

106. He to Chiang, January 20, 1940, ibid., 368; for He's shopping list, see ibid., 374-375, 532.

107. Chiang's conversation with the chief of Soviet advisers, January 22, 1940, ibid., 369-370.

108. Chiang to He, January 24, ibid., 371.

109. Shao Li-zi, "Reminiscences on Being Ambassador in the Soviet Union," in *Renwu* [People] 1 (1983): 165-173.

110. Shao, "Reminiscences," 166. According to Shao, Chiang nodded agreement to his proposal, but on his way to the Soviet Union, Shao received a telegram from the chairman of Gansu Province, Zhu Shao-liang, saying that Chiang Kai-shek telephoned him that the suggestion about Germany should not be mentioned. For Chiang's opinion of Germany and the Soviet Union in July and August, see Qin Xiao-yi, ed., *DSCB,* 4, part 2: 551, 567-568.

111. Record of Chiang's interview with Johnson, October 30, *SLCB,* 3, part 1: 105; see Garver, *Chinese-Soviet Relations,* 104-105.

112. Shao to Chiang, September 28, *SLCB,* 3, part 2: 379.

113. Chiang to Stalin, September 29, ibid., 379; Keiji, *The Secret Records,* 12: 54, 61.

114. Stalin to Chiang, October 16, ibid., 382-383.

115. Chiang to Shao, October 22, ibid., 383-384; Shao, "Reminiscences," 169-170.

116. Garver, *Chinese-Soviet Relations,* 108; Chiang to Hu, December 11, *HSDG,* 88.

117. Chiang's conversation with the Soviet ambassador, Paniushkin, January 22, *SLCB,* 3, part 2: 386-388; also see Shao's recollection in "Reminiscences," 170.

118. See Qin Xiao-yi, ed., *DSCB,* 4, part 2: 677.

119. Steven I. Levine, "Introduction" in *Along Alien Roads* by Alexander Ya. Kalyagin (New York: East Asian Institute, Columbia University, 1983), 9.

Notes to Chapter 7

1. For a description of American policy, see Borg, *The United States and the Far Eastern Crisis,* 293-309.

2. Gauss's summary of Shanghai local press in August; see State Department decimal file, 711.93/375.

3. Memo of conversation with Wang Zheng-ting, September 17, 1937, Hull Papers, microfilm reel no. 28, Library of Congress.

4. Hankou *Dagongbao,* September 28, 1937.

5. Wang Ji-yuan, "An Analysis of Recent American Attitudes," *Kang Zhan* (September 26, 1937), 5-6.

6. Robert Dallek, *Franklin D. Roosevelt and American Foreign Policy, 1932-1945* (New York: Oxford University Press, 1979), 148; John M. Haight, Jr., "Franklin D. Roosevelt and a Naval Quarantine of Japan," *Pacific History Review* 40 (1971), 203-226; John Morton Blum, *From the Morgenthau Diaries: Years of Crisis, 1928-1938* (Boston: Houghton Mifflin Co., 1959), 486-490.

7. For the Chinese reaction to the Quarantine Speech, see *Eastern Miscellany* 34, no. 18 (October 1, 1937): 79; "Comments on Current Events, October 5-18, 1937," microfilm reel no. 2, *U.S. Military Intelligence Reports: China, 1911-1941* (Frederick, Md.: University Publications of America, 1983). Hereafter cited as *USIR.* Gauss to Secretary of State, November 8, 1937, State Department decimal file, 711.93/381; also see Naval Attaché Reports, October 13, RG 38, Box 455, National Archives.

8. Fu to Hu, October 11, 1937, *Selected Letters of Hu Shi,* 2: 368.

9. For example, see editorial, "America and the Far East," Shanghai *Dagongbao,* November 28, 1937.

10. "Comments on Current Events, July 3-16, 1937," microfilm reel no. 2, *USIR;* Naval Attaché Reports, August 13, 1937, RG 38, Box 455, National Archives; for American government opinions, see Jonathan G. Utley, "Cordell Hull and the Diplomacy of Inflexibility," in Hilary Conroy and Harry Wray, eds., *Pearl Harbor Reexamined: Prologue to the Pacific War* (Honolulu: University of Hawaii Press, 1990), 76.

11. Carlson to Le Hand, August 27, September 11 and 22, and November 1, 1937, Presidential Personal File, 4951, Franklin D. Roosevelt Library, Hyde Park, New York.

12. Yarnell to Admiral Leahy, September 12, October 15, and October 16, Yarnell Papers, Box 3, Library of Congress; Leahy to Yarnell, November 10, ibid., and Leahy Diary, August 24, 1937, microfilm reel no. 1. Actually Leahy viewed the war as "a wonderful opportunity . . . to insure Western trade supremacy in the Orient for another century."

13. "Comments on Current Events, November 27-December 20, 1937," microfilm reel no. 2, *USIR;* Johnson to Hull, March 4, 1938, *FRUS,* 1938, 3: 115-116.

14. Situation Reports, April 6 and May 5, reel no. 10, *USIR.*

15. Carlson to Le Hand, March 31 and April 15, 1938, PPF 4951, Roosevelt Library; Yarnell to Leahy, April 15 and May 10, 1938, Box 3, Yarnell Papers; "Political-Military Situation," March 28, 1938, Box 2, f-12; McHugh to Holcomb, April 12, and Holcomb to McHugh, July 19, Box 1, f-1, James McHugh Papers, Cornell University Library, Ithaca, New York; For Leahy's remarks, see his conversation with Morgenthau on September 28 in which Morgenthau asked Leahy to thank McHugh for his reports, *Morgenthau Diary,* book 143, 144-149, Roosevelt Library, Hyde Park, New York.

16. Harold Ickes Diary, March 4 and May 1, 1938, Library of Congress. For Hull's thoughts, see Utley's article "Cordell Hull" in Conroy and Wray, eds., *Pearl Harbor Reexamined,* 76.

17. The best analysis of American aid to China is Michael Schaller, *The U.S. Crusade in China, 1938-1945* (New York: Columbia University Press, 1979). Also see Arthur N. Young, *China and the Helping Hand, 1937-1945* (Cambridge: Harvard University Press, 1963).

18. *Morgenthau Diary,* June 1, 1938, book 127, 109.

19. Blum, *From the Morgenthau Diaries,* 508.

20. *Morgenthau Diary,* July 12, 1938, book 134, 43.

21. Interview with Li Zong-ren, August 27, *Morgenthau Diary,* book 138, 185.

22. Situation Reports, June 25, reel no. 10, *USIR*; J. Lossing Buck to Morgenthau, September 6 and his interviews with Carlson, August 29 and Stilwell, August 30, *Morgenthau Diary,* book 138, 167-168, 187-189; for McHugh's urge for support, see McHugh to Admiral (?), Box 1, f 1; Report of September 14, Box 2, f 13, McHugh Papers. Also see Barbara W. Tuchman, *Stilwell and the American Experience in China, 1911-1945* (New York: Bantam Books, 1972), 240-241.

23. *Morgenthau Diary,* book 142, 176, 352.

24. October, 17, 1938, microfilm reel no. 1, *Presidential Diaries of Henry Morgenthau* (Frederick, Md.: University Publications of America, n.d.).

25. February, *Memoirs,* 67; See Michael Barnhart, *Japan Prepares for Total War,* 130-132; Dallek, *Franklin D. Roosevelt,* 193.

26. Cited in McCarty, "Hornbeck," 170-171; Hornbeck's memo on the tung oil project, November 14, Presidential Secretary's File, Box 26, Roosevelt Library.

27. *Morgenthau Diary,* 435-436; Chiang to Roosevelt, November 9, Presidential Secretary's File, Box 26, Roosevelt Library; also see Adams, 85. The loan was increased to $25 million later.

28. Aron Shai, *Origins of the War in the East: Britain, China and Japan, 1937-1939* (London: Croom Helm, 1976), 192.

29. Zheng Yun-kong, "The Change of the Anglo-American Attitude to Japan," *Eastern Miscellany* 36, no. 1 (January 1, 1939): 1-2; Schaller, *The U.S. Crusade,* 28-29; Guo Bin-jia, "The Present Sino-American Relations," and Ma Xing-ye, "The United States Is Not Isolationist," *Diplomatic Studies* 1, no. 2 (March 15, 1939): 37-43, 54-57; see Comments on Current Events, January 8, 1939, *USIR,* reel no. 3.

30. Wu Yan-jun, "Kangzhan Shiqi De Guoji Xuanchuanchu," [The International Propaganda Bureau during the Resistance War], *Republican Archives* 2 (1990): 118-122.

31. See *Morgenthau Diary,* book 109, 131 and State Department decimal file, 793.94/12892.

32. Foreign Ministry to Hu, October 1, 1938, *HSDG,* 1.

33. Wang's memo to Chiang, Second Historical Archives, 761.152. Wang was one of the key officials in Chiang's Personal Attendance Office.

34. Wang Shi-jie to Hu, January 19, 1939; Hu to Wang Shi-jie, January 30, *HSDG,* 7, 10-11.

35. Policy recommendation by Gan Jie-hou and Zhang Zhong-fu; see Second Historical Archives, 761.152.

36. Betty Glad, *Key Pittman, the Tragedy of a Senate Insider* (New York: Columbia University Press, 1986), 258-262.

37. Wang Shi-jie, "Report on the Problem of Neutrality Acts," March 1939, Second Historical Archives, 761.152.

38. Foreign Ministry to Hu, March 25, 1939, *Kangzhan Qijian Fengsuo Yu Jinyun Shijian* [Blockade and Embargo during the Resistance War], vol. 6, Diplomatic Materials Series. (Taibei: n.p., 1967). Hereafter cited as *FSJY,* 183; Wang Shi-jie to Hu, March 23, Foreign Ministry to Hu, April, 1, 1939, *HSDG,* 14.

39. Hu to Pittman, March 25, and Hu's memo, no date, Chen Guang-pu Papers, Columbia University, Box 2, F-F3.

40. Embassy in China to Secretary of State, March 27, 1939, State Department decimal files, 811.044/362.

41. Hu to Kung, March 28, and Hu to Foreign Ministry, March 31, 1939, *FSJY,* 184, 186.

42. Secretary of State to Grew, April 27, and Peck to Secretary of State, May 2, 1939, *FRUS,* 1939, 3: 534-535; also see Glad, *Key Pittman,* 263.

43. For the Committee's activities, see Donald J Friedman, *Road from Isolationism* (Cambridge: Harvard University Press, 1968); for the close coordination between China and the Committee, see Zhang Peng-chun (Chinese coordinator with the Committee) to Foreign Ministry, April 11 and July 28, 1939, *FSJY,* 196 and 221-222; Chiang Kai-shek to T. V. Soong, July 17, 1940, *HSDG,* 55. Zhang's predecessor was Qian Duan-sheng and his successor was Yu Jun-jie. Harry Price's brother Frank was in Sichuan during this period and often acted as a channel between Chiang and the Committee. For some financial contributions to the Committee, see its file under Chen Guang-pu (Chen Kwang-pu) and also Hu to Kung, October 13, 1940, *HSDG,* 75. Interview with Harry Price, April 1991; according to Harry Price, Hu encouraged his friends, Americans as well as Chinese, to contribute to the Committee.

44. Hu to Chiang Kai-shek, August 3, Chen Guang-pu Papers, Box 3, F-H.

45. For Chinese foreign minister and press reactions, see, *FSJY,* 226-228; Weng Wen-hao, economic minister, to Hu, July 31, *HSDG,* 19.

46. See Chiang's diary entries, February 10, 14 and his statement on February 11, Qin Xiao-yi, ed., *DSCB,* 4, part 1: 301-302.

47. Peck to Secretary of State, February 12 and 21, 1939, *FRUS,* 1939, 3: 105-107, 111.

48. Guo to Chiang, February 24, 1939, *SLCB,* 3, part 2: 207.

49. Yang to Chiang, February 23, *SLCB,* 3, part 2: 31; also see Clifford, *Retreat from China,* 133; Foreign Ministry to Hu, April 10, *HSDG,* 15; Halifax to Clark Kerr, April 13, *DBFP,* 3rd series, 9: 5-7; Koo, *Memoirs,* 413-414.

50. For the Chinese memo to State Dept., see ibid., 525; for Chiang Kai-shek and Wellington Koo's hopes for U.S. support, see Bullitt to Secretary of State, April 18, 1939, ibid., 526-528.

51. Chiang's diary entry, April 18, Qin Xiao-yi, ed., *DSCB,* 4, part 1: 345; Foreign Ministry to Hu, April 24, 1939, *HSDG,* 16; State Department to Chinese Embassy, May 1, 1939, *FRUS,* 1939, 3: 533-534; Hu to Foreign Ministry, May 2, Koo Papers, Box 37.

52. Foreign Ministry to Koo, Koo Papers, Box 37.

53. Diary entry, August 26, *Diary of Wang Shi-jie,* 2: 140, 142; See Weekly Reports of the Far East, August 24 and 31, State Department decimal file, RG 59, 890.00/159; also see Chapter Six.

54. Chiang to Hu, August 29, *SLCB,* 3, part 1: 86-87. Chiang asked Hu to pass this message to Roosevelt.

55. Johnson to Secretary of State, August 30, 1939, *FRUS,* 1939, 3: 217-18.

56. Hu to Chiang and Kung via Foreign Ministry, August 29, Chen Papers, Box 3, F-H.

57. Hu to Chiang, September 2, *SLCB,* 3, part 1: 87.

58. Chiang to Hu, September 3, ibid., 88.

59. See Chinese records of Chiang's conversation with Johnson on August 30, Foreign Ministry to Koo, August 30, Koo Papers, Box 37; also see Johnson to Secretary of State, September 6, 1939, *FRUS,* 1939, 3: 233-234.

60. Koo to Chiang, September 1, and Chiang to Koo, September 2 (?), Koo Papers, Box 23. Koo reported to Chiang Bullitt's idea that if the Soviet Union attacked Poland as specified in the Nazi-Soviet understanding, Britain and France would regard the Soviets as an enemy country and by then there might be a possibility that the United States, Britain, France, China and Japan form a bloc. If such a scenario happened, the Sino-Japanese conflict might be mediated. But in Chiang's reply, Japan was simply dropped.

61. Keiji, *The Secret Records,* 12: 17.

62. Chiang to Koo, September 13, Koo Papers, Box 37.

63. Johnson to Secretary of State, May 29 and June 19, 1939, *FRUS,* 1939, 3: 173, 187; Kung to Chen, July 4, Chen Papers, Box 2, F3.

64. Weekly Review of the Far East, State Department, 890.00/164.

65. Sun, Koo, Guo and Li Shi-Zeng to Chiang (September-October?), Koo Papers, Box 23.

66. Hu to Chiang, October 16, Chen Papers, Box 3, G-2; also see Chen's diary, August 31, Box 3, I.

67. Koo to Chiang and Kung, August 26 and 27, Koo Papers, Box 40.

68. Boyle, *China and Japan,* 289-293; Kirby, *Germany and Republican China,* 248; Garver, *Chinese-Soviet Relations,* 110-111.

69. Chiang to Koo, August 27, Koo Papers, Box 37.

70. Hu to Kung, September 8, Chen Papers, Box 3, F-H; Schaller, *The U.S. Crusade,* 31-32; Young, *China and the Helping Hand,* 130-131.

71. Chen to Kung, October 8, *SLCB,* 3, part 1: 257; Chiang to Hu, December 19, ibid., 260.

72. Hu to Kung, March 25 and Kung to Hu, March 27, ibid., 268-269; Chen to Kung, April 9, *HSDG,* 34-35.

73. Chen's Report, Chen Papers, Box 2, F-E.

74. For Chinese disappointments, see "The Far East in the Summer of 1940, confidential notes on visits made by Eugene E. Barnett on behalf of International Committee of YMCA, May-September 1940," State Department decimal file, 711.93/466, 28-50; for pro-German influences, see Kirby, *Germany,* 249-251; for criticism of U.S. policy, see He Jong-ji, "Gentleman's Diplomacy," September 1, 1940, *Zhan Tuan Biweekly,* in He Jong-ji, *Wei Zhongguo Xunqiu Guoji Heping* [Seeking International Peace for China] (Changsha: Shangwu Yinshuguan, 1941), 9-21; for talks of peace, see Johnson to Secretary of State, July 27, 1940, *FRUS,* 1940, 4: 409.

75. Hu to Chiang, July 16; Chiang to Hu and Soong, July 17, 1940, *HSDG,* 54-56.

76. Soong to Chiang, September 23 and 26; Chiang to Soong, September 26, *SLCB,* 3, part 1: 277-281.

77. Hu to Chen Bu-lei (Chiang's secretary), October 12; Zhu Jia Hua to Hu, October 16; Chen to Hu, October 17; and Wang Shi-jie to Hu, October 23, *HSDG,* 74-76, 80.

78. See Chiang's diary, October 31, Keiji, *The Secret Records,* 12: 61-62

79. Chiang's diary, September 29, ibid., 52, 61; Diary, September 22, *DSCB,* 4, part 2: 576.

80. Chiang's conversation with Johnson, October 18; Chiang to Soong, October 20, *SLCB,* 3, part 1: 100-103; Johnson to Secretary of State, October 21, 1940, *FRUS,* 1940, 4: 674-676.

81. Hu to Chen Bu-lei, October 24, *SLCB,* 3, part 1: 104.

82. Chiang to Soong and Hu, November 1, ibid., 107-108.

83. Kung to Hu, November 8, *HSDG,* 82.

84. For this letter of November 6, see, State Department decimal file, 711.93/460.

85. Soong to Chiang, November 9, *SLCB,* 3, part 1: 112-113; for Chiang's interview with Johnson, November 9, and his plan, see *FRUS,* 1940, 4: 688-692.

86. Ibid., 689.

87. Cyril Rogers to Soong, November 18, Soong Papers, Box 8.

88. Johnson to Secretary of State, November 27, 1940, *FRUS,* 1940, 4: 446-447.

89. For the American response, see Hornbeck's memo, November 12, State Department decimal file, 711.93/467; Wells to Johnson, November 18, 1940, *FRUS,* 1940, 4: 693-694.

90. Chen Jie to Chiang, November 11, *SLCB,* 3, part 2: 698-700.

91. Xu Mo's conversation with Johnson, November 19, ibid., 114-115.

92. Dallek, *Franklin D. Roosevelt,* 270; Johnson to Secretary of State (two telegrams), November 22, 1940, *FRUS,* 1940, 4: 694-695; Chiang to Soong, November 21, *SLCB,* 3, part 1: 119.

93. Soong to Chiang, November 30, *SLCB,* 3, part 1: 285; Chiang's conversation with Johnson, December 1, ibid., 125; see Schaller, *The U.S. Crusade,* 36-37.

94. Chiang to Soong, December 10; Chiang to Soong and Hu, December 11, *HSDG,* 87-88.

95. See Johnson to Secretary of State, January 2 and 24, 1941, *FRUS,* 1941, 5: 456, 473.

96. Soong to Chiang, January 20, *SLCB*, 3, part 1: 533. Currie's trip was paid for by the Chinese government, including salaries for him and his aide. Total expenses—$3,363, see Currie Papers, Archives Division, Hoover Institution on War and Peace, Box 4.
97. Roosevelt to Currie, January 11, 1941, Currie Papers, Box 5.
98. See Schaller, *The U.S. Crusade,* 42-43. For a typical argument of Chiang, see his conversation with Johnson, *SLCB*, 3, part 1: 100-103.
99. See Schaller, *The U.S. Crusade,* 43-45; for the link between American aid and the Kuomintang intention to use it to buttress its position against Communists, see Wang Shi-jie to Hu, October 23, *HSDG*, 80.
100. Chiang's interview with Currie, February 8, 1941, *SLCB*, 3, part 1: 542-545
101. Roosevelt's conversation with T. V. Soong, see Soong to Chiang, April 15, and Chiang to Soong, April 17, ibid., 129, 135.
102. Councillors Mo De-hui, etc., to Currie, February 15, and People's Foreign Relations Association to Currie, February 2, Currie Papers, Box 3.
103. Chiang to Soong, February 27. An English translation of the letter is in Currie Papers, Box 3. For Chiang's dislike of the U.S. State Department, see Owen Lattimore, *China Memoirs: Chiang Kai-shek and the War Against Japan* (Tokyo: University of Tokyo Press, 1990), 87-88.
104. For a good description of Currie's visions of the American role in China and his influence on future U.S. policy, see Schaller, *The U.S. Crusade,* 48-51.
105. Lattimore to Currie, 1941, Currie Papers, Box 5.
106. For Chiang's repeated request for 500 airplanes, see Chiang to Roosevelt via Soong, *SLCB*, 3, part 1: 427-429; for the story of Chennault and his American Volunteer Groups (AVG), see Boyd H. Bauer, "General Claire Lee Chennault and China, 1937-1958," Ph.D. dissertation, American University, 1973, and Wanda Cornelius and Thayne Short, *Ding Hao, America's Air War in China, 1937-1945* (Gretna, La.: Pelican Publishing Co., 1980), Chapter Three.
107. See Chiang's diaries, February 20 and 22 and March 8, 1941, Qin Xiao-yi, ed., *DSCB*, 4, part 2: 642-644, 670.
108. Gauss to Johnson, March 29, 1937, State Department decimal file, 793.003/864; also for a brief Chinese account, see Chen Guo-huang, "The Formation and Abrogation of Consular Jurisdiction in China," master's thesis, National Taiwan University, Taiwan, 1971, Chapter Nine.
109. Wang Shi-jie to Hu, December 18, 1940, *Selected Letters of Hu Shi,* 505-506.
110. For Wang's speech at Weekly Memorial Meeting, see State Department decimal file, 893.00/14606.
111. Guo to Hu, April 20, *HSDG*, 102.
112. Guo to Wang Chong-hui, April 29; Guo to Foreign Ministry, May 5, *HSDG*, 103-104; memo by Hornbeck, May 14, 1941, *FRUS*, 1941, 5: 776.
113. For the exchanges of letters, see State Department decimal file, 711.93/471.
114. Chiang's conversation with Gauss, the new American ambassador who replaced Johnson in May, June 24, *SLCB*, 3, part 1: 141-144; also see Zhou En-lai's conversation with Vincent, Service, and Drumright, June 30, 1941, *FRUS*, 1941, 5: 519.

115. Chiang to Currie, July 8 and Currie to Chiang, July 12, Currie Papers, Box 1.
116. Chiang to Soong, July 27, *SLCB,* 3, part 1: 461-462; also see Chiang's diary, July 31, Qin Xiao-yi, ed., *DSCB,* 4, part 2: 710.
117. Excerpts of a letter from Frank Price, September 16, State Department decimal file, 711.93/480.
118. Lattimore to Currie and memo by Currie, August 2, State Department decimal file, 711.93/473 2/1; also see memo by Major McHugh, August 17, Currie Papers, Box 5.
119. Memo by Currie for Roosevelt, August 25, Currie Papers, Box 5.
120. Lattimore to Currie, August 20, Currie Papers, Box 5.
121. Hull to Gauss, September 2, and Hull's conversation with Hu, September 4, *FRUS,* 1941, 4: 419-422; for Chinese press reaction, see State Department decimal file, 893.00/14800. Also see memo by Currie for Roosevelt, September 13, Currie Papers, Box 5.
122. Chiang's diary, September 12, Keiji, *The Secret Records,* 12: 1171-1172.
123. See Chiang's interviews with Magruder, October 27 and 31, *SLCB,* 3, part 1: 467-478.
124. For Chiang's requests, see Senate Judiciary Committee, *Morgenthau Diary,* 528-529.
125. Hu to Foreign Ministry, November 22, ibid., 148; also see memo by Secretary of State, November 22, 1941, *FRUS,* 1941, 4: 640.
126. Guo to Chiang, Chiang to Hu and Hu to Foreign Ministry, November 24, *SLCB,* 3, part 1: 147, 149-150.
127. Lattimore to Currie, November 25, Currie Papers, Box 5; Chiang to Soong, November 25, ibid., Box 3.
128. David Klein and Hilary Conroy, "Churchill, Roosevelt, and the China Question in Pre-Pearl Harbor Diplomacy," in Conroy and Wray, eds., *Pearl Harbor Reexamined,* 135-136.
129. Diary December 27, Qin Xiao-yi, ed., *DSCB,* 4, part 2: 762.
130. Han Suyin, *Birdless Summer* (New York: G. P. Putnam's Sons, 1968), 235.

Notes to Epilogue

1. See Iriye's bibliographical essay, *The Origins of the Second World War in Asia and the Pacific,* (London: Longman, 1987), 190.
2. The pre-1937 American policy of acquiescing to Japan's new position in the Far East is convincingly documented by Dorothy Borg in her *United States and the Far Eastern Crisis of 1933-1938.*
3. For example, Lord Halifax said specifically that China was fighting their battles; see Iriye, "Japanese Aggression and China's International Position 1931-1949," in John K. Fairbank and Albert Feuerwerker, eds., *Cambridge History of China,* vol. 13, (Cambridge: Cambridge University Press, 1986), 524. Hornbeck used similar terms to describe China's resistance, see Chapter

Seven. Of course the Soviet support for China was based, it can be safely assumed, on the same logic.

4. For example, see Warren Cohen, *America's Response to China*, 3rd. ed., (New York: Columbia University Press, 1990), 124, and Waldo Heinrichs, "1900-1945: The Question of U.S. Policy for East Asia," in Warren Cohen, ed., *New Frontiers in American-East Asian Relations*, (New York: Columbia University Press, 1983), 100.

5. See the description of the views of Michael Schaller, Frederick C. Adams, etc., Heinrichs, "1900-1945," 99-100. For an up-to-date bibliographical essay regarding the origins of the war, consult pages 187-190 of Iriye's *The Origins* book.

6. For Hull's positions, see Jonathan Utley, "Cordell Hull and the Diplomacy of Inflexibility," in Conroy and Wray, eds., *Pearl Harbor Reexamined: Prologue to the Pacific War* (Honolulu: University of Hawaii Press, 1990), 75-84. For detailed views, see his *Going to War with Japan*.

BIBLIOGRAPHY

Documents

China. Party History Committee of the Kuomintang Central Committee. *Zhonghua Minguo Zhongyao Shiliao Chubian: Duiri Kangzhan Shiqi* [Important Historical Documents on the Republic of China during the Anti-Japanese War]. Vol. 2, 2 parts: War Operations. Taibei: Party History Committee, 1981.

———. Vol. 3, 3 parts: Wartime Diplomacy. Taibei: Party History Committee, 1981.

———. Vol. 5, 4 parts: Truth of the Chinese Communist Party's Activities. Taibei: Party History Committee, 1981.

———. Vol. 6, 4 parts: Puppet Regimes. Taibei: Party History Committee, 1981.

———. Supplementary volume, 3 parts. Taibei: Party History Committee, 1981.

China. Party History Committee of the Kuomintang Central Committee. *Geming Wenxian* [Revolutionary Documents]. Vol. 15. Taibei: Zhongyang Wenwu Gongyingshe, 1956.

———. Vols. 33-40. Taibei: Zhongyang Wenwu Gongyingshe, 1964-67.

———. Vol. 72. Taibei: Zhongyang Wenwu Gongyingshe, 1977.

China. Second Historical Archives. Nanking.

Institute of Diplomatic Studies, Taiwan. *Lugouqiao Shibian Qianhou De Zhongri Guanxi* [Sino-Japanese Relations around the Marco Polo Bridge Incident]. Vol. 4, Diplomatic Materials Series. Taibei: n.p., 1966.

———. *Kangzhan Qijian Fengsuo Yu Jinyun Shijian* [Blockade and Embargo during the Resistance War]. Vol. 6, Diplomatic Materials Series. Taibei: n.p., 1967.

Institute of Modern History, Chinese Academy of Social Sciences. *Hu Shi Ren Zhumei Dashi Qijian Wanglai Diangao* [Telegraphic Correspondences of Hu Shi during His Ambassadorship to the United States]. Vol. 3, *Zhonghua Minguo Shi Ziliao Conggao* [Collection of Materials on the Republic of China]. Peking: Zhonghua Shuju, 1978.

Institute of History, Shanghai Academy of Social Sciences. *"9.18" — "1.28" Shanghai Jun Min Kang Ru Yundong Shiliao* [Materials on the Resistance Movements by Shanghai Army and People during the Period from September 18 (1931) to January 28 (1932)]. Shanghai: Academy of Social Sciences Press, 1986.

Soviet Union. Komissiia po izdaniiu diplomaticheskinkh dokumentov. *Dokumenty Vneshnei Politiki SSSR* [Documents on Soviet Foreign Policy, 1936-38]. Vols. 18-21. Moscow: Political Literature Publishing House, 1973-77.

U.K. Foreign Office. *Documents on British Foreign Policy, 1919-1939.* 2nd Series. Vol. 11. London: Her Majesty's Stationery Office, 1970.

————. 2nd Series. Vols. 20-21. London: Her Majesty's Stationery Office, 1984.

————. 3rd Series. Vols. 8-9. London: Her Majesty's Stationery Office, 1955.

University Publications of America. *U.S. Military Intelligence Reports: China, 1911-1941.* Microfilm. Frederick, Md.: University Publications of America, 1983.

U.S. Department of State. *Foreign Relations of the United States, Diplomatic Papers,* 1930-41. Vols. 2-4. Washington, D.C.: GPO, 1945-56.

————. *Papers Relating to the Foreign Relations of the United States: Japan, 1931-1941.* 2 vols. Washington, D.C.: GPO, 1943.

————. Decimal files. National Archives. Washington, D.C.

Personal Papers and Diaries

Chen Guang-pu Papers. Columbia University. New York.

Currie, Laughlin Papers. Hoover Institution. Stanford, California.

Hornbeck, Stanley Papers. Hoover Institution. Stanford, California.

Hu Shi De Riji [Diary of Hu Shi]. Vol. 2. Peking: Chonghua Shuju, 1985.

Hu Shi Laiwang Shuxin Xuan [Selected Letters of Hu Shi]. edited by Institute of Modern History, Chinese Academy of Social Sciences. Peking: Zhonghua Shuju, 1979.

Huang Fu Papers (directory). Hoover Institution. Stanford, California.

Huang Fu Papers. Columbia University. New York.

Huang Yanpei Riji Zhailu [Selected Diaries of Huang Yan-pei]. edited by Institute of Modern History, Chinese Academy of Social Sciences. Supplement, vol. 5, *Zhonghua Minguo Shi Ziliao Cong Gao* [Collection of Materials on the Republic of China]. Peking: Zhonghua Shuju, 1979.

Johnson, Nelson Papers. Library of Congress. Washington, D.C.

Koo, Wellington Papers. Columbia University. New York.

Leahy, William Diary. Library of Congress. Washington, D.C.

McHugh, James Papers. Cornell University. Ithaca, New York.

Morgenthau, Henry Papers. FDR Presidential Library. Hyde Park, New York.

Roosevelt, Franklin D. Papers. FDR Presidential Library. Hyde Park, New York.

Soong, T.V. Papers. Hoover Institution. Stanford, California.

Wang Shijie Riji (Diary of Wang Shi-jie). ed. by Modern History Institute, Academica Sinica. Taibei: Modern History Institute, 1990.

Yarnell, Harry Papers. Library of Congress. Washington, D.C.

Zhou Fuohai Riji [Diary of Zhou Fuo-hai]. Hong Kong: Chuangken Chubanshe, 1955.

Memoirs, Articles, Pamphlets, Books, and Periodicals

Bin, Fu. *Zhongguo Kangzhan Yu Guoji Xingshi* [China's Resistance and International Situation]. Shanghai: Guangming Shudian, December 1937.

Braun, Otto. *A Comintern Agent in China.* Translated by Jeanne Moore with an introduction by Dick Wilson. Stanford: Stanford University Press, 1982.

Bulletin on China's Foreign Relations and Public Events in the Far East, 1931-35. Nanking: International Relations Club, 1931-1935.

Bullitt, Orville H., ed. *For the President, Personal and Secret: Correspondence between Franklin D. Roosevelt and William C. Bullitt.* Boston: Houghton Mifflin Co., 1972.

Cai, Ting-kai. *Cai Tingkai Zizhuan* [An Autobiography of Cai Ting-kai]. Harbin: Heilongjiang Renmin Chubanshe, 1982.

Chang, Peng-chun. "The Second Phase of China's Struggle," in *Pamphlets on China.* Vol. 3. John Regenstein Library, University of Chicago, 1939.

Chen, Bin-he. *Zhongsu Fujiao Wenti* [The Problem of Restoring Sino-Soviet Diplomatic Relations]. n.p: Liangyou Tushu Yinshua Gongci, January 1933.

Chen, Bu-lei. *Chen Bulei Huiyilu* [Memoirs of Chen Bu-lei]. Shanghai: 20th Century Chubanshe, 1949.

Chen, Cheng. *Diyu Waihui Yu Fuxing Minzu* [Resisting Foreign Humiliations and Restoring the Nation]. Chongqing: Huangpu Chubanshe, June 1940.

Chen, Du-xiu. *Cong Guoji Xingshi Guancha Zhongguo Kangzhan Qiantu* [The Future of Chinese Resistance in View of the International Situation]. Canton: Yadong Tushuguan, April 1938.

Chen, Gong-bo. *Ku Xiao Lu: Chen Gong-bo Huiyilu, 1925-1936* [Record of Bitter Smile: Memoirs of Chen Gong-bo, 1925-1936]. Edited by Wang Rui-jiong, Li E, and Zhao Ling-yang. Hong Kong: Center of Asian Studies, University of Hong Kong, 1979.

Chen, Jia-geng. *Nanqiao Huiyilu* [Memoir of a Southern Overseas Chinese]. Singapore: Nanyang Yinshua She, 1946.

Chen, Li-fu. "Canjia Kangzhan Zhunbei Gongzuo De Huiyi" [Recollections about Participating in Preparations for the Resistance War]. *Zhuanji Wenxue* [Biographical Literature] 31, no. 1 (July 1977): 45-51.

Chen, Percy. *China Called Me: My Life Inside the Chinese Revolution*. Boston: Little, Brown and Co., 1979.

Chen, Shao-xian, *Zhongri Wenti Zhi Yanjiu: Yubei Jianglai Juedou De Zhishi* [A Study of the Sino-Japanese Question: The Knowledge for the Final Struggle in the Future]. Shanghai: Commercial Press, 1935.

Chen, Tian-xi, ed. *Dai Jitao Xiansheng Wencun* [Works of Mr. Dai Ji-tao]. Taibei: Central Committee of the Kuomintang, 1959.

Chen Tong-he. *Diguozhuyi Qinlue Zhongguo Sh*i [A History of Imperialist Aggression in China]. Shanghai: Commercial Press, 1928.

Chen, Xiao-cen. "Xian Shibian Qian Guogong Liangdang Tanpan Pianduan De Huiyi" [Recalling Some Negotiations between the KMT and the CCP Prior to the Sian Incident]. *Dangshi Yanjiu Ziliao* [Study Materials on Party History]. Vol. 3. [Chongqing:] Sichuan Renmin Chubanshe, 1982.

Chen, Xiao-ling. "Diguo Zhuyi De Lilun" [Theories on Imperialism]. Taibei: Pamier Shudian, 1977.

Chen, Xiao-wei, ed. *Kangzhan Disannian* [The Third Year in Resistance]. [Hong Kong]: Tianwentai Semiweekly Review, 1939.

Chen, Xie-cheng. *Guomin Jiuguo Lun* [On People's Duty of Saving the Nation]. Shanghai: Guanghua Shuju, 1927.

Cheng, Tian-fang. *Shi De Huiyilu* [Recalling My Days as Ambassador to Germany]. Taibei: National Political University, 1967.

Cherepanov, A. I. *As Military Adviser in China*. Moscow: Progress Publishers, 1976.

Chiang Kai-shek. *Kangzhan Bisheng Shi Jiang* [Ten Speeches on the Certainty of Victory of the Resistance]. Shanghai: Shanghai Xinyun Cujinhui, 1938.

————. *Kangzhan Yu Jianguo* [Resistance and Reconstructing the Nation]. Chongqing: n.p., 1939.

Chiang Kai-shek, et al. *Minzu Fuxing Zhilu* [The Way of National Regeneration]. 1935.

China Forum. Shanghai: 1932-1934.

China Weekly Review. Shanghai: 1931-1941.

China Quarterly. Shanghai: 1935-1941.

Chinese Affairs. Nanking: 1928-1934.

Chongqing, Dongjing, Henei [Chongqing, Tokyo, and Hanoi]. Edited by Xiandai Shiliao Yanjiuhui. Hong Kong: Magnet Publishing Co., January 1939.

Chu, Yu-kun. *Dongdang Zhong De Zhongsu Guanxi* [The Shaky Sino-Soviet Relations]. Wuhan: Dagongbao, May 1938.

Cui, Shu-qin (Shu-Chin Tsui). "The Influence of the Canton-Moscow Entente Upon Sun Yat-sen's Political Philosophy." *The Chinese Social Political Science Review* (Peking) 18, no. 1 (1934): 96-145.

———. "Yazhou Menluo Zhuyi Yu Menhu Kaifang" [Asian Monroe Doctrine and the China Open Door Policy]. *Waijiao Yuebao* [Diplomatic Monthly] 5, no. 1 (July 1934): 30-33.

Dai, Ji-tao. *Tai Jitao Xiansheng Liangge Zhongyao De Jianghua* [Two Important Speeches of Mr. Dai Ji-tao]. n.p.: Huangpu Military Academy, 1927.

———. *Zhongguo Duli Yundong De Jidian* [The Foundation of China's Independence Movement]. Canton: Minzhi Shuju, 1925.

De Wang (King De). "Kangzhan Qian Wo Goujie Rikou De Zuie Huodong" [My Evil Colluding Activities with the Japanese before the Resistance War]. *Wenshi Ziliao* 63 (1979): 24-52.

Deng, Wen-yi. *Congjun Baoguo Ji* [Joining the Army and Requiting the Nation]. Taibei: Zhengzhong Shuju, 1979.

Diguo Zhuyi [Imperialism]. Edited by Pamier Shudian. Taibei: Pamier Shudian, 1977.

Ding, Yong-nian. "Guanyu Wo Dang Heping Jiejue Xian Shibian De Fangzhen" [About Our Party's Policy of Peaceful Solution of the Sian Incident]. *Dangshi Yanjiu Ziliao* 11 (1982).

Dong, Lin (William Tung). *Diguo Zhuyi Yu Zhonghua Minzu* [Imperialism and the Chinese Nation]. Shanghai: Guangming Shuju, 1930.

Dongfang Zazhi [Eastern Miscellany]. Shanghai: 1931-1941.

Dongfang Zazhi Zongmu [Index of Eastern Miscellany]. N.p., n.d.

Dou Niu. "The Changes of the American Far Eastern Policy and Our Diplomacy to the United States." *Waijiao Pinglun* [Diplomatic Review] 3, no. 6 (May 1934): 26-28.

Du, Cheng-xiang. *Guoji Yuanhua Yundong* [The International Movement for Aid to China]. Chongqing: Youth Chubanshe, 1938-1939.

Du Chong-yuan. *Yuzhong Zagan* [Thoughts in Prison]. 1936. Reprint. Hong Kong: 1975.

Du, Ruo-jun. *Ouju Yu Yuandong* [The European Situation and the Far East]. [Chongqing]: Shenghuo Shudian, December 1939.

Dui Yue Gui Yidong Zhi Renshi [An Analysis of the Guangdong and Guangxi Rebellion]. 1936. Reprint. Hong Kong: 1975.

Duli Pinglun [Independent Review]. Peking: 1932-1937.

Fan, Qi. *Zhongguo Guomin Geming Zhi Shiming* [The Mission of Chinese National Revolution]. Shanghai: Minzhi Shuju, 1928.

Fan, Zhong-yun. "Riben Duihua Xuanyan Zhihou Guoji Xingshi Yu Zhongguo" [The International Situation and China after the Japanese Declaration on China]. *Shenbao Yuekan* [Shenbao Monthly] 3, no. 5 (May 1934): 15-18.

———. *Kangzhan Yu Guoji Xingshi* [Resistance and the International Situation]. Changsha: Commercial Press, 1938.

Fang, Le-tian. *Taipingyang Dashi* [General Situation in the Pacific]. Shanghai: Commercial Press, 1934.

————. *Dongbei Guoji Guanxi* [International Relations in the Northeast]. Shanghai: Commercial Press, 1935.

Feng, Jie. *Guogong Hezuo De Weilai* [The Future of KMT-CCP Cooperation]. Shanghai: n.p., 1937.

Feng, Yu-xiang. *Fan Guolian Diaocha Baogaoshu* [Opposing the League of Nations' Report]. N.p., 1932.

————. *Feng Yuxiang Huiyilu* [Memoirs of Feng Yu-xiang or The Chiang Kai-shek I Know]. Shanghai: Wenhua Chubanshe, 1949.

————. *Zhongguo Yu Erci Dazhan* [China and the Second World War]. Tientsin: Shishi Chubanshe, 1935.

Fu, Si-nian. *Fu Sinian Quanji* [Complete Works of Fu Si-nain]. Vol. 5. Taibei: Lianjing Chuban Shiye Gongsi, 1980.

————. "The Possibility of a Japanese-Soviet Conflict." *Duli Pinglun* [Independent Review] 116 (1934).

Fu, Yu-chen. *Guogong Tuanjie Yu Zhongguo Qiantu* [The KMT-CCP Unity and the Future of China]. Hankou: Qunli Shudian, 1938.

Fuxing Yuekan [Revival Monthly]. Shanghai: Xin Zhongguo Jianshe Xuehui, 1932-1937.

Gan, Jie-hou. *Kangzhan Zhong Junshi Waijiao De Zhuanbian* [Changes in Military and Diplomatic Affairs during the Resistance War]. Shanghai: Qianjinshe, January 1938.

————. *Sue Weishenmo Haiwei Canzhan?* [Why Hasn't the Soviet Russia Joined the War Yet?]. Shanghai: Qianjinshe, July 1938.

Gao, Er-song. *Diguozhuyi Yu Zhongguo* [Imperialism and China]. N.p.: Qingnian Zhengzhi Xuanchuanhui, 1926.

Gao, Qian-ping and Gong Bin. *Lieqiang Yu Zhongguo* [The Powers and China]. Shanghai: Beixin Shuju, 1929.

Ge, Sui-cheng. *Taipingyang Wenti Zhi Jiepao* [An Anatomy of the Pacific Problem]. N.p. 1937.

Geng, Dan-ru. "A Perspective on Anglo-American-Japanese Competition in the Pacific." *Shishi Yuebao* [Current Events Monthly] 12, no. 6 (1936): 5-7.

Gong, De-bo. *Jiepao Riben De Yinmou* [Exposing Japan's Plot]. Shanghai: Taipingyang Shudian, 1929.

Guanyu Wang Jingwei Panguo [About Wang Jing-wei's Treason]. 1939. Reprint. Hong Kong: 1976.

Guoji Ruhe Yuanzhu Zhongguo [How the World Should Aid China]. Edited by Guoji Shishi Yanjiuhui. Shanghai: Yiban Shudian, November 1937.

Guolian Diaocha Baogaoshu Yu Gefang Yanlun [The League of Nations Report and Various Comments]. Shanghai: Nanking Qiushi Zazhishe, 1933.

Guolian Diaochatuan Baogaoshu Pingyi [Comments on the League of Nations Report]. N.p. 1932.

"Guolian Bali Jueyian De Piping Ji Guomin Duiyu Diaocha Weiyuanhui Yingqu De Taidu" [Criticisms on the Paris League of Nations Resolution and the Correct Attitude Citizens Should Adopt toward the League of Nations' Committee of Inquiry]. *Eastern Miscellany* 29, no. 3 (February 1932): 3-36.

Guomin Canzhenghui Jishi [Records of People's Political Council]. Edited by Meng, Guang-han, et al. 2 vols. Chongqing: Chongqing Chubanshe, 1985.

Guonan Wenxuan [Selected Articles about the National Crisis]. Edited by Jiang Bin-xin. N.p.: Junshi Xinwenshe, 1934.

Guowen Zhoubao [National News Weekly]. Tientsin: 1931-1937.

Guowen Zhoubao Zongmu [Index of National News Weekly]. Peking: Sanlian Shudian, 1957.

Han, Qing. "The Second World War and Its Impact on Russia and China." *Sue Pinglun* [Soviet Russia Review] 2-3, 2 (1932).

He, Han-wen. *Zhonge Waijiaoshi* [Sino-Soviet Diplomatic History]. Shanghai: Zhonghua Shuju, 1936.

He, Jie-cai. "Fuxing Yu Waijiao" [Restoration and Diplomacy]. *Fuxing Yuekan* [Fuxing Monthly] 1, no. 1 (1932): 123-132.

———. "Du Jiuguo Gongyue Zhi Jinxi Ganxiang" [Thoughts after Reading the Nine Power Treaty]. Fuxing Monthly 1, no. 3 (1932): 139-152.

He, Jiong-ji. *Wei Zhongguo Mou Guoji Heping* [Seeking International Peace for China]. Chongqing: Commercial Press, 1941.

He, Li. "The KMT-CCP Relations during the Resistance War." *Jindaishi Yanjiu* [Studies on Modern History] 3 (1983): 27-53.

Heping Fangong Jianguo Wenxian [Documents on Peace, Anticommunism and Reconstruction of the Nation]. 3 vols. Compiled by the Propaganda Department of Wang Jing-wei's regime. Nanking: Propaganda Department, 1941.

Heping Huiyi Zhongyao Yanlunji [Important Speeches of the Peace Conference]. Shanghai: n.p., 1931.

Hong, Jun-pei. *Guomin Zhengfu Waijiaoshi* [Diplomatic History of the National Government]. Shanghai: Huadong Shuju, 1930.

Hu, Han-min. *Hu Hanmin Xiansheng Zhenglun Xuanbian* [Selected Political Articles of Mr. Hu Han-min]. Canton: Canton Xiandaoshe, 1934.

———. *Yuandong Wenti Yu Da Yaxiya Zhuyi* [The Far Eastern Problem and Pan-Asianism]. Canton: Zhongxing Xuehui, 1935.

Hu, Han-min, et al. *Heping Xiezuo De Zhenwei* [The Truth and Falsehood in Peaceful Cooperation]. 1935. Reprint. Kong Kong: 1981.

Hu Hanmin Yanxinglu [Speeches and Actions of Hu Han-min]. Edited by Shi Xi-sheng. N.p.: Guangyi Shuju, 1929.

Hu, Huan-yong. "Studying China's Foreign Relations from a Geopolitical Perspective." *Waijiao Pinglun* [Diplomatic Review] 3, no. 7 (July 1934).

Hu, Lan-cheng. *Zuijin Yingguo Waijiao De Fenxi* [An Analysis of Recent British Diplomacy]. Changsha: Commercial Press, 1838.

————. *Zhan Nan He Yi Buyi* [To Fight Is Difficult and So Is to Make Peace]. Shanghai: Chonghua Ribao, 1940.

Hu, Qiu-yuan. *Dongbei Guoji Zibenzhan* [Struggle among Foreign Capitals in the Northeast]. N.p.: Dongbei Guomin Jiuguojun, 1932.

————. *Shifeng Yu Xuefeng* [Official Style and Scholarly Style]. Vol. 3, *Shidai Ribao Shelun* [Editorials of the Shidai Daily]. Hankou: 1938.

————. , ed. *Sujian Yu Chengtan* [Punish Treason and Corruption]. Vol. 2, *Shidai Ribao Shelun* [Editorials of the Shidai Daily]. Hankou: 1938.

Hu, Shi. "Chinese Diplomacy in the New World Situation." *Duli Pinglun* [Independent Review] 78 (November 1933).

————. "Guoji Xin Xingshi Li De Zhongguo Waijiao Fangzhen" [Chinese Diplomatic Policy in the New World Situation]. *Independent Review* 78 (November 26 1933): 1-5.

Hu, Shi-jie. "Japanese-German Alliance, Anti-Sovietism and the World War." *Soviet Russia Review* 10, no. 1 (1936):5-7.

Hu, Yu-zhi. "Wei Quanmin Kangri Benzou Huhao" [Working for National Resistance War]. *Wenshi Ziliao Xuanji* 106 (1986).

————. "Zhongsu Hubu Qinfan Tiaoyue De Huigu Yu Qianzhan" [Retrospect and Prospect of Sino-Soviet Nonaggression Pact]. *Eastern Miscellany* 34, Nos. 16-17 (September 1937):15-16.

Huang, Fu. *Ouzhan Zhi Jiaoxun Yu Zhongguo Zhi Jianglai* [Lessons of the European War and the Future of China]. Shanghai: Zhonghua Shuju, 1922.

————. *Zhanhou Zhi Shijie* [The World after the War]. Shanghai: Xin Zhongguo Jianshe Xuehui, 1935.

Huang, Shao-hong. "Changcheng Kangzhan Gaishu" [A Brief Description of the Great Wall Resistance]. *Wenshi Ziliao Xuanji* 14 (1961).

Huang Xiao-xian. *Diguozhuyi Qinlue Zhongguo Shi* [A History of Imperialist Aggression in China]. Shanghai: Shijie Shuju, 1927.

Hull, Cordell. *Memoirs of Cordell Hull.* 2 vols. New York: Macmillan Co., 1948.

Jia, Cun-de. "Kong Xiangxi Yu Rikou Goujie Huodong Pianduan" [Sketches of H.H. Kung's Colluding Activities with Japanese Bandits]. *Wenshi Ziliao Xuanji* 29 (1962): 67-78.

Jiang Feng Shujian [Jiang (Kai-shek)-Feng (Yu-xiang) Correspondences]. Shanghai: Zhongguo Wenhua Xintuo Fuwushe, November 1946.

Jiang, Gong-huai and Zhang Yue-hua. "An Analysis on the Pacific Situation." *Shenbao Yuekan* [Shenbao Monthly] 3, no. 7 (July 1934).

Jiang, Jian-ren. *Jianglai Dazhan Yu Zhongguo* [The Future World War And China]. Hangzhou: Dafengshe, November 1935.

———. *Kangzhan Zhong De Jige Genben Wenti* [Several Fundamental Questions during the Resistance War]. Hankou: Chinese Air Force Press, 1938.

———. "Weilai Zhanzheng Yu Zhongguo Qiantu" [The Coming War and China's Future]. *Kongjun* [Airforce] 141 (August 1935).

Jiang, Ting-fu. "A Recollection of Participating in the National Conference on Crisis." *Jiang Tingfu Xuanji* [Selected Works of Jiang Ting-fu]. Taibei: Qingwen Chubanshe, 1968.

———. *Jiang Tingfu Xuanji* [Selected Works of Jiang Ting-fu]. 6 vols. Taibei: Qingwen Chubanshe, 1968.

———. *Jiang Ting-fu Huiyilu* [Memoirs of Jiang Ting-Fu]. Taibei: Zhuanji Wenxue, 1979.

———. "Jiuyiba Shibian Yu Duli Pinglun" [The September 18 Incident and the Independent Review]. *Zhuanji Wenxue* [Biographical Literature] 31, no. 5 (November 1977): 103-110.

———. "On Foreign Aid." *Waijiao Yuebao* [Diplomatic Monthly] 1, no. 3 (September 1932).

Jiang Zongtong Ji [Works of President Chiang]. Compiled by Guofang Yanjiuyuan. Taibei: Lianhe Chuban Zhongxin, 1968.

Jiang, Zuo-bin. *Jiang Zuobin Huiyilu* [Memoirs of Jiang Zuo-bin]. Taibei: Zhuanji Wenxue, 1967.

Jiao, Ji-hua. "Zhang Xueliang Yu Sushi De Mimi Huiwu" [Zhang Xue-liang's Secret Talks with the Soviet Ambassador]. *Xian Shibian Qin Li Ji* [Witnesses to the Sian Incident]. Peking: Wenshi Chubanshe, 1986.

Jiaotu Kangzhan [Scorched Earth Resistance]. Nanning: Zhujiang Ribao, October 1937.

Jindaishi Yanjiu [Studies of Modern History]. Peking: 1979 to present.

Jindaishi Ziliao [Materials on Modern History]. Peking: 1954 to present.

Jindai Zhongguo Waijiao Gaiguan [An Overview of Modern Chinese Diplomacy]. Edited by *Waijiao Pinglun* [Diplomatic Review]. Nanking: Zhengzhong Shuju, 1936.

Jin, Wen-si. *Cong Bali Hehui Dao Guolian* [From the Paris Peace Conference to the League of Nations]. Taibei: Zhuanji Wenxue, 1967.

———. "Jiu Guolian Ruhe Chuli Woguo Duiri De Qisu" [How Did the Old League of Nations Deal with Our Appeals against Japan.] *Zhuanji Wenxue* 9, no. 5 (November 1966): 31-36 and 10, no. 4 (April 1967): 90-97.

Jin, Zhao-zi. *Xiandai Zhongguo Waijiao Shi* [Modern Diplomatic History of China]. Shanghai: Commercial Press, 1930.

Jin, Zhong-hua, et al. *Guoji Xingshi Yu Zhongguo* [International Situation and China]. Shanghai: Yixin Shudian, December 1937.

Jiuyiba Xuehui. *Jiuyiba Xuehui Dui Guolian Diaochatuan Baogaoshu Zhi Yijian* [9.18 Association's Opinion about the League of Nations Report]. Tientsin: n.p., October 1932.

Jiuyiba-Yierba Shanghai Junmin Kangri Yundong Shiliao [Materials on Shanghai People and Army Resistance to Japan from September 18 Incident to January 28 Incident]. edited by History Institute of Shanghai Academy of Social Sciences. Shanghai: Academy of Social Sciences Press, 1986.

Kangzhan Daodi [Resisting to the Very End]. Shanghai: Shenghuo Shudian, 1938.

Kangzhan Qian Shinian De Zhongguo [China during the Ten Years Prior to the Sino-Japanese War]. Shanghai: Commercial Press, 1939.

Kangzhan Sanrikan [Resistance Tri-Daily]. [Shanghai and Wuhan]: 1937-1938.

Kangzhan Zhong De Zhongguo Zhengzhi [Chinese Politics during the Resistance War]. [Yenan]: Shishi Wenti Yanjiuhui, 1940.

Kiang, Kan-li, ed. *Public Opinion towards the Report of the League Enquiry Commission on the Sino-Japanese Dispute.* Nanking: International Relations Committee, 1932.

Kong Ruzhi Xiansheng Jiangyan Ji [Speeches of Mr. H. H. Kung]. Edited by Liu Zhen-tong. New York: China-America Cultural Association, 1960.

Kong, Xiang-xi. "Xian Shibian Huiyilu" [Recalling the Sian Incident]. *Zhuanji Wenxue* 9, no. 6 (December 1966): 54-57, 10, no. 3 (March 1967): 83-89 and no. 6 (June 1967): 115-121.

Koo, Wellington. *Gu Weijun Huiyilu* [Memoirs of Wellington Koo]. 3 vols. Translated by Institute of Modern History, Chinese Academy of Social Sciences. Peking: Zhonghua Shuju, 1985.

Kwong, Edward. "The Powers' Part in the Sino-Japanese War." *China Quarterly* 4 (Spring 1939): 410.

Lattimore, Owen. *China Memoirs: Chiang Kai-shek and the War Against Japan.* Tokyo: University of Tokyo Press, 1990.

Li, Tsung-jen (Li Zong-ren) and Tong Te-kong. *Memoir of Li Tsung-jen.* Boulder, Colo.: Westview Press, 1979.

Liang Guang Panluan Neimu [The Inside Story of Rebellion in Two Guang Provinces]. N.p. 1936.

Liang, Qi-chao. "Big Trust in the 20th Century," *Yinbingshi Heji.* Peking: Zhonghua Shuju, 1989.

———. "On the General Situation of National Competition." *Yinbingshi Heji.* Peking: Zhonghua Shuju, 1989.

———. "On the Development of Imperialism and the Future of the World in the 20th Century." Vol. 1, *Xinhai Geming Qianshinian Jian Shilun Xuanji* [Selected Articles in the Ten Years Prior to the Republican Revolution]. Hong Kong: Sanlian Shudian, 1963.

Liang, Xi-hua, comp. *Hu Shi Micang Shuxinxuan* [Selected Secret Letters of Hu Shi]. Taibei: Yuanjing Chuban Shiye Gongsi, 1982.

Liao, Kuang-sheng. *Anti-foreignism and Modernization in China, 1860-1980*. Hong Kong: Chinese University Press, 1984.

Liao Zhongkai Ji [Works of Liao Zhong-kai]. Peking: Zhonghua Shuju, 1983.

Lin, Bo-sheng. *Duiri De Liangtiao Luxian* [Two Lines Regarding Japan]. Shanghai: Zhonghua Ribao, 1935.

———. , ed. *Wang Jingwei Xiansheng Zuijin Yanlunji*. 3rd ed. Shanghai: Zhonghua Ribaoshe, 1938.

Lin, Quan, ed. *Kangzhan Qijian Feichu Bupingdeng Tiaoyue Shiliao* [Materials on the Abolition of the Unequal Treaties during the Resistance War]. Taibei: Zhengzhong Shuju, 1983.

Lishi Dangan [Historical Archives]. Peking: 1981 to present.

Liu, Guang-yan. *Xin Zhongguo De Duiwai Zhengce* [The Foreign Policy of the New China]. Taibei: Pamier Shudian, 1953.

Liu, Feng-han. *Kanri Zhanshi Lunji* [Analysis of the War of Resistance]. Taibei: Datong Tushu Youxian Gongsi, 1987.

Liu, Jing. "Huiyi Jiuyiba Shibian Shi De Xuesheng Yundong" [Recalling Student Patriotic Movement during 9.18 Incident]. *Zhongguo Xiandaishi*. Compiled by People's University, China. 6 (1982): 79-85.

Liu Qun. *Zhongguo Zai Tongyi Zhong* [China in the Process of Unification]. 1937.

Liu, Wen-hai. *Jinshi Daguojia Zhuyi* [Big Countryism in Modern Age]. Shanghai: Commercial Press, 1925.

Liu, Xin-Xian. "Mei Zhonglifa Zhi Tantao" [A Discussion about the American Neutrality Act]. *Waijiao Pinglun* [Diplomatic Review] 5, no. 5 (1935): 44-61.

Liu, Yu-wan. *Zuijin Taipingyang Wenti* [The Recent Problems in the Pacific]. Shanghai: Pacific International Association of China, 1932.

Lou, Zhuang-xing. *Guoji Xianshi Yu Zhongguo Diwei* [The Present International Situation and China's Status]. Shanghai: Yaxiya Shuju, 1935.

Lu Yi-ying, ed. *Guoji Fan Qilue Yundong Yu Zhongguo Kangzhan Qiantu* [The International Anti-aggression Movement and the Future of China's Resistance War]. Shanghai: 1938.

Lu, Zhen-yu. *Zhongguo Waijiao Wenti* [China's Diplomatic Problems]. Peking: Cunzhi Monthly, 1929.

———. "Nanjing Tanpan Shimo" [The Beginning and the End of Nanking Negotiations]. *Qunzhong Yusi* [Mass Forum] 3 (1980).

Ma, Xing-ye. "The American Attitude during the Second World War." in Zhang Nai-qi, ed., *Dierci Shijie Dazhan Yu Zhongguo* [The Second World War and China]. Shanghai: Qingnian Xiehui Shuju, 1936.

Mao Zedong Shuxin Xuanji [Selected Letters of Mao Ze-dong]. Peking: Renmin Chubanshe, 1983.

Minguo Dangan [Republican Archives]. Nanking: 1985 to present.

Mu, Chao. *Zhongguo Cunwang De Genben Wenti* [The Fundamental Question for China's Survival]. Nanking: Zhonghua Zhengyituan Choubeichu, 1933.

Public Opinion toward the Report of the League Enquiry Commission on the Sino-Japanese Dispute. Nanking: International Relations Committee, 1932.

Qian, Duan-sheng. *Jianguo Tujing* [The Road to Reconstruction of the Nation]. Chongqing: Guomin Tushu Chubanshe, March 1942.

Qian Jia-ju, Hu Yu-zhi and Zhang Tie-sheng. *Kangzhan De Jingyan Yu Jiaoxun* [Experiences and Lessons in the Resistance War]. Chongqing: n.p., 1939.

Qian, Yi-shi. *Jinji Shiqi De Shijie Yu Zhongguo* [The World and China during the Emergency Period]. Shanghai: Shenghuo Shudian, February 1937.

Qian, Zhi-guang. "Luochuan Tanpan Qianhou" [Around the Luochuan Negotiations]. Vol. 10, *Zhonggong Dangshi Ziliao* [Materials on the History of the Chinese Communist Party]. Compiled by CCP Committee on Historical Materials. Peking: n.p., 1984.

Qin, De-chun. "Jicha Zhengwu Weiyuanhui Shiqi De Huiyi" [Recollections on the Period of Hebei-Chahar Political Council]. *Zhuanji Wenxue* 2, no. 1 (June 1963): 20-22.

———. *Qin Dechun Huiyilu* [Memoirs of Qin De-chun]. Taibei: Zhuanji Wenxue, 1967.

Qinghua Zhoukan [Qinghua Weekly]. Peking: 1931-1937.

Qing Tai. "My Views on Crisis Diplomacy." *Waijiao Yuebao* [Diplomatic Monthly] 2, no. 2 (August 1932).

Qing, Wei, ed. *Wang Jingwei Yu Riben* [Wang Jing-wei and Japan]. N.p., 1939.

" 'Qiqi Shibian' Zhi Pingjin Lunxian Jiang He Deng Midian Xuan" [Secret Telegrams between Jiang (Jie-shi) and He (Ying-qin) and others from the July 7 Incident to the Loss of Peking and Tientsin]. *Lishi Dangan* [Historical Archives] 1 (1985): 51-75.

Ren Zhuo-xuan (Ye Qing). *Kangzhan Zhong De Wenti* [Problems during the Resistance War]. Taihe, Jiangxi: Shidai Sichao She, 1938.

Renmin Zhenxian Tantao Ji [Discussion about the Popular Front]. Nanking: Tiba Shudian, January 1937.

Riben Dalu Zhengce De Zhenmianmu [The True Face of the Japanese Continental Policy]. Edited by Guonan Ziliao Bianjishe. Shanghai: Shenghuo Shudian, 1938.

Second Historical Archives. *Xian Shibian Dangan Shiliao Xuanbian* [Selected Archival Materials on the Sian Incident]. Peking: Archival Press, 1986.

Sha, Qian-li. *Qiren Zhi Yu* [Imprisonment of the Seven Gentlemen]. Shanghai: Shenghuo Shudian, 1937.

———. *Manhua Jiuguohui* [Recalling the Salvation Association]. Peking: Wenshi Ziliao Chubanshe, 1983.

Shao, Li-zi. "Chushi Sulian Huiyi" [Recalling My Days as Ambassador to the Soviet Union]. *Renwu* [People] 1 (1983): 165-173.

Shao, Yu-lin. "Su De Xieshou Yu Riben Waijiao De Dongxiang" [The Soviet-German Rapprochement and the Japanese New Diplomatic Moves]. *Waijiao Yanjiu* [Diplomatic Studies] 1, no. 5 (September 1939): 17-21.

Shen, Bo-chun. *Xian Shibian Jishi* [Records of the Sian Incident]. Hong Kong: n.p., 1980.

———. "Zhengqu Zhang Xueliang Kangri De Jingguo" [The Process of Winning Zhang Xue-liang to Join the Resistance]. *Xian Shibian Qinliji* [Witnesses to the Sian Incident]. Peking: Wenshi Chubanshe, 1986.

Shen Cheng, ed. *Zenyang Fuxing Zhongguo* [How to Regenerate China]. N.p. 1938.

Shen, Li-ren. *Zhongguo Yu Guolian De Jishu Hezuo* [Technical Cooperation between China and the League of Nations]. Shanghai: Shenghuo Shudian, 1933.

Shen, Wei-tai. *Zhong Ying Waijiao*. Changsha: Commercial Press, 1939.

Shen, Yi-yun. *Yiyun Huiyilu* [Memoirs of Yiyun]. Taibei: Zhuanji Wenxue Chubanshe, 1968.

Shen, Yun-long. "Guonan Huiyi Zhi Huigu" [Recalling the National Emergency Conference]. *Zhuanji Wenxue* 30, no. 6, (June 1977): 95-102 and 31, no. 1 (July 1977): 106-113.

Shen, Zhi-yuan. *Zhongsu Huzhu Lun* [On Chinese and Soviet Mutual Assistance]. Shanghai: Shanghai Zazhi Gongsi, April 1938.

Shenbao Yuekan [Shenbao Monthly]. Shanghai: 1932-1935.

Shi, Bu-jin. *Quanmian Kangzhan De Zhengzhi Xingshi* [The Political Situation of An All-out Resistance War]. N.p., 1938.

Shijie Dazhan Yu Zhongguo Kangzhan [The World War and Chinese Resistance]. Edited by Gonglunshe. Shanghai: Yibao Tushubu, October 1938.

Shi, Le-qu. "Jiang Jieshi Zai Kangzhan Qijian De Yige Touxiang Yinmou Huodong" [A Surrender Plot of Chiang Kai-shek during the Resistance War]. *Wenshi Ziliao Xuanji*, 1 (1960): 65-67.

Shishi Wenti Yanjiushe. *De Su Zhanhou Zhi Zhonggong* [The Chinese Communist Party after German-Soviet War]. Chongqing: n.p., 1941.

Shishi Yuebao [Current Events Monthly]. Nanking: 1929-1937.

Shi, Yi-zhi. *Taipingyang Wenti Zhi Guoqu Xianzai Yu Jianglai* [The Past, Present and Future of the Pacific Problem]. Tientsin: Zhongguo Yinwuju, 1936.

Shou, Kang, ed. *Wang Jingwei Chezhi Jingguo* [The Story of Wang Jing-wei's Being Fired]. N.p. 1939.

Snow, Helen Foster. *Notes on Chinese Student Movement, 1935-1936.* Madison, Conn.: n.p., 1961.

Song Qing-ling. *Zhongguo Buwang Lun* [China Will Not Be Destroyed]. Shanghai: Shenghuo Shudian, 1938.

Sue Pinglun [Soviet Russia Review]. Nanking: 1931-1937.

Sun, Ke (Zhe-sheng). *Zhongsu Guanxi* [Sino-Soviet Relations]. Shanghai: Zhonghua Shuju, 1946.

————. *Bashi Shulue* [A Summary at Eighty]. Taibei: n.p., 1970.

————. *Sun Ke Wenji* [Works of Sun Ke]. Taibei: Commercial Press, 1970.

Sun, Lin-sheng. "Zhong Ri Mei E Siguo Guanxi De Qiantu" [The Future of Relations among China, Japan, America and Russia]. *Eastern Miscellany*, 31, no. 3 (December 1934): 17-23.

Sun, Xiao-cun. "Huiyi Feng Yuxiang Jiangjun Dui Jiuguohui De Zhichi" [Recalling General Feng Yu-xiang's Support for the Salvation Association]. *Wenshi Ziliao Xuanji* 89 (1983): 47-50.

Sun, Xiao-lou and Zhao Ji-nian. *Lingshi Caipanquan Wenti* [The Problem of Consular Jurisdiction]. Shanghai: Commercial Press, 1937

Sun, Yat-sen. *San Min Chu I: The Three Principles of the People.* Calcutta: Chinese Ministry of Information, 1942.

Sun, Ye-fang. *Quanmin Kangzhan De Lilun Jichu* [The Theoretical Foundation for National Resistance]. Shanghai: n.p., November 1937.

Sun Zhesheng Zuijin Yanlunji [Recent Speeches of Sun Zhe-sheng]. Chongqing: Sino-Soviet Cultural Association, 1940.

Taipingyang Wenti Shijiang [Ten Lectures on the Pacific Problem]. Shanghai: Shijie Zhishishe, 1935.

Tang, Shou-chang. *Diguozhuyi Qinlue Zhongguo Tongshi* [A General History of Imperialist Aggression in China]. Shanghai: Dadong Shuju, 1929.

Tao, Ju-yin. *Guoji Manxie* [Notes on International Situations]. Vol. 1. Shanghai: Kun Lun Shudian, June 1939.

Tao, Xi-sheng. *Chaoliu Yu Diandi* [Currents and Drops]. Taibei: Zhuanji Wenxue Chubanshe, 1964.

————. *Jiti Anquan Yu Guoji Xin Junshi* [Collective Security and New International Equilibrium]. [Wuhan]: Wartime Culture Chubanshe, January 1938.

————. "Luan Liu" [Chaotic Currents]. *Zhuanji Wenxue* 2 (1964): 165-194.

————. *Ouzhou Junshi Yu Taipingyang Wenti: Dierqi Kangzhan Zhi Guoji Huanjing* [The European Equilibrium and the Pacific Problems: The International Environment during the Second Phase of Resistance War]. Yi Wen Series. Wuhan: Yi Wen Yanjiuhui, June 1938.

Taofen Wenji [Works of (Zou) Tao Fen]. Hong Kong: Sanlian Shudian, 1959.

Tian, Peng. *Zhong E Bangjiao Zhi Yanjiu* (Studies on Sino-Soviet Diplomatic Relations]. Shanghai: Zhengzhong Shuju, 1936.

Tung, William (Dong Lin). *Revolutionary China: A Personal Account, 1926-1949.* New York: St. Martin's Press, 1973.

Waijiao Pinglun [Diplomatic Review]. Nanking: 1932-1937.

Waijiao Yanjiu [Diplomatic Studies]. Chongqing: 1939-1943.

Waijiao Yuebao [Diplomatic Monthly]. Peking: 1932-1937.

Wang, Da-yi, ed. *Wangri Miyue* [The Secret Treaty between Wang (Jing-wei) and Japan]. N.p.: Lingnan Chubanshe, [1940?]

Wang, Diao-pu. "The Basic Diplomatic Policy and Attitudes that Should Be Adopted." *Waijiao Yuebao* [Diplomatic Monthly] 3, no. 4 (October 1933).

Wang, Ji-yuan. "Contradictions among the Imperialists and China's Political Diplomacy." *Shenbao Yuekan* [Shenbao Monthly] 3, no. 7 (July 1934): 25-29.

Wang, Jing-wei. *China's Problems and Their Solutions.* Shanghai: China United Press, 1934.

―――. *Guomin Huiyi Guoji Wenti Caoan* [The Draft Resolution of the National Congress]. Peking: Guoji Wenti Yanjiuhui, 1925.

―――. *Ruhe Jiuguo Cunwang* [How to Achieve National Salvation and Survival]. Edited by Lin Bo-sheng. 3rd edition. Hong Kong: South China Daily, 1938.

―――. "Wu Guo Waijiao Fangzhen" [Our Diplomatic Policy]. *Eastern Miscellany* 35, no. 21 (October 1938): 67-70.

―――. *Zeng Zhongming Xiansheng Xingzhuang* [Deeds of Mr. Zeng Zhong-ming]. Hong Kong: South China Daily, 1939.

Wang, Jing-wei, et al. *Bali Hehui Hou Zhi Shijie Yu Zhongguo* [The World and China after the Paris Peace Conference]. Shanghai: Minzhi Shuju, 1927.

Wang Jingwei Wencun [Works of Wang Jing-wei]. Shanghai: Qizhi Shuju, 1935.

Wang Jingwei Xiansheng Heping Yundong Yanlunji [Mr. Wang Ching-wei's Speeches about the Peace Movement]. Edited by Canton Zhongshan Ribao. Canton: Zhongshan Ribao, 1940.

Wang, Ming. *Zhonggong Banshiji Yu Pantu Mao Zedong* [Half a Century of the CCP and Traitor Mao Ze-dong]. Hong Kong: Wanhai Yuyan Chubanshe, 1980.

Wang Ming Xuanji [Selected Works of Wang Ming]. Tokyo: Jigu Shuyuan, 1970.

Wang, Xing-hun. "My Observations of the Second World War." *Duli Pinglun* [Independent Review] 187 (1936):7-14.

Wang, Ya-nan. *Xiandai Waijiao Yu Guoji Guanxi* [Modern Diplomacy and International Relations]. Shanghai: Zhonghua Shuju, 1933.

Wang, Zao-shi. *Guoji Lianmeng Yu Zhongri Wenti* [The League of Nations and the Sino-Japanese Problem]. Shanghai: Xinyue Shudian, 1932.

Wang, Zhong-shu, ed. *Zhanggufeng Shijian Niaokan* [A Birdseye View of the Zhanggufeng Incident]. Changsha: Commercial Press, July 1938.

Wei, Hong-yun, ed. *Zhongguo Xiandaishi Ziliao Xuanbian* [Selected Materials on Modern Chinese History]. Harbin: Heilongjiang Chubanshe, 1981.

Weng, Wen-hao. "Yijiusanqi Nian Fangwen Ying De He Sulian De Huiyi" [Recollections on Visits to England, Germany and the Soviet Union in 1937]. *Wenshi Ziliao Xuanji* 1 (1960): 57-64.

Wenshi Ziliao Xuanji [Selected Historical Materials]. Edited by Wenshi Ziliao Yanjiu Weiyuanhui. Peking: Zhonghua Shuju, 1960 to present.

Wu, Ke-jian and Pan Zi-nian. *Sulian Zhi Chengbai Yu Zhongguo Zhi Kangzhan* [The Soviet Success or Failure and China's Resistance]. N.p.: Chuangzao Wencuishe, September 1941.

Wu, Qian-yao. "The Crisis of World War and Redivision of the World." *Shenbao Yuekan* [Shenbao Monthly] 3, no. 7 (July 1934): 15-18.

Wu, Tie-cheng. *Wu Tiecheng Xiansheng Huiyilu* [Memoirs of Mr. Wu Tie-cheng]. N.p. 1957.

Wu, Zhi-hui. *Dui Wang Jingwei Ju Yigeli De Jinyijie* [Further Explanation of Wang Jing-wei's "Take One Example"]. Guilin: Zhanwang Shudian, 1939.

"Xian Shibian Qianhou Wang Jingwei Yu Chen Bijun Deng Laiwang Dianhan" [Correspondences between Wang Jing-wei and Chen Bijun before and after the Sian Incident]. Edited by Cai De-jin. In *Jindaishi Ziliao* [Materials on Modern History] Vol. 60. Peking: Academy of Social Sciences Press, 1986.

Xian Shibian Ziliao Xuanji [Selected Materials on the Sian Incident]. Compiled by History Dept., Northeastern University, et al. N.p. 1979.

Xian Zongtong Jianggong Sixiang Yanlun Zongji [A Complete Collection of Former President Jiang's Thoughts and Speeches]. 40 vols. Edited by Qin Xiao-yi. Taibei: The Party History Committee of the Kuomintang, 1984.

Xie, Yi-zheng. "Su De Xieshou Yu Yuandong Waijiao" [The Soviet-German Joining of Hands and Far Eastern Diplomacy]. *Waijiao Yanjiu* [Diplomatic Studies] 1, no. 5 (September 1939): 13-16.

Xin Ren. "Lidun Baogaoshu Fabiao Hou Zhi Guoji Yulun" [The World Public Opinion after the Publication of the Lytton Report]. *Qinghua Zhoukan* [Qinghua Weekly] 38, no. 5 (October 1932): 5-11.

Xue, Mo-cheng and Zheng Quan-bei, eds. *Fujian Shibian Ziliao Xuanbian* [Selected Materials on the Fujian Incident]. Nanchang: Jiangxi Chubanshe, 1984.

Yan, Hui-qing. *Yan Huiqing Zizhuan* [Autobiography of Yan Hui-qing]. Taibei: Zhuanji Wenxue Chubanshe, 1973.

Yang, You-jiong. *Jinshi Guoji Wenti Yu Zhongguo* [Recent International Problems and China]. Shanghai: Taidong Tushuju, 1928.

Yao Ping. "The Conflicts among the Powers in the Far East and Our Diplomatic Principle." *Guofang Luntan* [National Defense Forum] 3, no. 11 (April 1935).

Ye Yu. "An Observation of China's Diplomatic Way out from the Perspective of World Realistic Situation." *Waijiao Yuebao* [Diplomatic Monthly] 3, no. 6 (December 1932).

Yierjiu Yundong Ziliao [Materials on the December 9 Movement]. Peking: Renmin Chubanshe, 1981.

Yierjiu Yundong [The December 9 Movement]. Vols. 1-2, *Zhongguo Xiandaishi Ziliao Cong Kan* [Materials on Contemporary Chinese History]. Peking: Renmin Chubanshe, 1954.

Yijiusanliu Nian De Guoji Zhengzhi Jingji Gaikuang [The International Political and Economic Situation in 1936]. Edited by Da Xia University. Changsha: Commercial Press, 1938.

Ying, De-tian. *Zhang Xueliang Yu Xian Shibian* [Zhang Xue-liang and the Sian Incident]. Hong Kong: n.p., 1981.

Yuan, Dao-feng. "Jinri Zhongguo Ying Qu Zhi Waijiao Fangzhen Yu Taidu" [The Diplomatic Policy and Attitude China Should Adopt Today]. *Waijiao Pinglun* [Diplomatic Review] 3, no. 7 (July 1934): 39-44.

————. "Ping Oumei Xuezhe Guanyu Weilai Shijie Dazhan De Yuyan" [A Comment on the Predictions of the Future War by European and American Scholars]. *Eastern Miscellany* 32, no. 1 (1935).

————. *Zhanhou Geguo Waijiao Zhengce* [Postwar Foreign Policies of Various Countries]. Edited by Wang Yun-wu. Wanyou Wenku Series. Shanghai: Commercial Press, 1933.

Zeng, Xu-bai. *Dawanbao Pinglunji* [A Collection of Editorials of the Great Evening Daily]. Shanghai: Sishe Chubanbu, 1933.

Zenyang Zhengqu Zuihou Shengli [How to Win the Final Victory]. Shanghai: n.p., 1937.

Zhang, Dao-xing. *Meiguo Zhongli Yu Weilai Zhanzheng* [American Neutrality and the Future War]. Chongqing: Commercial Press, May 1939.

Zhang, Feng-qi. "Riben Xuanyan Yu Yuandong Wenti" [The Japanese Declaration and the Far Eastern Question], *Waijiao Pinglun* [Diplomatic Review] 3, no. 6 (May 1 1934): 56-58.

Zhang, Nai-qi. *Dierci Shijie Dazhan Yu Zhongguo* [The Second World War and China]. Shanghai: Qingnian Xiehui Shuju, 1936.

————. *Kangri Bisheng Lun* [On the Certainty of the Resistance War]. Hankou: n.p., 1937.

————. *Minzhong Jichu Lun* [On Masses as Basis]. Canton: Shanghai Zazhi Gongsi, 1937.

————. *Minzu Chulu Wenti Luncong* [On the Salvation of the Nation]. N.p.: Qingnian Wenhua Xiehui, 1937.

————. *Zhang Naiqi Wenxuan* [Selected Works of Zhang Nai-qi]. Shanghai: Shenghuo Shudian, 1934.

————. *Zhongri Wenti Jianghua* [Speeches on the Sino-Japanese Problem]. Shanghai: n.p., September 1935.

Zhang, Nai-wen. *1936*. Shanghai: Yuehua Tushushe, 1935.

Zhang, Qun. "Ren Waijiao Buzhang De Huiyi" [Recalling My Days as Foreign Minister]. *Zhuanji Wenxue* 31, no. 6 (December 1977): 50-56 and 32, no. 1 (January 1978): 51-58.

————. *Wo Yu Riben Qishinian* [Japan and I in the Past Seventy Years]. Taibei: Institute of Sino-Japanese Relations, 1980.

Zhang, Shi-zhang, ed. *Jiluan Wencun* [Collected Works of (Zhang) Ji-luan]. Jindai Zhongguo Shiliao Congkan Xubian, vol. 17, edited by Shen Yun-long. Taibei: Wenhai Chubanshe, 1975.

Zhang, Xue-liang, et al. *Kangri Jiuwang Yanlunji* [Speeches about Resisting Japan and Saving the Nation]. Xian: n.p., December 1936.

Zhang, Yi-ding. *Wo Guo Guoji Guanxi Yu Kangzhan Qiantu* [Our Foreign Relations and the Future of Resistance]. Yiwen Series. Wuhan: Yiwen Yanjiuhui, June 1938.

Zhang, Yun-fu. *Zhongsu Wenti* [The Sino-Soviet Problem]. Shanghai: Commercial Press, 1937.

Zhang, Zhong-fu. "Lun Zhongguo Zhi Waijiao Zhengce" [On China's Foreign Policy]. *Waijiao Yuebao* [Diplomatic Monthly] 1, no. 5 (November 1932): 1-6.

————. *Meiguo Zhanqian de Yuandong Waijiao* [The Prewar Far Eastern Diplomacy of the United States]. Chongqing: Duli Chubanshe, 1944.

————. *Mi Wang Ji* [Memoir of a Lost Person]. Hong Kong: n.p., 1968

————. "Sino-Soviet Restoration of Relations and the Future of China's Diplomacy." *Waijiao Yuebao* [Diplomatic Monthly] 2, no. 1 (August 1932).

————. *Zhongguo Guoji Guanxi* [China's International Relations]. Shanghai: Shijie Shuju, 1933.

Zhao, Rui. "Yan Xishan Tongdi Panguo Zuixing Jiyao" [Records of Yan Xi-shan's Colluding with the Enemy and Betraying the Nation]. *Wenshi Ziliao Xuanji*, 29 (1962):158-276.

Zheng, Gong-bi. *Xuyue Yu Feiyue* [Revision and Abolition of the Treaties]. Shanghai: Lizhi Shuju, 1929.

Zhongguo Jindai Duiwai Guanxishi Ziliao Xuanji [Selected Materials on Modern Foreign Relations of China]. Vol. 2. Compiled by History Department, Fudan University. Shanghai: Shanghai Renmin Chubanshe, 1977.

Zhongguo Kangzhan Yu Sulian [Chinese Resistance and the Soviet Union]. Vol. 1. Edited by Wei Ling. Wuhan: Dazhong Chubanshe, 1938.

Zhongguo Waijiao Nianjian [Yearbook of Chinese Diplomacy, 1933-1935]. Edited by Xue Dai-qiang and Zhang Jin. Nanking: Zhengzhong Shuju, 1934-1936.

Zhonghua Minguo Guonan Jiujihui. *Guolian Diaocha Baogao Jiqi Piping* [The League of Nations Report and Its Criticisms]. Nanking: n.p., 1934.

Zhonghua Minguoshi Jiyao [Records of the Republic of China]. 1928-1937. 8 vols. Taibei: Zhonghua Minguo Shiliao Yanjiu Zhongxin, 1978-1985.

Zhou, En-lai, et al. *Kangzhan De Xinxingshi Yu Xincelue* [New Situations and New Strategies during the Resistance War]. Edited by Zhang Yi-min. Wuhan: n.p., February 1938.

Zhou Enlai Nianpu [A Chronological History of Zhou En-lai]. edited by Chongyang Wenxian Janjiushi of the Chinese Communist Party. Peking: Renmin Chubanshe and Chongyang Wenxian Chubanshe, 1989.

Zhou Enlai Xuanji [Selected Works of Zhou En-lai]. Peking: Renmin Chubanshe, 1980.

Zhou Fuohai Xiansheng Wenji [Works of Mr. Zhou Fuo-hai]. Nanking: n.p., 1941.

Zhou, Geng-sheng. *Bupingdeng Tiaoyue Shi Jiang* [Ten Speeches on Unequal Treaties]. Shanghai: Taipingyang Shudian, 1928.

————. *Geming Waijiao Lun* [On Revolutionary Diplomacy]. Shanghai: Taipingyang Shudian, 1928.

————. *Jiefang Yundong Zhong Zhi Duiwai Wenti* [The Foreign Affairs in the Liberation Movement]. Shanghai: Taipingyang Shudian, 1927.

————. *Zhanshi Waijiao Wenti* [Wartime Diplomatic Problems]. Chongqing: Political Dept. of National Military Commission, September 1939.

————. *Zhongsu Guanxi Yu Zhongdong Tielu* [Sino-Soviet Relations and the Chinese Eastern Railway]. Shanghai: Commercial Press, 1933.

Zhou, Kai-qing. *Xianjieduan De Zhongri Wenti* [The Sino-Japanese Problem at the Present Time]. Nanking: Zhongyang Pinglunshe, 1936.

Zhou, Zi-ya. *Zhongguo Waijiao Zhilu* [The Way for China's Diplomacy]. [Chongqing]: Guomin Tushu Chubanshe, 1943.

Zhu, Zi-shuang. *Zhongguo Guomindang Waijiao Zhengce* [The Foreign Policy of the Kuomintang of China]. Chongqing: Guomin Tushu Chubanshe, 1942.

Zhuanji Wenxue [Biographical Literature]. Taibei: 1962 to present.

Zou, Lu. *Huigulu* [Memoirs]. Nanking: Duli Chubanshe, 1946.

Zou, Tao-fen. *Ji Bian* [Rapid Changes]. Wuhan: n.p., September 1938.

————. *Kangzhan Yilai* [Since Resistance]. Hong Kong: n.p., July 1941.

————. *Taofen Shishi Lunwenji* [Tao-fen's Articles on Current Affairs]. Shanghai: Zhongliu Shudian, 1938.

———— *Zongping Yiyu* [Travels Abroad]. Hong Kong: Shenghuo Shudian, 1941.

Zuo, Zhou. "Zhongdonglu Maimai De Tanpan" [Negotiations about the Sale of the Chinese Eastern Railway]. *Eastern Miscellany* 30, no. 15 (August 1 1933): 4-5.

Secondary Sources

Adams, Frederick C. *Economic Diplomacy: The Export-Import Bank and American Foreign Policy, 1934-1939.* Columbia, Mo.: University of Missouri Press, 1976.

Bauer, Boyd H. "General Claire Lee Chennault and China, 1937-1958." Ph.D. dissertation, American University, 1973.

Beloff, Max. *The Foreign Policy of Soviet Russia, 1929-1941.* 2 vols. London: Oxford University Press, 1947 and 1949.

Bernal, Martin. Chinese Socialism to 1907. Ithaca: Cornell University Press, 1976.

Boorman, Howard L., ed. *Biographical Dictionary of Republican China.* 4 vols. New York: Columbia University Press, 1967-1971.

Borg, Dorothy. *American Policy and the Chinese Revolution, 1925-1928.* New York: Macmillan Co., 1947.

————. *The United States and the Far Eastern Crisis of 1933-1938: From the Manchurian Incident through the Initial Stage of the Undeclared War.* Cambridge: Harvard University Press, 1964.

Borg, Dorothy, and Shumpei Okamoto, eds. *Pearl Harbor as History: Japanese-American Relations, 1931-1941.* New York: Columbia University Press, 1973.

Botjer, George F. *A Short History of Nationalist China, 1919-1949.* New York: Putnam, 1979.

Boyle, John Hunter. *China and Japan at War, 1937-1945: The Politics of Collaboration.* Stanford: Stanford University Press, 1972.

Bunker, Gerald. *The Peace Conspiracy: Wang Ching-wei and the China War, 1937-1945.* Cambridge: Harvard University Press, 1972.

Buss, Claude A. *War and Diplomacy in Eastern Asia.* New York: Macmillan Co., 1941.

Cai, De-jin. "Wang Jingwei Jituan Panguo Toudi De Qianqian Houhou" [The Story of Betraying the Nation and Surrendering to the Enemy by the Wang Jing-wei Clique]. *Jindaishi Yanjiu* [Studies on Modern History] 2 (1983): 181-203.

Cao, Ju-ren. *Caifang Waiji* [Other Records of a Reporter]. Hong Kong: Chuangken Chubanshe, 1955.

Cao, Xi-zhen. *Zhongsu Waijiao Shi* [Sino-Soviet Diplomatic History]. Peking: Shijie Zhishi Chubanshe, 1951.

Chan, F. Gilbert, and Thomas H. Etzold, eds. *China in the 1920s: Nationalism and Revolution.* New York: New Viewpoints, 1976.

Chan, F. Gilbert, ed. *China at Crossroads: Nationalists and Communists, 1927-1949.* Boulder, Colo.: Westview Press, 1980.

Chan, K. C. "The Abrogation of British Extraterritoriality in China, 1942-43." *Modern Asian Studies* 11, no. 2 (1977):257-291.

Chang, Hsu-hsin. "Kuomintang Foreign Policy, 1925-1928." Ph.D. dissertation, University of Wisconsin, 1967.

Chang, Kai, and Cai De-jin. "On Hebei-Chahar Political Council," *Jindaishi Yanjiu"* [Studies on Modern History] 4 (1985):140-161.

Chang, Kuo-tao. *The Rise of the Chinese Communist Party, 1928-1938.* Lawrence, Kans.: University Press of Kansas, 1971.

Chang, Maria Hsia. "The Blue Shirt Society: Fascism and Developmental Nationalism." Ph.D. dissertation, University of California, Berkeley, 1983.

Chen, Guo-huang. *Lingshi Caipanquan Zai Zhongguo Zhi Xingcheng Yu Feichu* [The Formation and Abolition of the Consular Jurisdiction in China]. Taibei: Jiaxin Cement Company Cultural Foundation, 1971.

Chen, Hong-min. "Hu Hanmin Nianbiao" [A Chronology of Hu Han-min]. *Minguo Dangan* [Republican Archives] 3 (February 1986): 119-133 and 4 (May 1986): 112-120.

Ch'en, Jerome. "The Communist Movement, 1927-1937." Chap. 4 in Fairbank, John K., and Albert Feuerwerker, eds. *Cambridge History of China: Republican China, 1912-1949.* Vol. 13. Cambridge: Cambridge University Press, 1986.

Chen, Ji-ying. *Baoren Zhang Jiluan* [Zhang Ji-luan, the Journalist]. Taibei: Wenyou Chubanshe, 1957.

Chen, Ming-zhong. "Jiuyiba Shibian Baofa Zhi Husong Tingzhan Xueding Qianzi Qijian De Jiang Ri Guanxi" [The Jiang-Japan Relationship from the Outbreak of the Manchurian Incident to the Conclusion of the Shanghai Truce]. Vol 2, *Minguo Dangan* [Republican Archives]. 1988.

Chen, Po-da. *Zhongguo Si Da Jiazu* [Four Big Clans in China]. Shanghai: Xinhua Shudian, 1949.

Chen, Shu-xiang. *Kangzhan Qijian Meiguo Duihua Zhengce Zhi Yanjiu* [A Study of American Policy toward China during the Resistance War]. Taibei: n.p., 1974.

Chen, Xing-tang. "Jiuyiba Qianhou De Feng Jiang Jun" [General Feng around the September 18 Incident]. *Lishi Dangan* [Historical Archives] 3 (1982): 110-115.

Chen, Zhi-mai. *Jiang Tingfu De Zhishi Yu Shengping* [Jiang Ting-fu's Aspirations and His Life]. Taibei: Zhuanji Wenxue Chubanshe, 1967.

Cheng, Tai-sheng. *Hu Hanmin de Zhengzhi Sixiang* [Hu Hanmin's Political Thoughts]. Taibei: Liming Wenhua Shiye Gongsi, 1981.

Ch'eng, T'ien-fang. *A History of Sino-Russian Relations.* Washington, D.C.: Public Affairs Press, 1957.

Ch'i, Hsi-sheng. *Nationalist China at War: Military Defeats and Political Collapse, 1937-45.* Ann Arbor: University of Michigan Press, 1982.

Chiang, Kai-shek. *Soviet Russia in China: A Summing-Up at Seventy.* New York: Farrar, Straus, and Cudahy, 1957.

Chien, Tai. *China and the Nine Power Conference at Brussels in 1937*. New York: St. John's University Press, 1964.

Chu, Pao-chin, V. K. *Wellington Koo: A Case Study of China's Diplomat and Diplomacy of Nationalism, 1912-1966*. Hong Kong: Chinese University Press, 1981.

Clifford, Nicholas R. *Retreat from China: British Policy in the Far East, 1937-1941*. Seattle: University of Washington Press, 1967.

Coble, Parks. *Facing Japan: Chinese Politics and Japanese Imperialism, 1931-1937*. Cambridge: Harvard East Asian Council, 1991.

Cohen, Warren I. *America's Response to China: An Interpretative History of Sino-American Relations*. 2nd ed. New York: John Wiley, 1980.

————. *The Chinese Connection*. New York: Columbia University Press, 1978.

————. "The Development of Chinese Communist Attitudes towards the United States, 1934-45." *Orbis* 11 (Spring 1967): 219-237.

Cong *"Jiuyiba" Dao "Qiqi" Guomindang De Touxiang Zhengce Yu Renmin De Kangzhan Yundong* [The KMT's Policy of Surrender and People's Resistance Movement from the Manchurian Incident to the Marco Polo Bridge Incident]. Shanghai: Renmin Chubanshe, 1959.

Coox, Alvin D. *The Anatomy of a Small War: The Soviet-Japanese Struggle for Changkufeng/Khasan, 1938*. London: Greenwood Press, 1977.

————. *Nomonhan: Japan against Russia, 1939*. 2 vols. Stanford: Stanford University Press, 1985.

Coox, Alvin D., and Hilary Conroy, eds. *China and Japan: Search for Balance Since World War I*. Santa Barbara, Calif.: ABC-Clio, 1978.

Cornelius, Wanda, and Thayne Short. *Ding Hao: America's Air War in China, 1937-1945*. Gretna, La.: Pelican Publishing Company, 1980.

Crowley, James B. *Japan's Quest for Autonomy: National Security and Foreign Policy, 1930-1938*. Princeton: Princeton University Press, 1966.

Crowley, James B., ed. *Modern East Asia: Essays in Interpretation*. New York: Harcourt, Brace & World, 1970.

Dallek, Robert. *Franklin D. Roosevelt and American Foreign Policy, 1932-1945*. New York: Oxford University Press, 1979.

Dallek, Robert, ed. *The Roosevelt Diplomacy and World War II*. American Problems Studies. Huntington, N.Y.: Robert E. Krieger Publishing Co., 1978.

Dallin, David J. *Soviet Russia's Foreign Policy, 1939-1942*. Translated by Leon Dennen. New Haven: Yale University Press, 1942.

Doenecke, Justus D., comp. *The Diplomacy of Frustration: The Manchurian Crisis of 1931-1933 as Revealed in the Papers of Stanley K. Hornbeck*. Stanford: Hoover Institution Press, 1981.

Dorn, Frank. *The Sino-Japanese War, 1937-1941: From the Marco Polo Bridge to Pearl Harbor*. New York: Macmillan Co., 1974.

Han, Suyin. *Birdless Summer.* New York: G. P. Putnam's Sons, 1968.

He Jun. "Lun Yijiuerjiu-Yijiusanjiu Nian de Zhongsu Guanxi" [On Sino-Soviet Relations, 1929-1939]. Master's thesis, Nanking University, 1986.

Herzog, James H. *Closing the Open Door: American-Japanese Diplomatic Negotiations, 1936-1941.* Annapolis, Md.: Naval Institute Press, 1973.

Hu Sheng. *Imperialism and Chinese Politics.* Peking: Foreign Languages Press, 1955.

Huang, Mei-zhen. *Wang Jingwei Guomin Zhengfu Chengli: Wangwei Zhengquan Ziliao Xuanbian* [The Establishment of Wang Jing-wei's Regime: Selected Materials on Wang's Puppet Regime]. Shanghai: Renmin Chubanshe, 1985.

Huang, Zheng-ming, et al. *Zhongguo Waijiaoshi Lunji* [Collection of Articles on Chinese Diplomatic History]. Taibei: Zhonghua Wenhua Shiye Weiyuanhui, 1957.

Hunt, Michael H. *Frontier Defense and the Open Door.* New Haven: Yale University Press, 1973.

———. *The Making of a Special Relationship: China and the United States to 1914.* New York: Columbia University Press, 1984.

Hussey, Harry. *My Pleasures and Palaces: An Informal Memoir of Forty Years in Modern China.* Garden City, N.Y.: Doubleday & Co., 1968.

Iriye, Akira. *Across the Pacific: An Inner History of American-Eastern Asian Relations.* New York: Harcourt Brace Jovanovich, 1967.

———. *After Imperialism.* Cambridge: Harvard University Press, 1965.

———. "Imperialism in East Asia." James B. Crowley, ed. *Modern East Asia: Essays in Interpretation.* New York: Harcourt, Brace & World, 1970.

———. "Japanese Aggression and China's International Position 1931-1949." In John K. Fairbank and Albert Feuerwerker, eds. *Cambridge History of China.* Vol. 13. Cambridge: Cambridge University Press, 1986.

———. *The Origins of the Second World War in Asia and the Pacific.* London: Longman, 1987.

———, ed. *The Chinese and the Japanese: Essays in Political and Cultural Interactions.* Princeton: Princeton University Press, 1980.

Israel, John. *Student Nationalism in China, 1927-1937.* Stanford: Stanford University Press, 1966.

Jiang, Yong-jing. *Hu Hanmin Xiansheng Nianpu* [A Chronological History of Mr. Hu Han-min]. Taibei: Kuomintang Party History Committee, 1978.

Jin, Chong-ji. *Zhou En-lai Zhuan* [A Biography of Zhou En-lai]. Peking: Renmin Chubanshe, 1989.

Jin, Xong-bai. *Wang Zhengquan De Kanchang Yu Shouchang* [The Beginning and End of Wang's Regime]. 5 vols. Hong Kong: Chunqiu Zazhishe, 1959-1964.

Jonas, Manfred. *Isolationism in America, 1935-1941.* Ithaca: Cornell University Press, 1966.

Jordan, Donald A. "China's Vulnerability to Japanese Imperialism: The Anti-Japanese Boycott of 1931-1932." In F. Gilbert Chan, ed. *China at the Crossroad: Nationalists and Communists, 1927-1949*. Boulder, Colo.: Westview Press, 1980.

————. *The Chinese Boycotts and Japanese Bombs*. Ann Arbor: University of Michigan Press, 1991.

————. *The Northern Expedition: China's National Revolution of 1926-1928*. Honolulu: University Press of Hawaii, 1976.

————. "Place of Chinese Disunity in Japanese Army Strategy during 1931." *China Quarterly* 109 (March 1987):42-63.

Kalyagin, Aleksandr Ya. *Along Alien Roads*. Translated with an Introduction by Steven I. Levine. New York: East Asian Institute, Columbia University, 1983.

Kangzhan Qian Shinian Zhi Zhongguo [China in the Ten Years before the War]. Edited by Zhongguo Wenhua Jianshe Xiehui. Hong Kong: Longmen Shudian, 1965.

Kapp, Robert A. *Szechwan and the Chinese Republic: Provincial Militarism and Central Power, 1911-1938*. New Haven: Yale University Press, 1970.

Kataoka, Tetsuya. *Resistance and Revolution in China: Communists and the Second United Front*. Berkeley: University of California Press, 1974.

Keiji Furuya. *Jiang Zongtong Milu* [Secretary Records of President Chiang]. 15 vols. Translated by Central Daily. Taibei: Central Daily, 1974-1978.

Kirby, William C. *Germany and Republican China*. Stanford: Stanford University Press, 1984.

Kitts, Charles R. "An Inside View of the Kuomintang: Ch'en Li-fu, 1926-1949." Ph.D. dissertation, Johns Hopkins University, 1978.

Lary, Diana. *Region and Nation: The Kwangsi Clique in Chinese Politics, 1925-1937*. London: Cambridge University Press, 1975.

Lee, Bradford A. *Britain and the Sino-Japanese War, 1937-1939*. Stanford: Stanford University Press, 1973.

Lee, Chong-sik. *Revolutionary Struggle in Manchuria: Chinese Communism and Soviet Interest, 1922-1945*. Berkeley: University of California Press, 1983.

Lensen, George Alexander. *The Damned Inheritance: The Soviet Union and the Manchurian Crisis, 1924-1935*. Tallahassee, Fla.: Diplomatic Press, 1974.

Levi, Werner. *Modern China's Foreign Policy*. Minneapolis: University of Minnesota Press, 1953.

Li, Jin-zhou. *Xian Shibian Qinliji* [Personal Experiences at the Sian Incident]. Taibei: Zhuanji Wenxue, 1972.

Li, Yun-han. *Jiuyiba Shibian Shiliao* [Materials on the September 18 Incident]. Taibei: Zhengzhong Shuju, 1977.

————. *Kangzhan Qian Huabei Zhengju Shiliao* [Materials Regarding the North China Political Situation before the Resistance War]. Taibei: Zhengzhong Shuju, 1982.

————. *Xian Shibian Shimo Zhi Yanjiu* [The Study of the Sian Incident]. Taibei: Jindai Zhongguo Press, 1982.

————. *Zhongguo Xiandai Shilun He Shiliao* [Articles and Materials on Modern Chinese History]. Taibei: Commercial Press, 1979.

Li, Zhen-hua, comp. *Jindai Zhongguo Guoneiwai Dashiji* [Chronological Events inside and outside Modern China, 1932-1941]. Vol. 67, Shen Yun-long, ed., Jindai Zhongguo Shiliao Series. Taibei: Wen Hai Press, 1979.

Liang, Han-bing, and Wei Hong-yun, eds. *Zhongguo Xiandaishi Dashiji* [Chronological Events in Modern Chinese History]. Harbin: Heilongjiang Renmin Chubanshe, 1984.

Liang, Jing-dun. *Jiuyiba Shishu* [A History of the September 18 Incident]. Taibei: Shijie Shuju, 1968.

Liang, Sheng-jun. *Jiang Li Douzheng Neimu* [The Inside Story of Chiang (Kai-shek)-Li (Zong-ren) Struggle]. Hong Kong: Yalian Chubanshe, 1954.

Liao, Kuang-sheng. *Anti-foreignism and Modernization in China, 1860-1980*. New York: St. Martin Press, 1984.

Liao Tie-jun. *Tanggu Xieding Hou De Huabei Jushi* [The North China Situation after the Tanggu Truce]. Taibei: n.p., 1977.

Lilley, Charles R. "Tsiang T'ing-fu: Between Two Worlds, 1895-1935." Ph.D. dissertation, University of Maryland, 1979.

Lin, Han-sheng. "A New Look at Chinese Nationalist 'Appeasers.'" in Coox, Alvin D., and Hilary Conroy, eds. *China and Japan: Search for Balance Since World War I*. Santa Barbara, Calif.: ABC-Clio, 1978.

————. "Wang Ching-wei and the Japanese Peace Efforts." Ph.D. dissertation, University of Pennsylvania, 1967.

Little, Richard, and Steve Smith, eds. *Belief Systems and International Relations*. Oxford: Basil Blackwell, 1990.

Liu, F. F. *A Military History of Modern China, 1924-1949*. Princeton: Princeton University Press, 1956.

Liu, Feng-han. *Kangri Zhanshi Lunji* [Papers on the History of the Resistance War]. Taibei: Dadong Tushuju, 1987.

Louis, Wm. Roger. *British Strategy in the Far East, 1919-1939*. Oxford: Clarendon Press, 1971.

Lowe, Peter. *Great Britain and the Origins of the Pacific War: A Study of British Policy in East Asia 1937-1941*. Oxford: Clarendon Press, 1977.

Luo, Rui-qing, Lu Zheng-cao, and Wang Bin-nan. *Xian Shibian He Zhou Enlai Tongzhi* [The Sian Incident and Comrade Zhou En-lai]. Peking: Renmin Chubanshe, 1978.

Luo, Xiang-lin. *Fu Bingchang Yu Xiandai Zhongguo* [Fu Bing-chang and Modern China]. Hong Long: Zhongguo Xueshe, 1973.

Luo, Yun-shu, and Wang Jin-xia. "Shilun Zhongguo Gongchandang Yu Liangguang Shibian" [On the Chinese Communist Party and the Southwest Revolt]. *Guangxi Shehui Kexue* 4 (1988).

Ma, Zhong-lian. *Jiuyiba Dao Qiqi* [From September 18 Incident to July 7 Incident]. Peking: Zhongguo Qingnian Chubanshe, 1985.

Mancall, Mark. *China at the Center: 300 Years of Foreign Policy.* New York: Free Press, 1984.

Marsh, Susan H. "Chou Fo-hai: The Making of a Collaborator." In Akira Iriye, ed. *The Chinese and the Japanese: Essays in Political and Cultural Interactions.* Princeton: Princeton University Press, 1980.

May, Ernest. *American Imperialism: A Speculative Essay.* New York: Atheneum, 1968.

May, Ernest R., and James C. Thompson, Jr., eds. *American and East Asian Relations.* Cambridge: Harvard University Press, 1972.

McCormick, Gaven. *Chang Tso-lin in Northeast China, 1911-1928: China, Japan and the Manchurian Idea.* Stanford: Stanford University Press, 1977.

MacKinnon, Stephen R., and Oris Friesen. *China Reporting: An Oral History of American Journalism in the 1930s and 1940s.* Berkeley: University of California Press, 1987.

McLane, Charles B. *Soviet Policy and the Chinese Communists, 1931-1946.* New York: Columbia University Press, 1958.

Mi, Zhan-chen. *The Life of General Yang Hucheng.* Translated by Wang Zhao. Hong Kong: Joint Publishing Co., 1981

Moore, Harriet L. *Soviet Far Eastern Policy, 1931-1945.* Princeton: Princeton University Press, 1945.

Morley, James William, ed. *The China Quagmire: Japan's Expansion on the Asian Continent, 1933-1941.* New York: Columbia University Press, 1983.

————, ed. *Deterrent Diplomacy: Japan, Germany and the U.S.S.R., 1935-1940.* New York: Columbia University Press, 1976.

Mu, Xin. *Zou Taofen.* Hong Kong: Sanlian Shudian, 1959.

Pelz, Stephen E. *Race to Pearl Harbor: Failure of the Second London Naval Conference and Onset of World War II.* Cambridge: Harvard University Press, 1974.

Pickler, Gordon Keith. "U.S. Aid to the Chinese Nationalist Air Force, 1931-1949." Ph.D. dissertation, Florida State University, 1971.

Pollard, Robert Thomas. *China's Foreign Relations, 1917-1931.* New York: Macmillan Co., 1933.

Pye, Lucien W. *Warlord Politics: Conflict and Coalition in the Modernization of China.* New York: Praeger, 1971.

Qin, Xiao-yi, ed. *Zongtong Jianggong Dashi Changbian Chugao* [Major Events in the Life of Former President Chiang]. 8 vols. Taibei: n.p., 1978.

Reardon-Anderson, James. *Yenan and the Great Powers: The Origins of Chinese Communist Foreign Policy, 1944-46.* New York: Columbia University Press, 1980.

Rock, William R. *British Appeasement in the 1930s.* New York: W. W. Norton & Co., 1977.

Rue, John E. *Mao Tsetung in Opposition, 1927-1935.* Stanford: Stanford University Press, 1966.

Schaller, Michael. *The U.S. Crusade in China, 1938-1945.* New York: Columbia University Press, 1979.

Schram, Stuart R. *The Political Thought of Mao Tse-tung.* New York: Praeger, 1963.

Schroeder, Paul W. *The Axis Alliance and Japanese-American Relations, 1941.* Ithaca: Cornell University Press, 1958.

Selle, Earl Albert. *Donald of China.* New York: Harper & Brothers, 1948.

Shaheen, Anthony Joseph. "The China Democratic League and Chinese Politics, 1939-1947." Ph.D. dissertation, University of Michigan, Ann Arbor, 1977.

Shai, Aron. *Origins of War in the East: Britain, China and Japan, 1937-1939.* London: Croom Helm, 1976.

Shao, Yu-lin. "Kangzhan Qianhuo Di Wo Ruogan Celue Zhi Jiantao" [A Discussion of both Our and the Enemy's Strategies before and after the Resistance War]. In vol. 4, *Zhongguo Xiandaishi Zhuanti Yanjiu Baogao* [Special Research Papers on Contemporary Chinese History]. Edited by Zhonghua Minguo Shiliao Yanjiu Zhongxin. Taibei: Zhonghua Minguo Shiliao Yanjiu Zhongxin, 1974.

Shao, Zhi-rui, and Li Wen-rong. "Guanyu Hemei Xieding De Jige Wenti" [Several Problems about the He-Mei Agreement]. *Jindaishi Yanjiu* [Studies on Modern History]. 3 (1982): 114-124.

Sharman, Lyon. *Sun Yat-sen, His Life and Its Meaning: A Critical Biography.* Hamden, Conn.: Archon Books, 1934.

Shen, Jia-shan. "Wang Jingwei Panguo Toudi Yuanyin Tantao" [An Inquiry on the Causes of Wang Jing-wei's Betraying the Nation and Surrendering to the Enemy]. In *Zhongguo Xiandaishi.* Compiled by People's University, 12 (1982): 107-112.

Shen Shu-yang. *Aiguo Laoren Shen Junru* [The Patriotic Old Man: Shen Jun-ru]. Zhejiang Renmin Chubanshe, 1981.

Shen, Yun-long. *Jindai Shishi Yu Renwu* [Events and Personages in Modern History]. Taibei: Ziyou Taipingyang Wenhua Shiye Gongsi, 1965.

————. *Huang Ying-bai Xiansheng Nianpu Changbian* [A Chronological History of Mr. Huang Ying-bai]. Taibei: Lianjing Chuban Shiye Gongsi, 1976.

Sheridan, James E. *Chinese Warlord: The Career of Feng Yu-hsiang.* Stanford: Stanford University Press, 1966.

————. *China in Disintegration: The Republican Era in Chinese History, 1912-1949.* New York: Free Press, 1975.

Shewmaker, Kenneth. *Americans and Chinese Communists, 1927-1945: A Persuasive Encounter.* Ithaca: Cornell University Press, 1971.

Shi, Zhen-ding. *Guofu De Waijiao Zhengce* [The Founding Father's Diplomatic Policy]. Taibei: Youshi Shudian, 1965.

―――. *Zongtong Waijiao Sixiang Yu Shijian* [President's Diplomatic Thoughts and Practices]. Yangmingshan, Taibei: Sanmin Zhuyi Yanjiusuo, 1966.

Shih, Paul K. T., ed. *Strenuous Decade: China's Nation-building Efforts, 1927-1937.* Baltimore: Johns Hopkins University Press, 1970.

Shirley, James. "Political Conflicts in the Kuomintang: The Career of Wang Ching-wei to 1932." Ph.D. dissertation, University of California, Berkeley, 1962.

Shum, Kui-kwong. *The Chinese Communist Road to Power: The Anti-Japanese United Front, 1935-1945.* New York: Oxford University Press, 1988.

Shyu, Lawrence Nae-lih. "The People's Political Council and China's Wartime Problems, 1937-1945." Ph.D. dissertation, Columbia niversity, 1972.

Smith, Sara R. *The Manchurian Crisis, 1931-1932: A Tragedy in International Relations.* New York: Columbia University Press, 1948.

Snow, Edgar. *Red Star Over China.* New York: Grove Press, 1968.

Soviet Volunteers in China: 1925-1945: Articles and Reminiscences. Moscow: Progress Publishers, 1980.

Stephen, John J. *Hawaii Under the Rising Sun: Japan's Plan for Conquest after Pearl Harbor.* Honolulu: University of Hawaii Press, 1984.

―――. "The Tanaka Memorial (1927): Authentic or Spurious?" *Modern Asian Studies* 7, no. 4 (1973): 733-745.

Tan, Chester C. *Chinese Political Thought in the Twentieth Century.* New York: Doubleday and Co., 1971.

Taofen De Taolu [Tao Fen's Road]. A Collection of Essays edited by Tao Fen Jinianguan. Hong Kong: Sanlian Shudian, 1979.

Thomson, James C., Jr. *While China Faced West.* Cambridge: Harvard University Press, 1969.

Thorne, Christopher. *The Limits of Foreign Policy: The West, the League and the Far Eastern Crisis of 1931-1933.* New York: Putnam, 1973.

Tien, Hung-mao. *Government and Politics in Kuomintang China, 1927-1937.* Stanford: Stanford University Press, 1972.

Trotter, Ann. *Britain and East Asia, 1933-1937.* Cambridge: Cambridge University Press, 1975.

Tsu, Susan Fu. "A Study of Chang Hsueh-liang's Role in Modern Chinese History." Ph.D. dissertation, New York University, 1980.

Tung, William (Dong Lin). *China and the Foreign Powers: The Impact of and Reaction to Unequal Treaties.* New York: Oceana Publications, 1970.

————, ed. *V. K. Wellington Koo and China's Wartime Diplomacy.* New York: Center for Asian Studies, St. John's University, 1977.

Upshur, Jiu Hwa-lo. "China Under the Kuomingtang: The Problem of Unification, 1928-1937." Ph.D. dissertation, University of Michigan, 1972.

Utley, Jonathan. *Going to War with Japan, 1937-1941.* Knoxville: University of Tennessee Press, 1985.

Van Slyke, Lyman P. *Enemies and Friends: The United Front in Chinese Communist History.* Stanford: Stanford University Press, 1967.

Varg, Paul A. *The Closing of the Door: Sino-American Relations, 1936-1946.* East Lansing, Mich.: Michigan State University Press, 1973.

Wang, Yi. "German Attitude to Mediating Sino-Japanese Relations in 1935." *Jindaishi Yanjiu* [Studies on Modern History] 5 (1984): 181-187.

Wang, Yun-sheng. "Yijiuerliu—Yijiusijiu De Jiu Dagongbao" [The Old Dagongbao from 1926-1949]. *Wenshi Ziliao Xuanji* 26 (1962): 208-277.

Wilbur, C. Martin. "Military Separatism and Process of Reunification under National Regime, 1927-1937." In Tsou Tang and Ho Ping-ti, eds. *China in Crisis.* Vol. 1. Chicago: University of Chicago Press, 1968.

Willoughy, Westel W. *The Sino-Japanese Controversy and the League of Nations.* Baltimore: Johns Hopkins University Press, 1935.

Wu, Aitchen K. *China and the Soviet Union: A Study of Sino-Soviet Relations.* New York: John Day Co., 1950.

Wu, Tien-wei. *The Sian Incident: A Pivotal Point in Modern Chinese History.* Ann Arbor: Center for Chinese Studies, University of Michigan, 1976.

Wu, Xiang-xiang. *Dierci Zhongri Zhanzheng Shi* [History of the Second Sino-Japanese War]. 2 vols. Taibei: Zonghe Yuekanshe, 1973.

Xian Shibian Ziliao Xuanji [Selected Materials on the Sian Incident]. Sian: Northwestern University, 1979.

Xian, Yi-shi, et al. *Jiuyiba Shibian Shi* [A History of the Manchurian Incident]. Shenyang: Liaoning Renmin Chubanshe, 1981.

Xiang Qing. *Gongchan Guoji Yu Zhongguo Geming Guanxi Shigao* [A History on the Relationship between the Comintern and the Chinese Revolution]. Peking: Peking University Press, 1988.

Xie, Guo-xing. *Huang Fu Yu Huabei Weiju* [Huang Fu and the North China Crisis]. Taibaei: Taiwan Normal University, 1984.

Yaacov, Y. I. Vertzberger. *The World in Their Minds: Information Processing, Cognition, and Perception in Foreign Policy Decision-making.* Stanford: Stanford University Press, 1990.

Yang, De-hui. "Lun Yang Jie De Minzhu Sixiang" [On Yang Jie's Democratic Thoughts]. *Sixiang Zhangxian* 6 (1984): 52-57.

Yang, Kui-song. "Guanyu 1936 Nian Guogong Liangdang Mimi Jiezhu Jingguo De Jige Wenti." [Several problems concerning the secret contracts between the KMT and the CCP in 1936]. *Jindaishi Yanjiu* [Studies on Modern History] 1 (1990).

————. "Zhongguo Gongchandang Kangri Minzu Tongyi Zhanxian Zhengce De Xingcheng Yu Gongchan Guoji" [The Formation of the Chinese Communist Party's United Front Policy and the Comintern]. *Jindaishi Yanjiu* [Studies on Modern History] 4 (1982): 69-95.

Yang, Shu. *Yierjiu Manyu* [About December 9]. Peking: Sanlian Shudian, 1981.

Yang, Zhong-zhou. *Xian Shibian* [The Sian Incident]. Shanghai: n.p., 1979.

Yi, Xian-shi, et al. *Jiuyiba Shibian Shi* [A History of the Manchurian Incident]. Shenyang: Renmin Chubanshe, 1981.

Yip, Ka-che. *Religion, Nationalism and Chinese Students.* Bellingham, Wash.: Center for East Asian Studies, Western Washington University, 1980.

Young, Arthur N. *China and the Helping Hand: 1937-1945.* Cambridge: Harvard University Press, 1963.

————. *China's Wartime Finance and Inflation, 1937-1945.* Cambridge: Harvard University Press, 1965.

————. *China's Nation-Building Effort, 1927-1937: The Financial and Economic Record.* Stanford: Hoover Institution Press, 1971.

————. "Cycle of Cathy: A Memoir." Unpublished manuscript.

Yu, Yi-fu. "Du Chongyuan Xiaozhuan" [A Short Biography of Du Chong-yuan]. In *Materials on the Sian Incident.* Compiled by Institute of Modern History, Academy of Social Sciences. Peking: Renmin Chubanshe, 1981

Zhang, Kai, and Cai De-jin. "Lun Jicha Zhengwu Weiyuanhui" [On Hebei-Chahar Political Council]. *Jindaishi Yanjiu* [Studies on Modern History] 4 (1985): 140-161.

Zhang, Tong-xin. *Jiang Wang Hezuo De Guomin Zhengfu* [The Nationalist Government under Jiang-Wang Cooperation]. Harbin: Heilongjiang Renmin Chubanshe, 1988.

Zhang, Xian-wen et al., eds. *Minguo Dangan Yu Minguoshi Xueshu Taolunhui Lunwenji* [Conference Papers on Republican Archives and Republican History]. Peking: Archival Press, 1988.

Zhang, Zhong-dong. *Cong Zhuzhang Heping Dao Zhuzhang Kangzhan De Hu Shi* [Hu Shi: From Advocating Peace to Advocating War]. [Taibei]: Institute of American Culture, Academia Sinica, 1983.

Zhongguo Jindai Xiandai Shilunji [Papers on Modern and Contemporary Chinese History]. Edited by its editing committee. Vol. 26. Taibei: Commercial Press, 1986.

Zhongguo Waijiao Shi [A Diplomatic History of China]. 2 vols. Edited by Diplomatic College. Peking: n.p., 1958.

Zhongguo Xiandaishi Dashiji [A Chronology of Major Events in Modern Chinese History]. Edited by Lian Han-bing and Wei Hong-yun. Harbin: Heilongjiang Renmin Chubanshe, 1984.

Zhou, Kai-qing. *Kangzhan Qian De Zhongri Guanxi* [The Prewar Sino-Japanese Relations]. Taibei: Taiwan Xuesheng Shuju, 1973.

Zhou, Tian-du. "Jiuguohui Shilue" [Short History of the Salvation Association]. *Jindaishi Yanjiu* [Studies on Modern History] 1 (1980): 161-198.

Zhou, Tian-du, ed. *Jiuguohui* [The Salvation Association]. Peking: Academy of Social Sciences Press, 1981.

Zhou, You-cun. *Zhongsu Guanxi Neimu* [Inside Story of Sino-Soviet Relations]. Hong Kong: Shidai Chubanshe, 1950.

————. *Sue Qinlue Zhongguo Shi* [History of Soviet Russian Aggression in China]. Taibei: Shidai Chubanshe, 1952.

INDEX

Amau Doctrine, 13, 14, 49-50.
American Committee for Non-participation in Japanese Aggression, 138-139, 198n.
American cotton and wheat loan, 45.
Anti-Comintern Pact, 74.
Ariyoshi, Ambassador, 60.
Axis Pact (Tripartite Alliance), 144, 147.

Bai Chong-xi, 67, 96, 99.
Bismarck, 12.
Blomburg, Defense Minister, 118.
Bogomolov, Domitri, 71-74, 80, 83-84, 88, 110-112, 181n, 191n.
Brest-Litovsk Treaty, 52.
Brussels Conference, 92-95, 113.
Buck, J. Lossing, 135.
Bullitt, William, 70, 135, 199n.
Bywater, H.C., 15.

Cai Ting-kai, 27, 65, 68.
Cai Yuan-pei, 20.
Carlson, Evans, 133, 134, 135, 148.
CC Clique, 42, 75.
Central Army, 13, 54-55, 82, 88, 91.
Central Political Council of the KMT, 29, 47, 93.
Chamberlain, Prime Minister, 56.
Chen Bu-lei, 104, 127.
Chen Gong-bo, 37, 107.
Chen Guang-pu, 134, 136, 140, 141, 142, 143.
Chen Ji-tang, 65, 66.

Chen Jia-geng, 106.
Chen Li-fu, 10, 71-72, 75, 81, 105, 110-111.
Chen Ming-shu, 9, 20, 25.
Chen Tong-he, 2.
Chen Xiao-qin, 75.
Chen Yi, 37, 58.
Chen You-ren, 9, 25-26, 27, 28, 29, 48, 105.
Cheng Qian, 9.
Cheng Tian-fang, 72.
Chennault, Claire, 150.
Chiang Kai-shek, 25, 34, 35-36, 37, 43, 44, 49, 51, 53, 60, 67, 84, 93-94, 99, 104, 106, 107, 128-129, 131-133, 136-137, 138, 139, 142-143, 146-147, 150, 152, 153, 158; and the article "Enemy and Friend"; and Axis Pact, 144-145; and decision for war, 88-90; and fear for an Anglo-Japanese alliance, 140-141; fear for a Soviet-Japanese rapprochement, 125-128; and German mediation, 96-97; and He-Umetsu Agreement, 54; and hopes for Anglo-Soviet cooperation, 120-122; and hopes for Soviet military intervention in war, 113-114, 116-120; and the League of Nations, 21-23, 34; and Nazi-Soviet Pact, 123; and negotiations for military alliance with Moscow, 70-74, 109-110; and negotiations with Japan, 76-78; and Nomura-Hull talks; and non-resistance policy, 20; and North China Autonomy, 58-60;